LEGENDARY LOCALS

OF

CARMEL

INDIANA

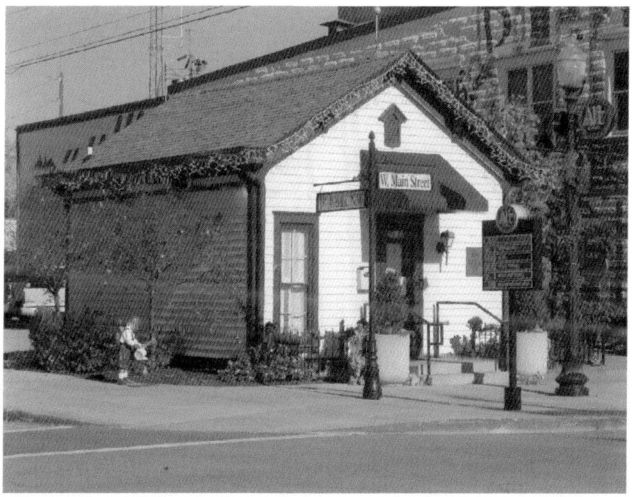

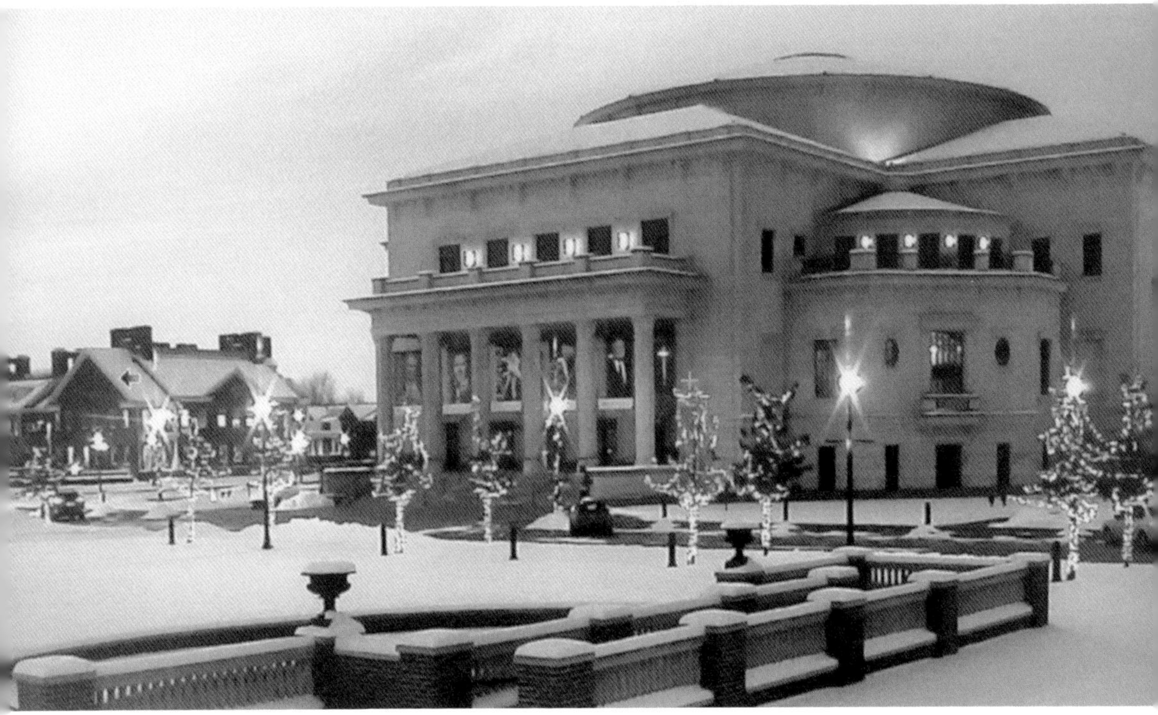

Carmel's Center for the Performing Arts
Carmel's Center for the Performing Arts consists of two theatrical venues and the crown jewel of the campus, the Palladium. The European-style, limestone building can host 1,600 patrons, has a 60-foot stage, and offers 360-degree seating. World-class performers fill the calendar year-round. (Courtesy of Bradley Johnson.)

Page 1: Carmel Arts Council
Once part of a home owned by one of Carmel's founding families and moved to its present location in 2005, this brightly painted, wood-framed building houses the World's Smallest Art Gallery, registered with the *Guinness Book of World Records* in 1999. The Carmel Arts Council displays schoolchildren's artwork in it from September to May of each year. (Author's collection.)

LEGENDARY LOCALS

OF

CARMEL

INDIANA

DEBRA HASKETT MAY

LEGENDARY LOCALS

ISBN 978-1-4671-0216-2

Legendary Locals is an imprint of Arcadia Publishing
Charleston, South Carolina

Printed in the United States of America

Library of Congress Control Number: 2015933425

For all general information, please contact Arcadia Publishing:
Telephone 843-853-2070
Fax 843-853-0044
E-mail sales@arcadiapublishing.com
For customer service and orders:
Toll-Free 1-888-313-2665

Visit us on the Internet at www.arcadiapublishing.com

Dedication
From a fur-trading post to a vibrant city, a sampling of Carmel's varied and interesting residents is respectfully honored in these pages.

On the Front Cover: Clockwise from top left:
Jeff and Shari Worrell, Carmelfest chairman (Photograph by Jennifer D. Hershberger; see page 100), Dick Ramsey, owner of Carmel Barber Shop (Courtesy of Janice Ramsey; see page 54), Eric Clark, basketball coach at Carmel High School (Courtesy of Deborah Clark Gangstad; see page 97), John Christy, justice of the peace (Courtesy of Dale Christy; see page 35), Doug Dolen, community volunteer (Photograph by Jennifer D. Hershberger; see page 107), Franklin Booth, artist and illustrator (Courtesy of a private collection; see page 30), Dave Dugan, comedian (Photograph by John Cinnamon; see page 119), Mary Davis, Carmel Police dispatcher (Courtesy of Dick Davis; see page 50), Don Huffer, golf coach at Carmel High School (Courtesy of Judy Huffer; see page 78).

On the Back Cover: From left to right:
John "Two Gun" Brunson, trash hauler (Courtesy of Carmel Clay Historical Society; see page 34), Ila and Jack Badger, community volunteers (Photograph by Jennifer D. Hershberger; see pages 122, 123).

CONTENTS

ACKNOWLEDGMENTS

While this book is certainly not an epic-length novel, a heartfelt memoir, or a detailed technical manual, the hours put into it seem like it could be any one or a combination of the above. My decision to write it changed my life and taught me that I am not too old to learn.

I agreed to serve as Carmel Clay Historical Society (CCHS) then president Jennifer Hershberger's vice president by blind invitation in 2013, and we soon learned that we shared a love of Carmel and a passion for history and preservation. A lasting friendship was born. You will see her beautiful photographs throughout this book. She was also a tireless cheerleader for me on this project, and her faith in me is incomprehensible. Former CCHS executive director Katherine Dill's encouragement as well as enthusiasm was a great catalyst in my decision to take this project on. My husband, Bradley May, worked hard to allow me the time to invest in this huge task. He listened to more than his fair share of my woes over the months, but he never stopped urging me on despite my frustrations. Lastly, my late parents, Loren and Emma Jane Haskett, instilled in me an appreciation and admiration of all those who came before me. Their stories and love of family, as well as a continued respect for family that came before them, gifted me with a sense of wonder and curiosity that fuels my need to uncover information to link people and events.

My gratitude to all will never be forgotten.

Unless otherwise noted, all photographs are from the author's collection.

INTRODUCTION

Fifteen miles due north from the heart of downtown Indianapolis is the city of Carmel, Indiana, known today for excellence in public education, numerous high school sports championship titles, appreciation of the arts, and home still to many whose descendants long ago settled the area.

Long before Indiana became a state, Bethlehem—or Carmel, as it is known today—was just a stop on a fur-trading route through wild and unsettled territory. Legend has it that its first white inhabitant was a French trapper and trader, Jean Brouillette, who built a trading post where two Indian trails crossed. The area was referred to as Tadpole's Glory.

By 1824, Clay Township had its first permanent white settlers in the family of Francis McShane. With the coming of more settlers, the downtown portion of Bethlehem was platted. In 1837, Seth Green, Alexander Mills, John Phelps, and Daniel Warren mapped out 14 lots. When application was made for a post office in 1847, it was discovered that there was already a town named Bethlehem in Indiana, so the name was changed to Carmel. This name being suggested by an early Quaker resident who thought Isaiah 35:2 was a perfect description for what the area should be. Many of the settlers that were flooding into the area were Quakers who left the East to escape the institution and stigma of slavery. Churches were built that doubled as schools. The Quakers had high respect for education, and that community-wide belief still holds today.

The little burg grew on pace with others being settled throughout the Midwest. Buildings popped up in town that housed places for folks to purchase necessary goods and services. One boon for Carmel would be the Monon Railroad that ran through the western section of the downtown area. Tracks were first laid in 1882 and that simplified the transporting of mail, livestock, grain, building supplies, and mercantile products. This brought farmers and outlying residents from the township into town on a regular basis and prompted the establishment of more downtown businesses. The railroad would also provide passenger service from Chicago to Louisville with ancillary service to attractions of the time such as French Lick and West Baden Springs. The Monon's tracks were not the only ones in town, however. The Interurban, an electric train-car passenger service that ran from Indianapolis to Anderson, would begin service in 1903. With the electricity that it required, one could say it was responsible for bringing that commodity to Carmel. The Interurban made more frequent stops than the Monon train, and residents would use it to visit family and friends nearby or take excursions to Indianapolis to conduct business or see the sights. Citywide water service would be in operation by 1930 and natural gas by 1933.

The invention of the automobile changed the landscape in numerous ways. Roads were paved, and the outlying ones were improved to accommodate the rapidly increasing number of cars in the township. With more cars on the road, the busier intersections caused confusion and wrecks. Carmel resident Leslie Haines invented a light to manage the traffic in downtown Carmel. In 1924, his "stop and go" light was installed at State Road 31 (now Rangeline Road) and Main Street. It was a different look for the intersection of those two Indian trails!

As municipal utilities found their way into being, so did municipal services. Carmel had early law enforcement—probably before there were too many actual laws—and it consisted of a justice of the peace with constables and marshals on the streets making arrests. In 1900, Carmel lost Constable William Carey in a gunfight at the livery stable. He is Carmel's only officer ever lost in the line of duty. His story holds intrigue that remains a mystery today. In 1921, when Carmel's fire department was a 10-member unpaid squad, the town's first fire truck was purchased. Under fire chief Donald Swails (who began as a volunteer and was eventually paid), the department would expand and become a municipal department in 1956.

Carmel's population explosion would not come until late in the 20th century, when Indianapolis executives and businessmen came to reside in Carmel. The commute was an easy one up Meridian Street or Keystone Avenue, taking less than 30 minutes to reach the slower pace of the suburbs. Carmel's population doubled from 1974 to 1990 and would more than double again between 2003 and 2013.

Albert Pickett became Carmel's first mayor when it became a city in 1975. Jim Brainard is the current mayor in his unprecedented sixth term and has revitalized the original downtown area and brought new life to old buildings with galleries, restaurants, specialty shops, and frequent highly attended events in the Arts & Design District.

Carmel continues on a path of economic growth, which breeds a need for residential growth. Technology companies are hearing about Carmel, and announcements are made regularly of new ventures locating within the city. This includes numerous foreign companies. Executives and employees need places to live, and Carmel's single- and multiple-family housing units continue to rise out of the fields that once grew corn and grazed livestock.

In 2008, Carmel was voted by *Forbes* magazine as one of the "Best Places to Raise a Family." *Money* magazine would follow up six years later in 2014 by naming Carmel as one of the "Best Places to Live." If you are already a resident, you know why you chose to live there. Visitors can look around and see how Carmelites love their community and embrace all that it has to offer. An area's people are the catalysts that share with outsiders a love of where they are, drawing in new businesses, residents, and visitors. A small selection of Carmel's people is featured in this book, *Legendary Locals of Carmel.*

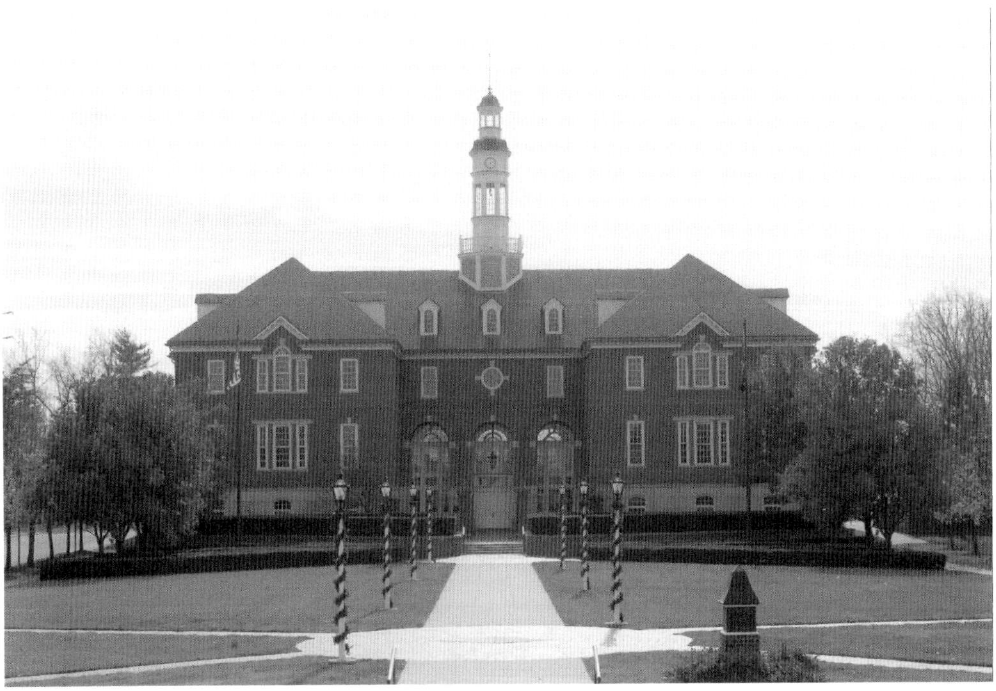

Carmel City Hall
As part of a centrally located government and community services campus with a beautiful fountain, green common area, and a public gazebo, city hall opened in 1990 as part of Carmel's civic center that also contains the main fire station and police headquarters. City hall houses the city's administration offices and traffic court.

CHAPTER ONE

Out of the Wilderness

As part of the Northwest Territory until it became a state in 1816, Indiana's main inhabitants were Indians of the Miami and Delaware tribes. Hamilton County was formed in 1823 when a group of settlers plotted the county seat of Noblesville. From a French trapper to Quakers from North Carolina and other points east, Carmel's—then Bethlehem's—first residents varied in origination and occupation. When it was decided to make the crossing of two Indian trails where Jean Brouillette's fur-trading cabin sat into a town, four men, Daniel Warren, Seth Green, John Phelps, and Alexander Mills, platted out 14 lots and registered them with the proper authorities in the county in 1837. All four of these men were originally from other states. There were a few hardy settlers that had arrived in the 1820s, and some of their descendants are still living in Carmel over 175 years later. Those family names are Moffitt and Kinzer.

People today can only imagine the challenges that early pioneers faced. Modern life makes inconveniences such as extreme weather tolerable. Even if daily life is disrupted, it is never for very long. Some of the illnesses that the pioneers were exposed to do not exist anymore. Pioneer homes, which were built with fewer tools and none of the mass-produced materials of today, are an enduring legacy of time gone by. Their windows invite us to wonder who might have peered out of them hoping for a loved one to return from a lengthy hunting trip. A porch creates a visual of who stood on the steps, perhaps receiving a gentleman caller or bad news from far away. An upstairs bedroom can bring to mind a person suffering from an illness, an injury, or perhaps the blessed occasion of childbirth.

Passed down by family or shared as town lore, some stories of these courageous individuals still make their way around. Even though gone for generations, their voices can still be heard.

Jean Brouillette (17??–1829)

Jean Brouillette was a French trapper from Vincennes, Indiana, who in 1819, upon passing through the lush, wooded land, decided to erect a cabin that would house a fur-trading business. His decision to build the cabin would launch the future settlement that was known as Tadpole's Glory, then Bethlehem, and eventually, Carmel in 1847. Jean would hire local settlers to trap the abundant wildlife and trade them goods and weapons for the fur pelts. The cabin was near where today is the intersection of Rangeline Road and Main Street, which were then two Indian trails. Jean was on friendly terms with the resident Indians that inhabited the area. Jean was related to Frances Slocum, who was an early settler taken from her Quaker family at age five by Delaware Indians in Pennsylvania and eventually raised by the Miami tribe outside of Peru, Indiana. (Courtesy of a private collection.)

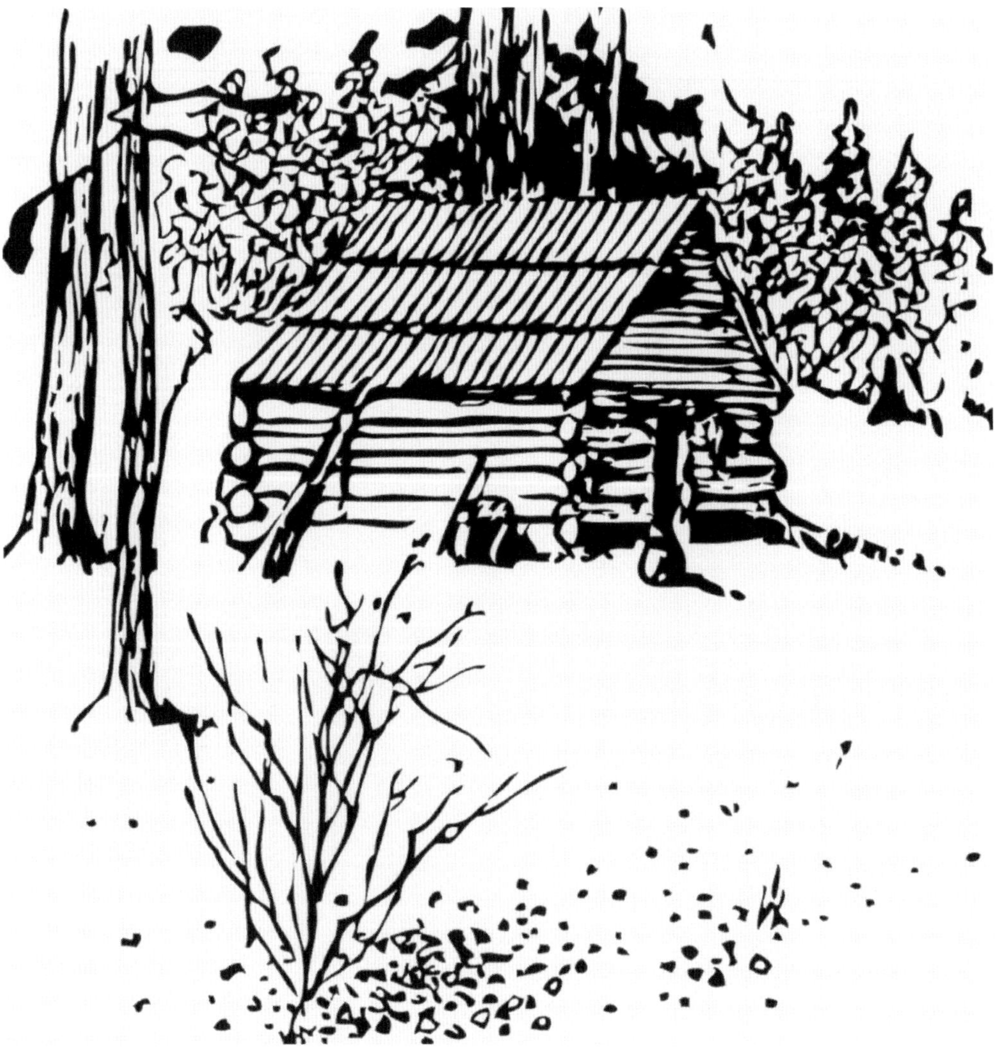

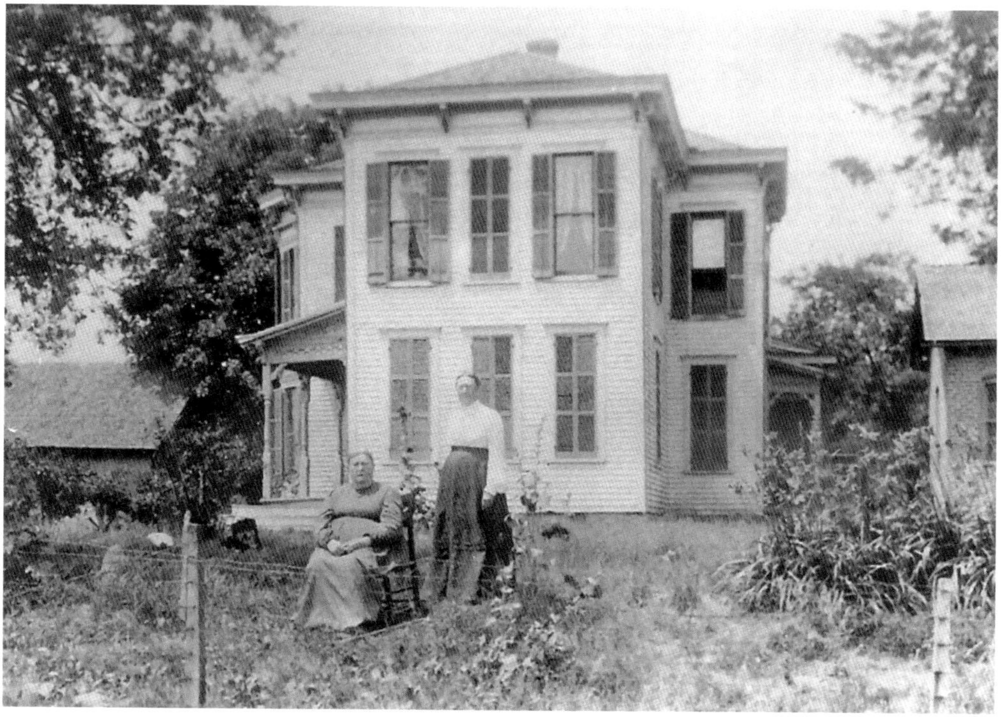

Francis McShane (1782–1842)
Much like many settlers of the time, Francis McShane arrived in the southern part of Hamilton County by horseback in 1824. He entered his land tract with the government and returned to his home in Kentucky. The following year, he brought his family to Indiana and settled near what is now the 10000 block of Westfield Boulevard where they lived in a cabin. His son James Gray McShane would build the beautiful home pictured that still stands today in 1883. The photograph above was taken in 1905, and photograph below was taken in 2014. It was recently purchased and restored, both inside and out. (Above, courtesy of Carmel Clay Historical Society; below, photograph by Jennifer D. Hershberger.)

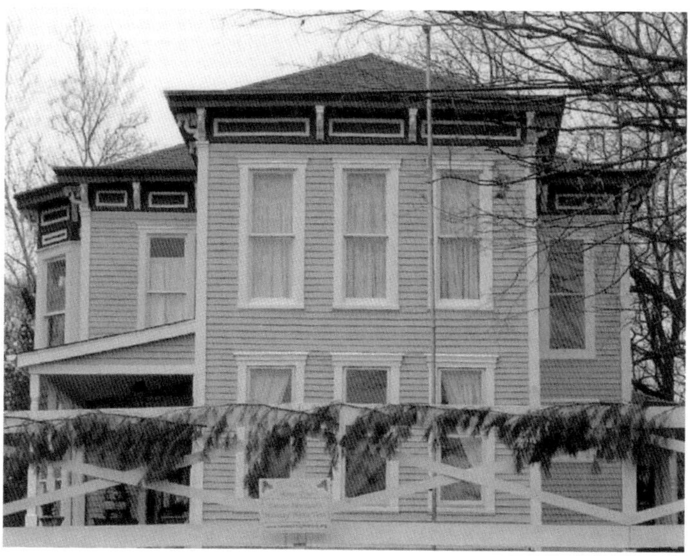

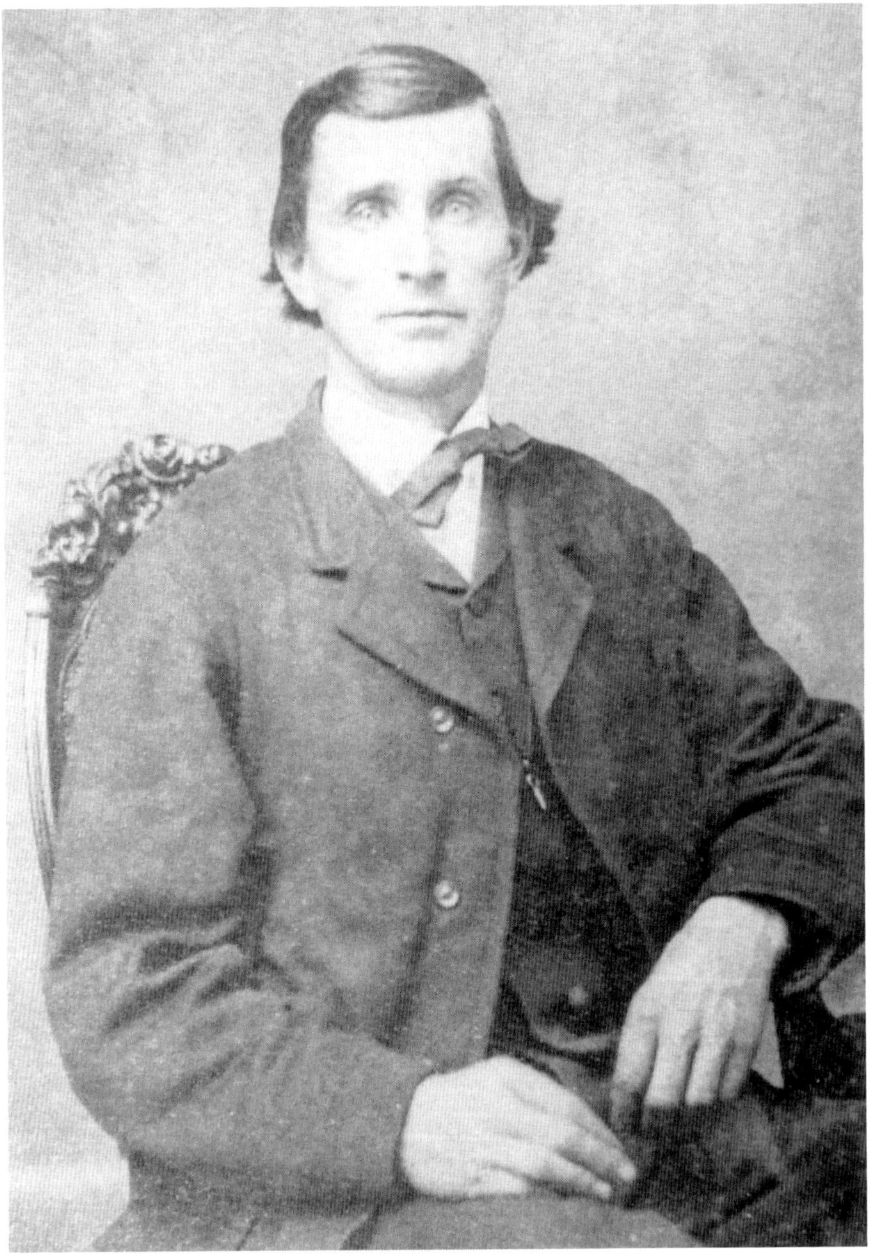

William J. Kinzer (1832–1914)

Born the eldest son of John and Ruth in the cabin mentioned in John's profile, William J. Kinzer resided in Carmel all of his 82 years. In those years, there were two marriages, the loss of one wife, the loss of a young son, five surviving children, years of farming to earn an income and eat the next year, plus his personal challenges. Because of his calling to record his daily life, he revealed his deepest feelings regarding life, love, and loss, as well as important events of the time, like the growth of a small Indiana Quaker community and the happenings in a young country experiencing its own trials of progress. William chronicled his thoughts and life events beginning in 1857 up through 1912, two years before his death. (Courtesy of Carmel Clay Historical Society.)

Warren, Green, Mills, and Phelps

The crossroads of Rangeline Road and Main Street in downtown Carmel were, in 1819, the intersection of two Indian trails where fur trader Jean Brouillette settled in his cabin to conduct business. As more and more Quakers came from the east and settled nearby, it was decided to plot the area, and in April 1837, John Stevenson, recorder for Hamilton County, met with residents Seth Green and Daniel Warren of North Carolina, Alexander Mills of South Carolina, and John Phelps of Virginia and entered Bethlehem as a town. The town was laid out in 14 plots divided evenly on the quarter sections of two 60-foot-wide cross streets both named Main Street at the time—one ran north to south and the other east to west.

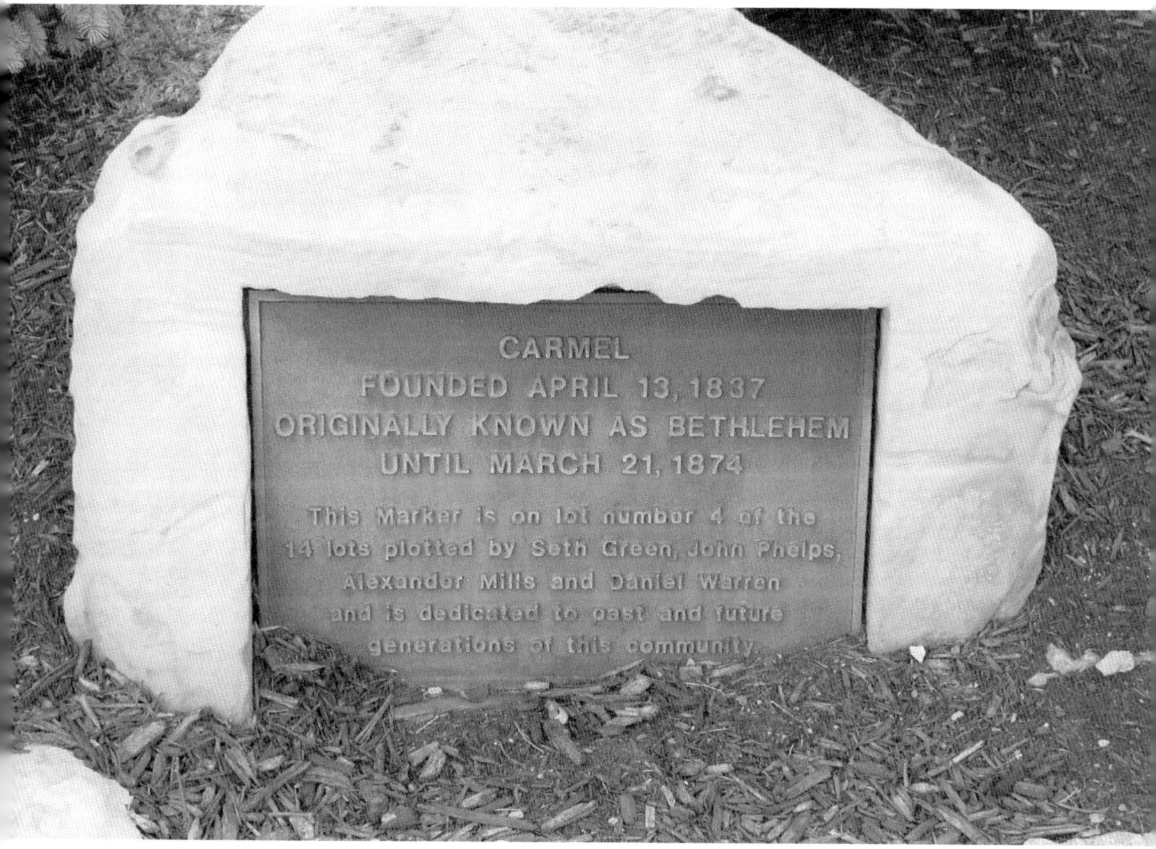

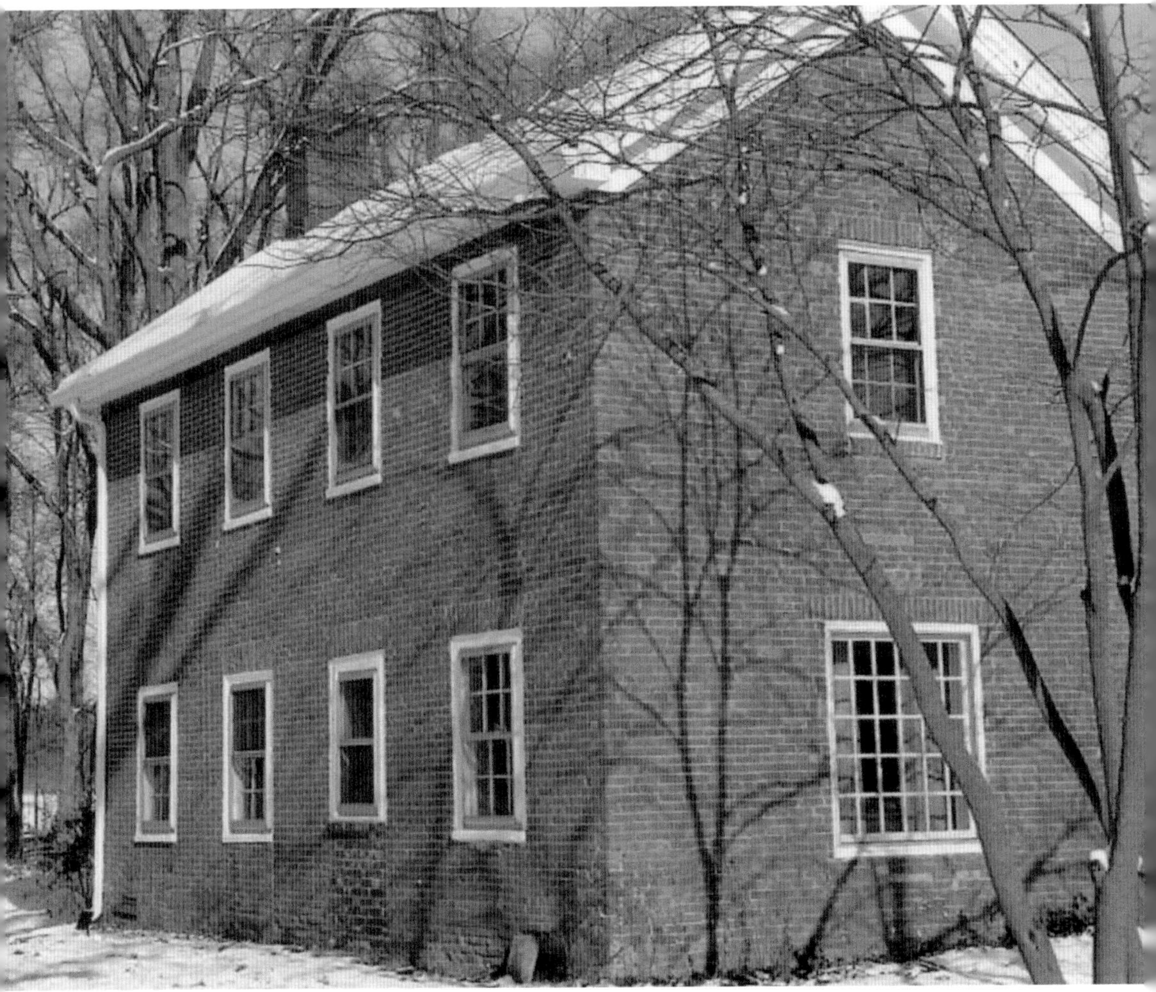

Silas Moffitt (1794–1873)

Silas and his wife, Hannah, who came from North Carolina in 1822, lived three years in a little, floorless cabin near White River in then Delaware Township. This land was lush with thick vegetation, abundant wildlife, and a wide, winding river fed by tributary creeks. A cache of clay was discovered on the property, and using the resources found nearby, Silas soon built a larger brick home for his quickly growing family. The family would flourish in that new home with a total of nine children. Descendants of Silas Moffitt still inhabit Carmel and the surrounding area. Having endured the changes that man and nature brought to it over nearly two centuries, the brick home that Silas built still stands stoically. (Photograph by Jennifer D. Hershberger.)

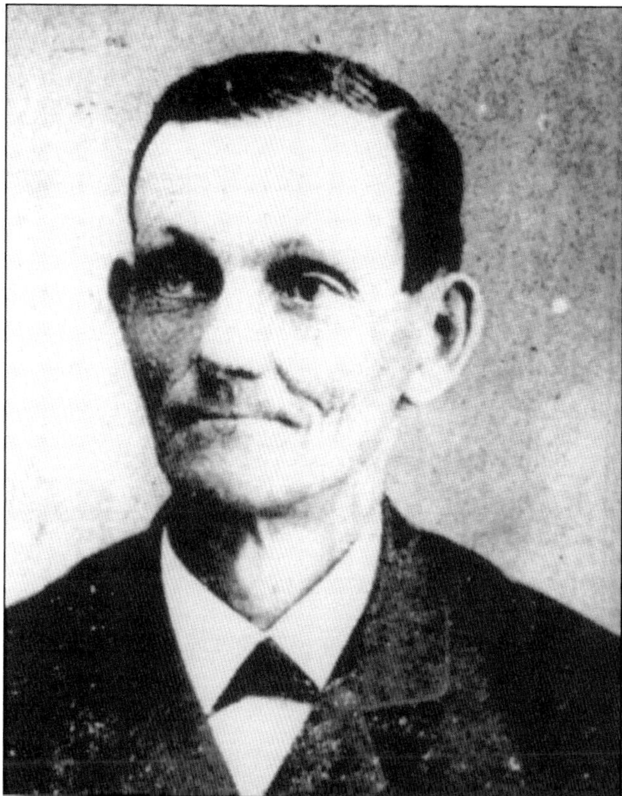

Zina Warren (1831–1911) Founding Carmel was only one legacy that Daniel Warren left behind. The second would be his son Zina, who would record his memories and recollections in writing for future generations. He was six years old when his father and three other men plotted the town of Bethlehem in 1837. Zina married Isabella Thomas of Pennsylvania in 1855. They settled down in Carmel, where they raised their family and resided their entire lives. In 1864, Zina was appointed postmaster of the Carmel Post Office and held that position for 33 years. Zina died in 1911, and published the same year was his book *Reminisces of the Long Ago*, which chronicled life in Bethlehem/Carmel over many decades. (Both, courtesy of Carmel Clay Historical Society.)

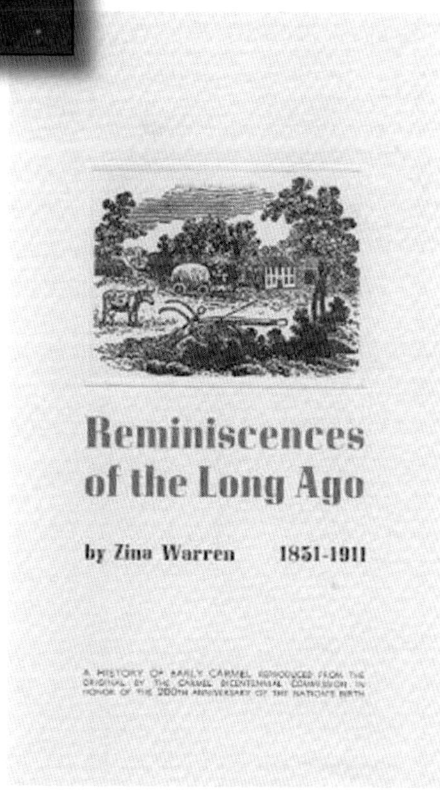

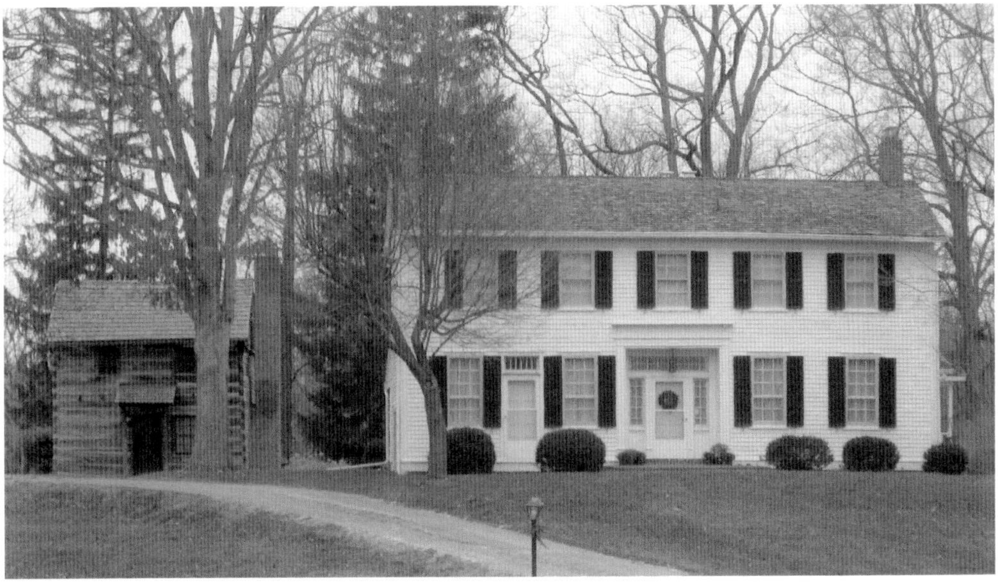

John D. Kinzer (1804–1850)

Carmel does not have many listings in the National Register of Historic Places, but one that it does have is the Kinzer homestead east of downtown on Main Street. It has been in the register since 1975. There is no sign, so many pass the historic farm every day unaware of the rich history that sits back up the gravel lane. The log cabin was built in 1828 by John D. Kinzer. He was born in Virginia and, like so many, came to Indiana when it was a young state to enter land in his name with the government. He and his wife, Ruth, whom he married in 1830, raised their first five children in the small, dirt-floored cabin. The larger frame, two-story home sits just a few feet from the cabin and was built in 1847. (Above, courtesy of the National Register of Historic Places; below, author's collection.)

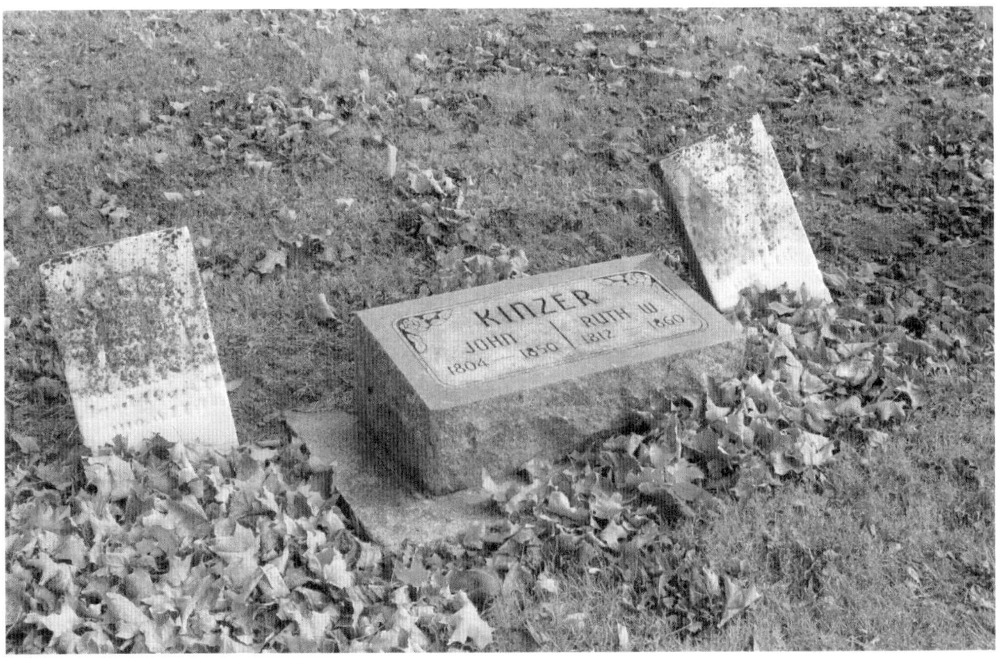

CHAPTER TWO

Fields to Foundations

During the late 1800s and early 1900s, Carmel's early foundations were being laid that would establish a farm town. Shops sprung up that included places to buy food, clothing, and household goods. There was enough demand for a blacksmith shop, so a man named Colonel Trester obliged. A lumber mill was in need for construction of the homes that would populate the tree-lined streets. The number of automobiles was on the rise, and traffic control was necessary. Electrician Leslie Haines would invent a device that is in use nationwide today, the stoplight.

In 1846, when application was made for a post office in town, it was discovered that there already was a Bethlehem, Indiana. A local resident decided the area was befitting of the following bible verse, Isaiah 35:2: "It shall blossom abundantly, and rejoice even with joy and singing: the glory of Lebanon shall be given unto it, the excellency of Carmel and Sharon, they shall see the glory of the Lord, and the excellency of our God." Application was made for the post office again with the name Carmel.

A need for city services arose, so law enforcement was organized with a justice of the peace and town constable. In 1900, Carmel would lose its first (and only to date) officer in the line of duty. After making an arrest and bringing the accused to the town's livery stable for arraignment, Constable William Frank Carey, as well as the man arrested, would end up dead.

The hidden talents of a few would take them great places in life. Places that many of Carmel's simple Quaker residents could not imagine. Franklin Booth and Worthington Hagerman, both artists, would travel the world to draw and paint its beauty.

With churches and schools comes the need for more people . . . people to teach, people to preach, and people to construct buildings. By 1900, Carmel's population was 498.

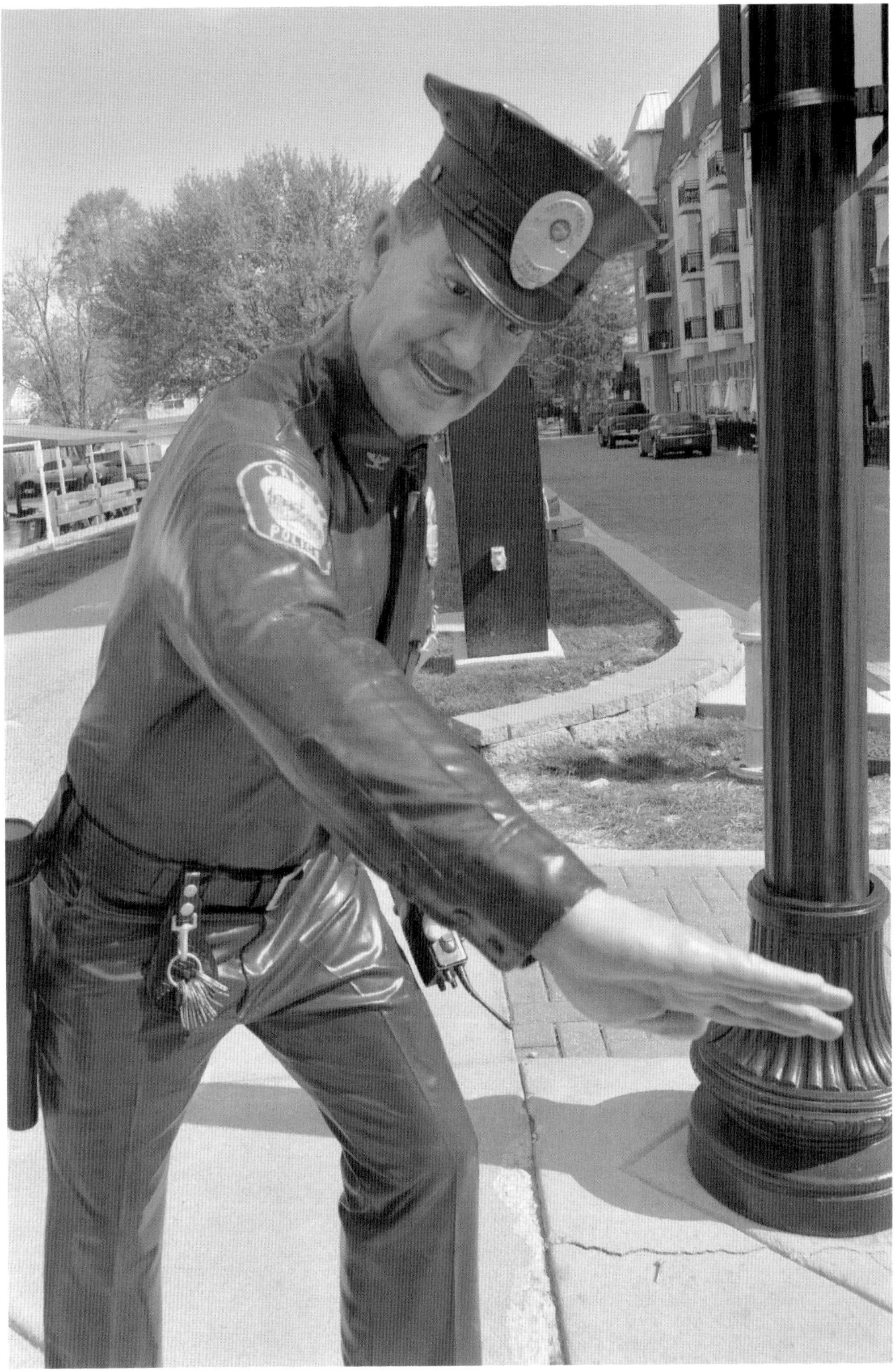

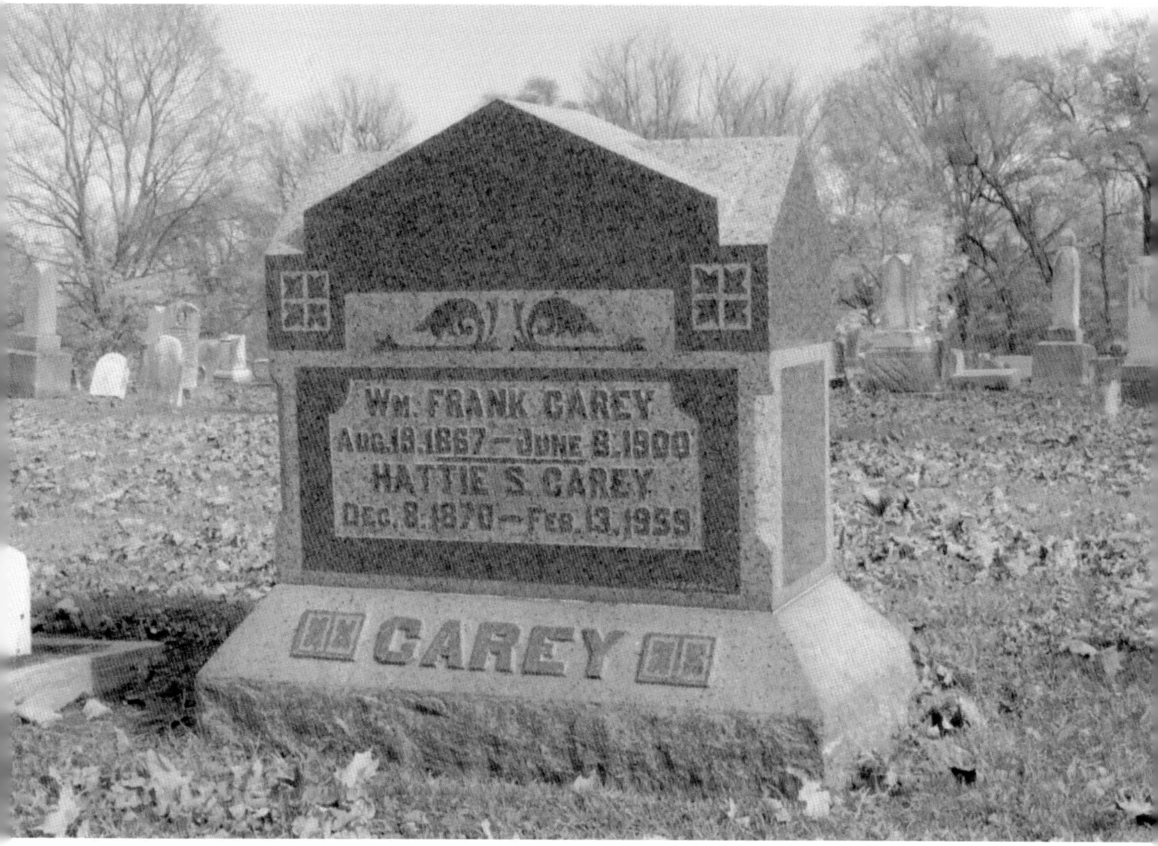

William Frank Carey (1867–1900)
In Carmel's more than 175-year history, it has only had one police officer killed in the line of duty. This officer was Constable William Frank Carey. On June 8, 1900, Carey was sent along with another constable to serve a warrant on a preacher who was known to have a volatile and uncertain temper. The two men removed the acclaimed evangelist Thomas "Cyclone" Johnson from his home and took him to the livery stable office for arraignment. Whether negligence on the part of the constables in failing to search his person or great concealment skills by the preacher, Johnson managed to carry two revolvers and a knife into the livery stable. Accusations got heated during the arraignment, and a crowd of onlookers assembled. Numerous folks in attendance had been victim of or witnessed Johnson's spirited nature. Shots were fired, and when the confusion cleared, two men, Johnson and Constable Carey, were dead. The coroner's inquest findings would be what today is termed as "inconclusive," and witnesses would not reveal who actually shot Johnson. It would be ruled that he was killed by someone unknown. The coroner stated that Constable Carey's assailant was Thomas Johnson. Over time, the story has taken on the air that the two men killed each other in a shoot-out.

The bronze statue of a police officer that sits along the Monon Trail at Main Street in downtown Carmel bears the name badge "Carey" as a tribute to the slain constable. Frank Carey is buried in the original Carmel Cemetery with no indication of his service or how he died. (Left, photograph by Jennifer D. Hershberger.)

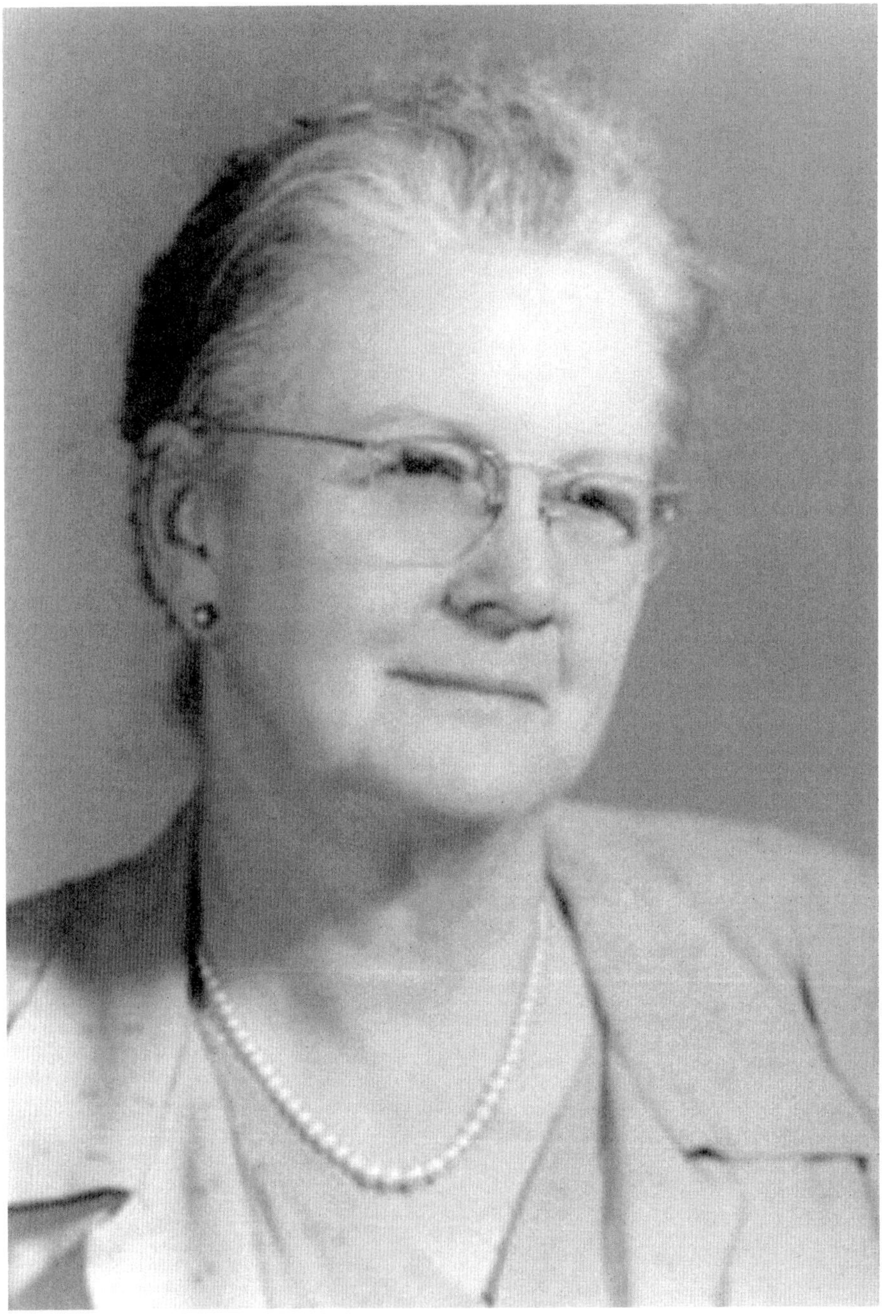

Olive (Brown) Brunner (1891–1988)

A 50-year Carmel High School (CHS) employee, as well as a 1909 Carmel graduate, Olive Brown Brunner also served on Carmel's library board for 49 years. She left Carmel when she married her husband but returned when he was killed in an accident. She taught multiple subjects at CHS, was a yearbook sponsor, and "retired" from teaching to begin a bookstore in the school. The school board requested her retirement in 1972 when it went to a rental system. Upon her death in 1988, Olive left a great many of her life's mementos to the Carmel Clay Historical Society. (Courtesy of Carmel Clay Historical Society.)

Colonel Neff Trester (1895–1970)

Four men pose in 1915 outside Colonel Trester's blacksmith shop in downtown Carmel. Colonel—yes, his given first name—was a longtime smithy and worked well into the age of the automobile. He shoed horses as well as repaired farm implements. His shop stood on Second Avenue SW and was demolished when the street was taken in the newer downtown development. (Courtesy of Carmel Clay Historical Society.)

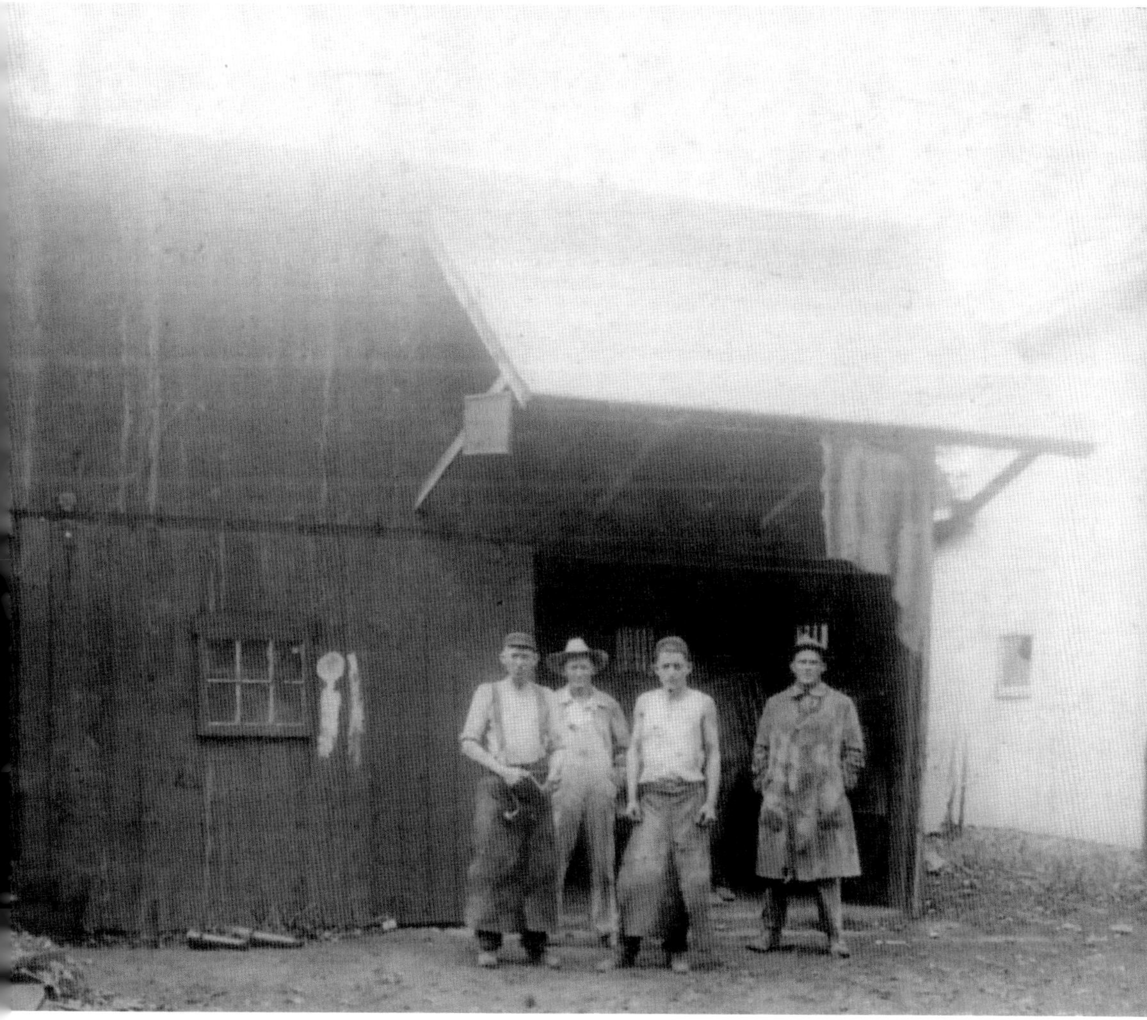

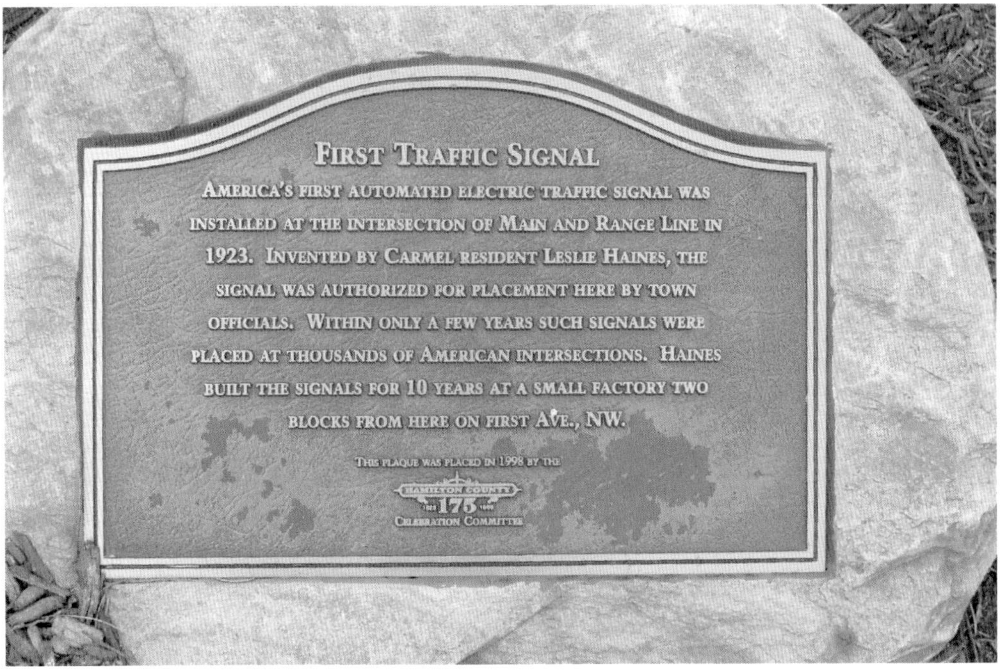

Leslie W. Haines (1883–1945)

Carmel had the first stoplight in the country, and it was invented by one of its residents. Leslie Haines was born in 1883 and was a resident of Carmel his whole life. Haines's invention, the pulley-system stoplight, did not require electricity and only had the words "stop" and "go" on it. A later version of one of Carmel's earliest stoplights sits in the Carmel Monon Depot Museum on the campus of the Carmel Clay Historical Society, while the concrete base that held it secure in the intersection of State Road 31 (now Rangeline Road) and Main Street is in one of the museum's gardens. Haines was also an influential factor regarding Carmel's geographical layout, but that acknowledgment did not come until after his death. (Right, photograph by Jennifer D. Hershberger.)

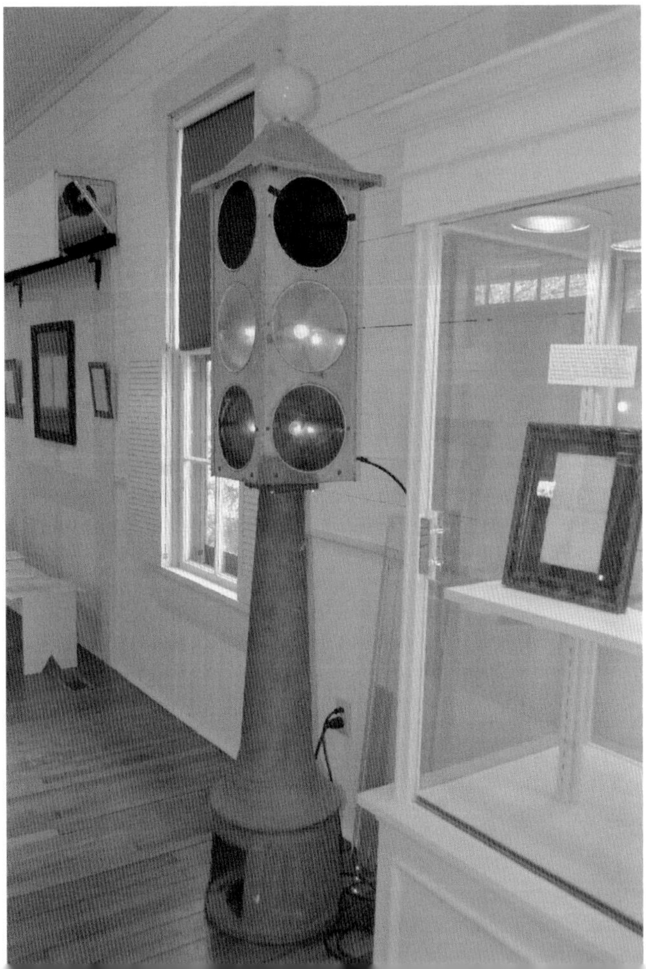

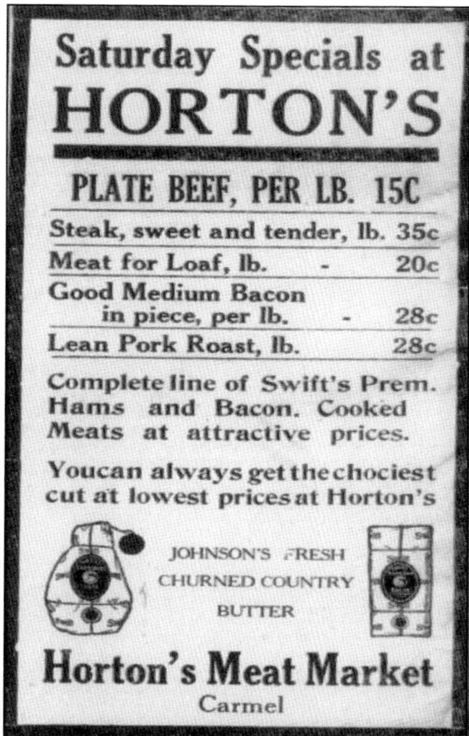

Saturday Specials at
HORTON'S

PLATE BEEF, PER LB. 15C

Steak, sweet and tender, lb. 35c
Meat for Loaf, lb. - 20c
Good Medium Bacon in piece, per lb. - 28c
Lean Pork Roast, lb. 28c

Complete line of Swift's Prem. Hams and Bacon. Cooked Meats at attractive prices.

Youcan always get the choiest cut at lowest prices at Horton's

JOHNSON'S FRESH CHURNED COUNTRY BUTTER

Horton's Meat Market
Carmel

Oakley G. Horton (1902–1989)

Oakley Horton stands outside his butcher shop/meat market in downtown Carmel, perhaps to cool off or to view something that caught his attention. The shop was in the first block of Main Street west of Rangeline Road. He opened it in 1926 in partnership with his brother Floyd. Oakley and his wife, Marge, would have two children, one of which is Phyllis Rockhill, a beloved teacher for many years with Carmel Clay Schools. (Above, from the 1928 *Carmel Standard*; below, courtesy of the Carmel Clay Historical Society.)

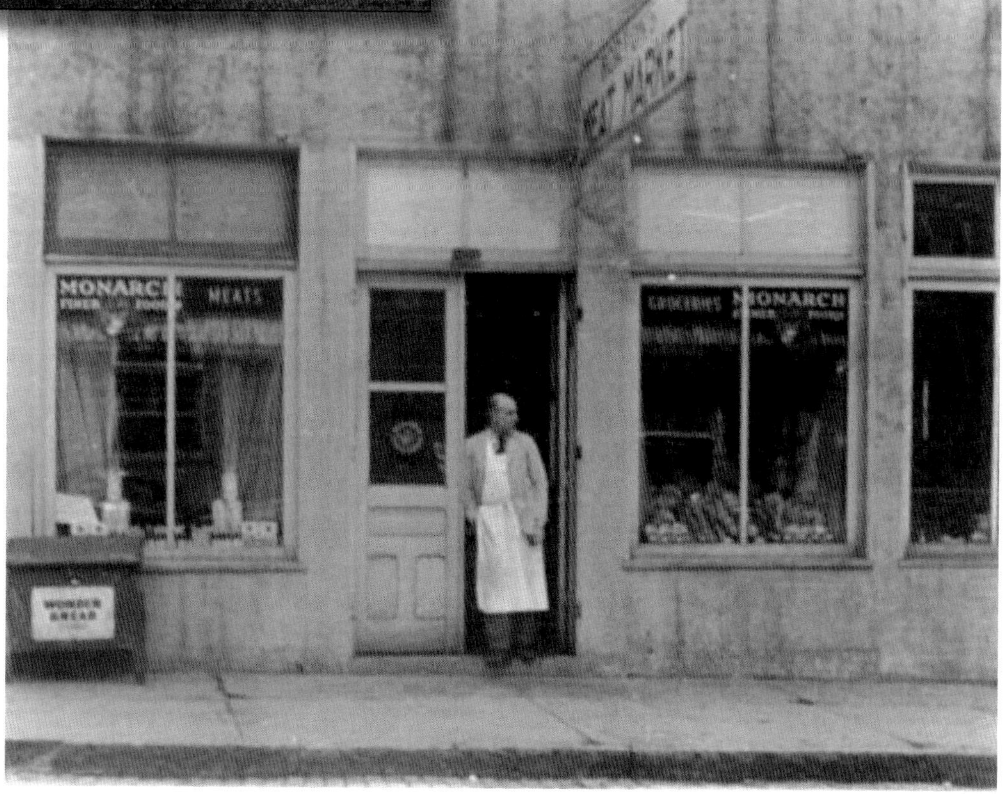

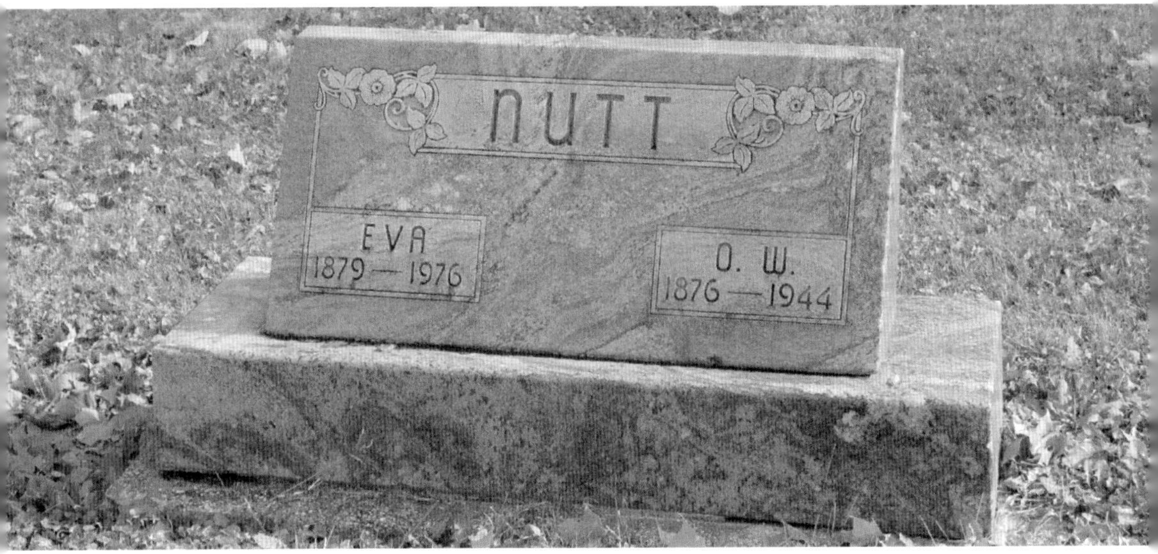

Otis W. Nutt (1876–1944)

O.W. Nutt had several businesses in early Carmel, but he was most noted for his hardware store, furniture store, and funeral home. He and his wife, Eva, lived in Carmel and raised their family there. Always trying to keep up with the times, the hardware store offered more than just the usual nuts, bolts, plumbing supplies, and lumber. In the first block south of the stoplight in downtown Carmel, the house that hosted the Nutt funeral business still grandly watches over the traffic of Rangeline Road. When opened in 1939, it was a well-appointed, modern funeral home with multiple rooms. As a young man, O.W. took an interest in the funeral business watching his father who was a casket maker. (Below, courtesy of the *Carmel Standard*, 1921.)

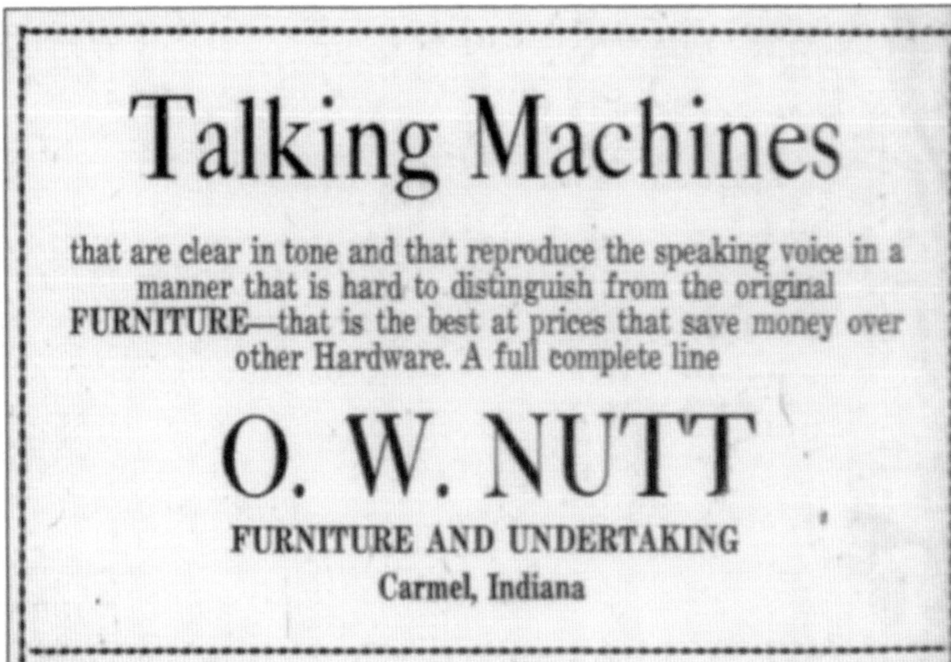

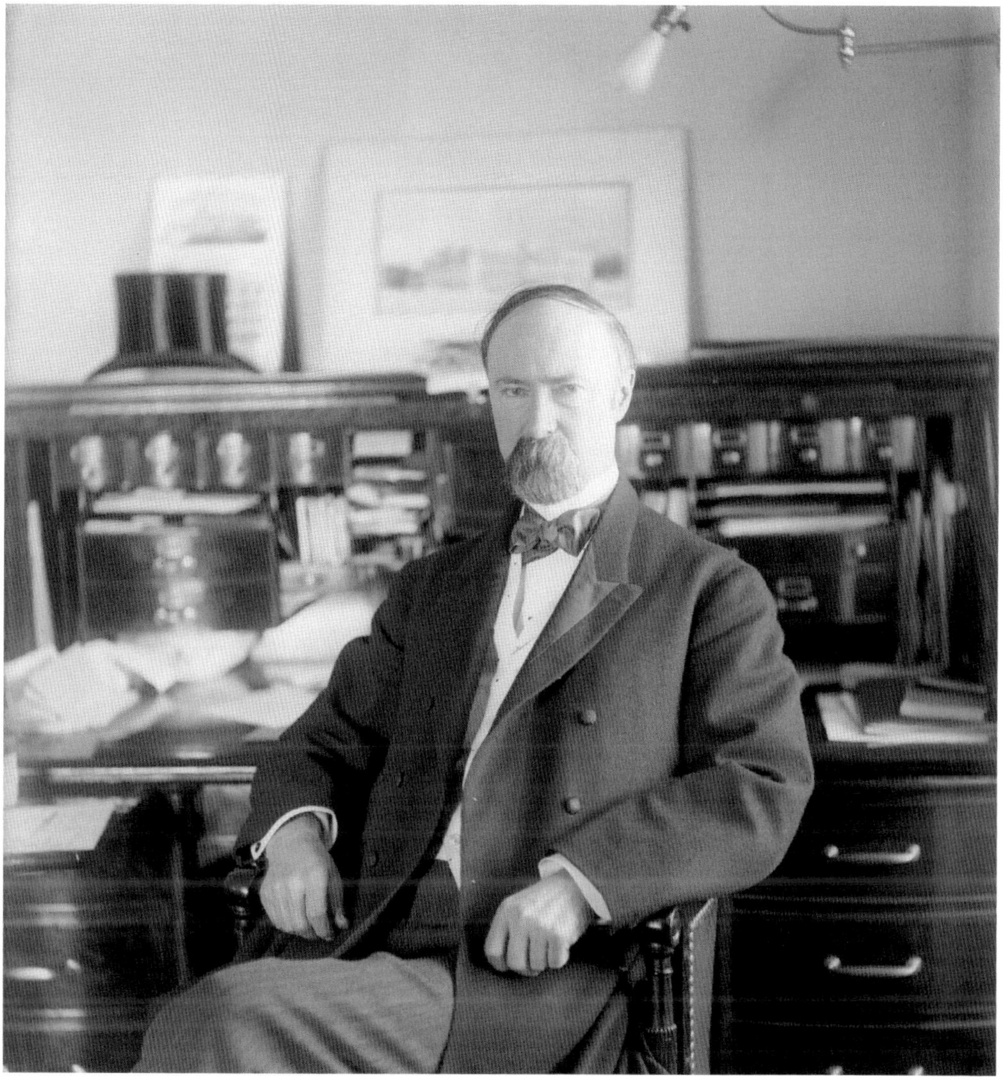

Charles W. Fairbanks (1852–1918)
Born in Ohio, Charles W. Fairbanks relocated to Indianapolis after passing the bar exam in 1874. He served as US senator from Indiana and went on to be Teddy Roosevelt's vice president from 1905 to 1909. When that term was completed, he returned to practicing law with a run for the presidency in 1916. Failing to win the nod of his party, he was named to run as vice president with Charles Hughes but lost to Woodrow Wilson. Fairbanks's daughter would marry a Carmel resident, and his grandson David Fairbanks Causey would found Cricklewood Farms in the low valley leading to Cool Creek and east. Adelaide, the vice president's daughter and David's mother, owned acres of farmland on present-day East Main Street where Carmel Christian Church is located. It was called Fairchild Farm. (Courtesy of the Library of Congress.)

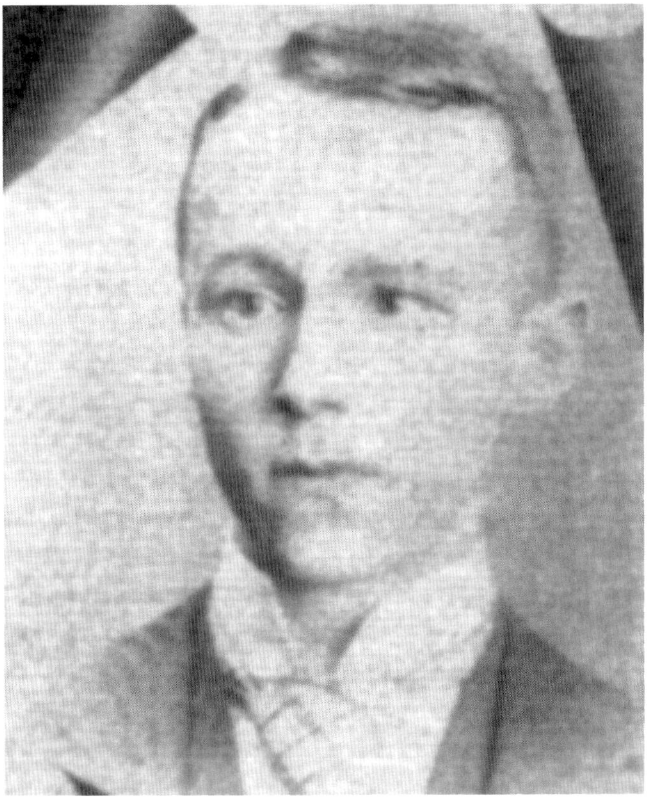

Worthington E. "Worthy" Hagerman (1878–1967)

If ever Carmel was to have someone dubbed as an "International Man of Mystery," Worthington Hagerman would fit the bill. Born into the Quaker church to Frank and Cordelia Hagerman in western Clay Township, he lost his mother, who was then just 24 years old, a few weeks shy of his second birthday. He was raised by his maternal grandparents and graduated from Carmel High School. Worthy attended the Art Institute of Chicago and then Penn College, a Quaker institution located in Oskaloosa, Iowa. Worthy left the United States in 1903 to live in Paris and practice the craft of oil painting. At the outbreak of World War I, he connected with the US State Department, and the intrigue begins. Identified in official documents as an artist and a singer, he traveled to European capitals extensively during World War I and World War II when travel was difficult for most. Details of his travel are virtually nonexistent. At one time, it was rumored that he may have aided Jews, as rare written documentation from a Frenchman commends Worthy for doing so. He received a civil service pension, but record of his service is not to be found. He did marry three times and was father to one daughter in his first marriage. He returned to the United States often enough to maintain his citizenship, spending much of that time in the artist colony of Taos, New Mexico.

After a fatal heart attack in 1967 in Lisbon, Portugal, his passport was destroyed immediately by the American consulate. He is buried in a British cemetery in Lisbon. While his art is obtainable and certainly not worthless today, little else about this mysterious man can be found besides basic information that could be deemed as "sterilized." The great question is: Why? (Courtesy of Julie Stevens.)

"Self Portrait" (OPPOSITE)
Worthy's sense of humor is revealed in his work titled "Self Portrait." The viewer believes that the painting is a mere still life of a vase until they notice Worthy in the reflection on the vase, a clever man and always mysterious. (Courtesy of John Graves.)

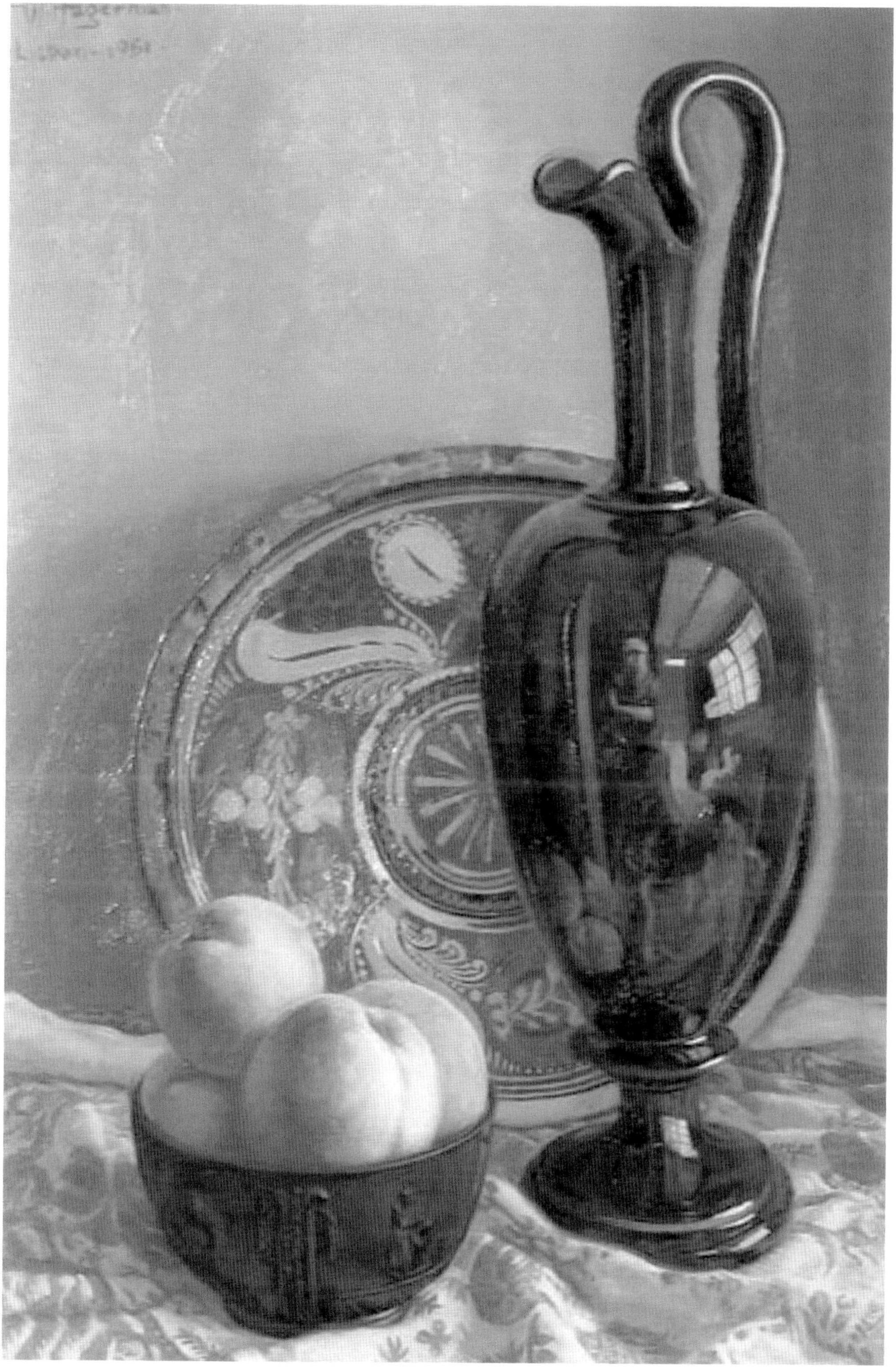

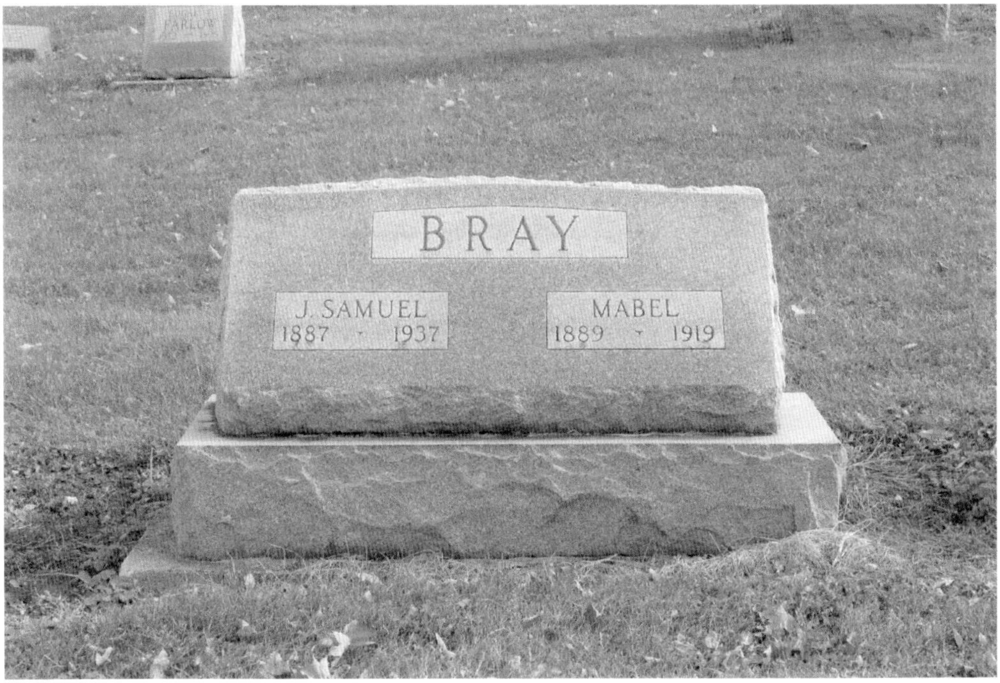

Trixie Ann (1932–1946)
James Samuel Bray passed away in 1937 and was laid to rest in the Carmel Cemetery next to his first wife and young son who had preceded him in death. James left behind at home his second wife, Nora, and his beloved Manchester terrier, Trixie Ann. Before he died, James had requested that when Trixie Ann's life on earth ended that she be interred next to him. Nine years later when his companion passed away, with cemetery board approval, Nora purchased a small casket and had Trixie Ann buried with James. All was well until the residents of Carmel decided that it was not the place for a dog, even a well-known, popular pup the people in town loved. A lawsuit was filed in Marion County Circuit Court against Nora and the cemetery trustees demanding the immediate removal of Trixie Ann. (Above, author's collection; below, courtesy of a private collection.)

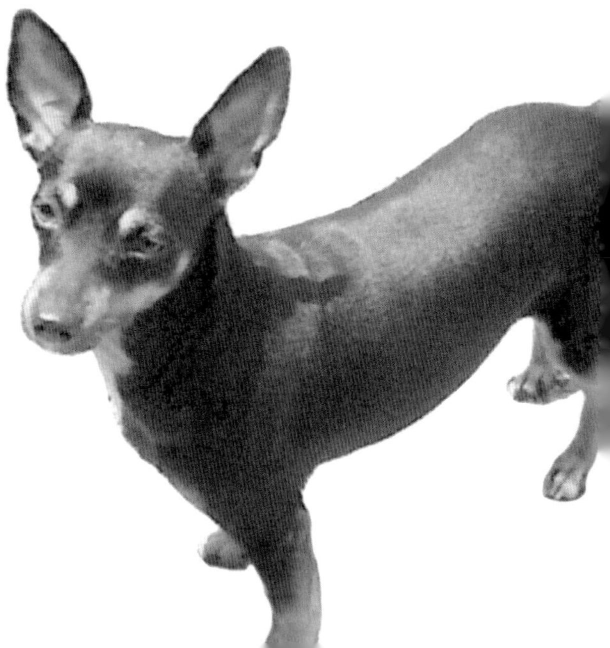

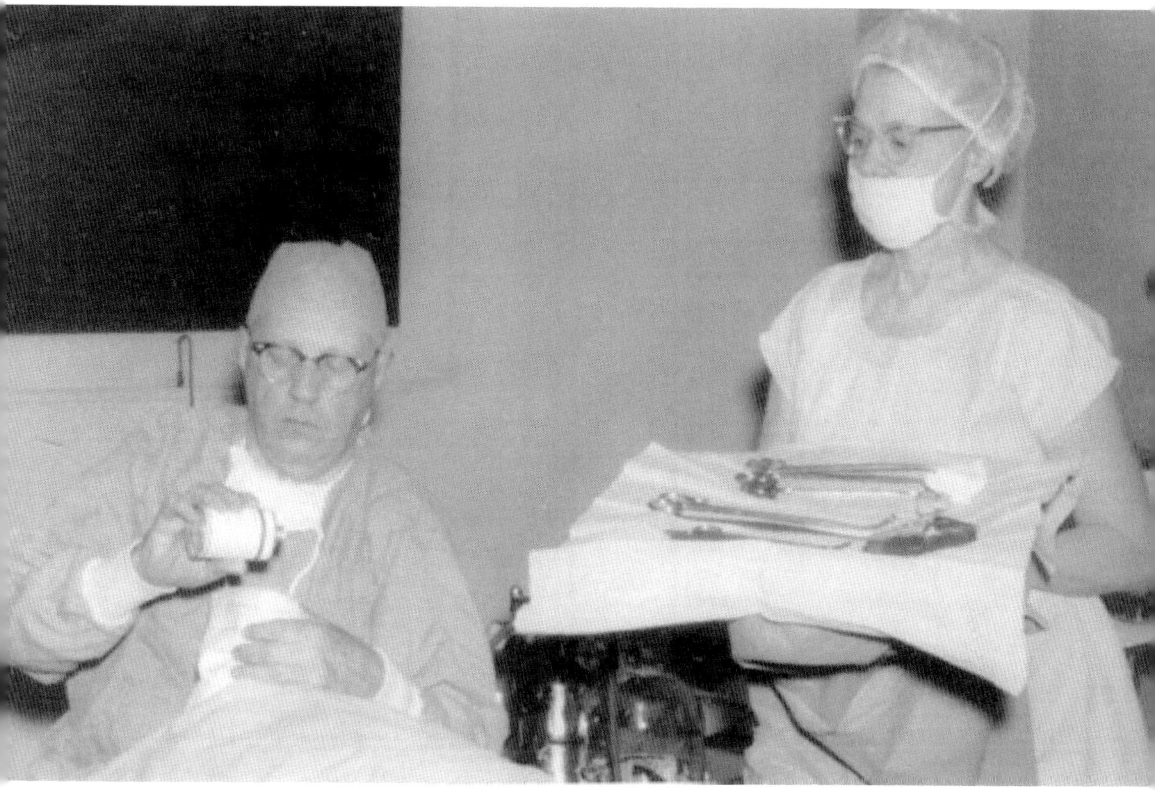

Claude M. Donahue (1895–1969)
Many Carmelites today can remember a visit to Doc Donahue's office for a vaccination or an antibiotic injection in their behind. Claude Donahue, son of Irish immigrants and native of Dubois County, was discharged from the US Navy after World War I and taught school there briefly. He enrolled and graduated from Indiana University School of Medicine and very shortly assumed the practice in Carmel of the late Dr. William Baker, who passed away in 1927. Dr. Donahue was a hard worker, rarely taking vacations. His respite was hunting and shooting and playing the occasional card game at the pool hall. Carmel's surrounding area was still very much undeveloped and provided great locations for the sports he loved. In 1932, he was elected Hamilton County coroner and served that term with little to nothing as pay. (Courtesy of Carmel Clay Historical Society.)

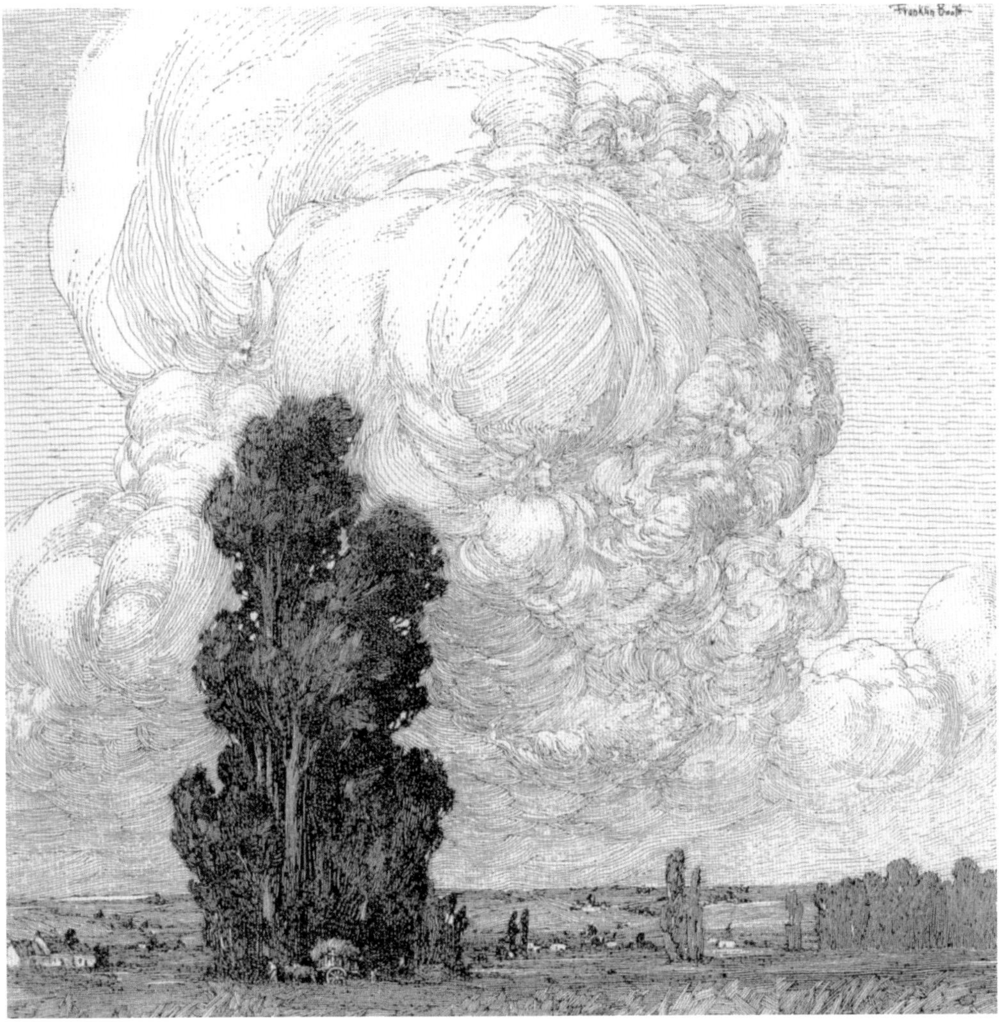
Franklin Booth

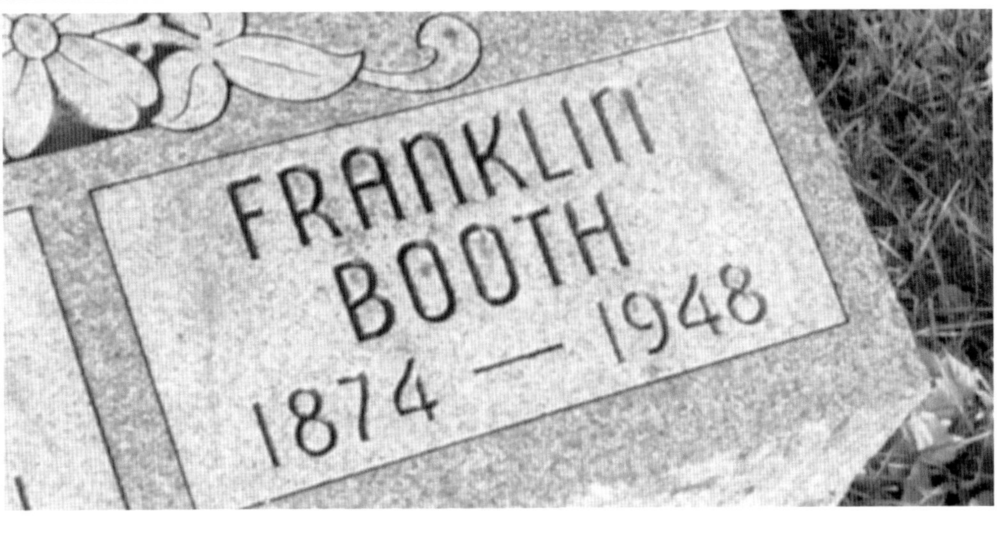
FRANKLIN
BOOTH
1874 — 1948

Jay Franklin Booth (1874–1948)

Born on a farm in Carmel in 1874 and never formally educated or trained, Jay Franklin Booth had a keen eye, inherent dexterity, and self-discipline. His intricate pen-and-ink drawings were exceptional with thousands of lines used for shading and images that drew the eye upward using tree trunks and cathedral columns. At 25 years old, Franklin landed in New York City and began illustrating advertisements, poems, and magazine articles. He illustrated literary works for Mark Twain, Theodore Dreiser, and Indiana's beloved poet, James Whitcomb Riley. Franklin and Dreiser agreed to travel by car from New York City to Terre Haute, Indiana, Dreiser's place of birth. Over the two-week trip, Dreiser would chronicle his observations with Booth and create over 30 sketches. *A Hoosier Holiday*—despite not being a work solely about Indiana as its title indicates—was published in 1916. (Clockwise from top left: courtesy of *Franklin Booth: American Illustrator*; courtesy of *Franklin Booth: American Illustrator;* author's collection.)

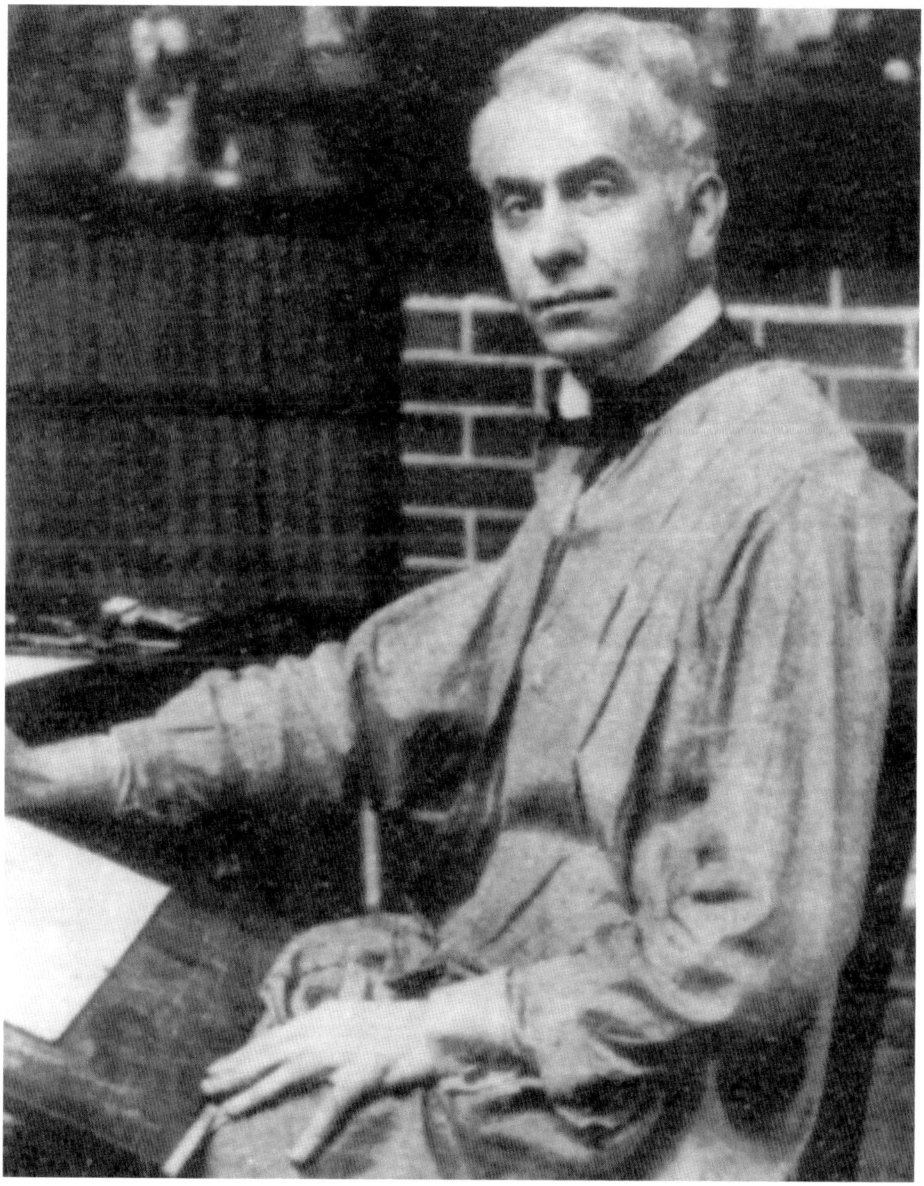

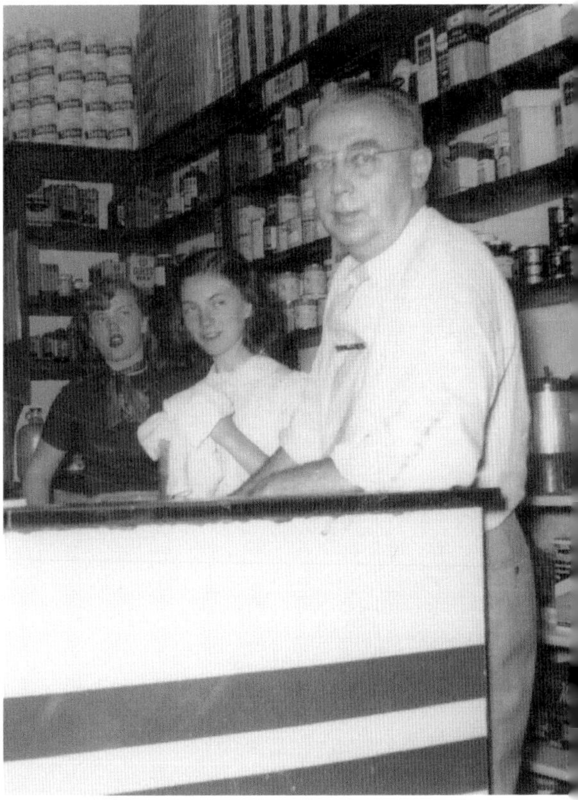

John W. Brown (1894–1980)

John Brown is seen behind the soda counter with employees in the late 1950s. John purchased the drugstore that bore his name on North Rangeline Road at auction in 1938. It was a place that Carmelites would hold in their hearts forever. The store was a pharmacy with a soda shop where students went after school and the adults went in the morning for coffee. (Courtesy of Rosalind Brown McCart.)

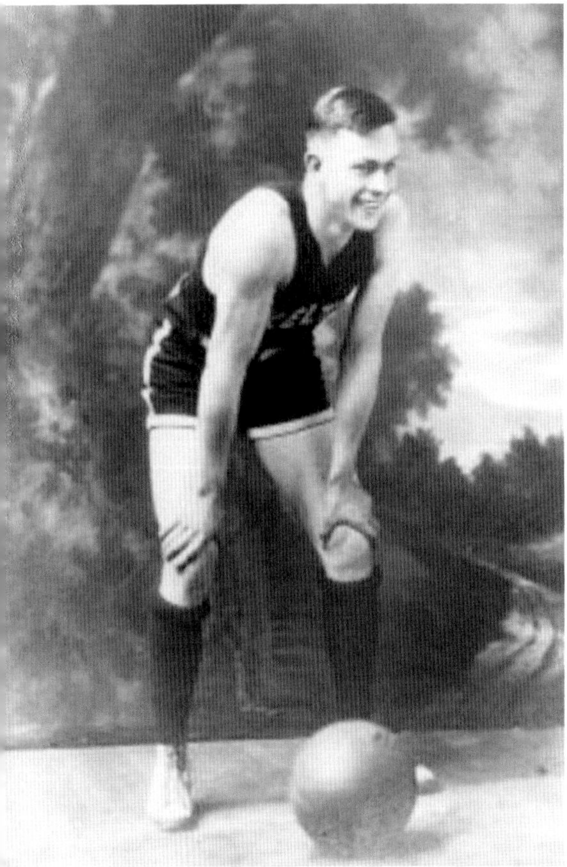

Sam H. Pursel (1897–1988)

A standout athlete of the Carmel High School class of 1916, Sam Pursel held the school record for a 4:52 mile in 1916. That record held for 10 years. Sam was owner of a gravel business and Delaware Township trustee in the 1950s. As trustee, one of his office's greatest accomplishments was the hiring of future CHS principal Dale Graham. (Courtesy of Carmel Clay Historical Society.)

CHAPTER THREE

The Quiet Years

Once Carmel was established with all of the amenities of small-town life, people settled in doing the business of the day. Life was peaceful. People were happy.

The Monon Railroad with cargo and passenger services ran from Louisville to Chicago through Indianapolis, thus giving it the name the CIL line. It had depots and made stops in most towns along its route, Carmel being one. With this regular service, farm and construction materials could be brought up from Indianapolis. The Monon, as it would be referred to, got its name from the Potawatomi Indian tribe and means "swift running." (In later years, after the service stopped and the tracks sat decades in disrepair, the city took it over and paved it, creating the Monon Greenway. It runs the entire length of the township and sees heavy use daily of walkers, joggers, and cyclists.)

In 1913, application was made by the Ladies' Wednesday Literary Club for a library, and the following year, a Carnegie library was built on East Main Street. (In 2013, multiple events celebrated the building's centennial year.) Also in 1913, there was a devastating flood across the middle United States that came after three days of heavy rain. Fatalities were reported in Indiana and Ohio, but none in Carmel. Businesses and homes that were damaged or destroyed were soon rebuilt.

By 1930, Carmel's population had increased to 682, and roads were more heavily traveled. In 1933, Meridian Street became US 31 taking the name away from the road that ran through downtown Carmel. It became Rangeline Road/Westfield Boulevard.

The population kept increasing but not at an alarming rate. Larger schools were in demand, especially by 1950 when the US census had Carmel with 1,009 residents. In 1957, the Metropolitan School District of Clay Township was formed. It would later become Carmel Clay Schools. In 1958, a new high was opened replacing the one later known as "Old North." Orchard Park Elementary opened in 1956, and Carmel Elementary followed it in 1961 with Tom Irvin at the helm as principal.

In 1962, plans would begin for what would change the face of Carmel—the construction of Keystone Avenue. It would run from 86th Street in Marion County to US 31 on the north side of town. The north side of town, where US 31 and Keystone met, would become known as "the Point." Don Dunkerly had built the Carmel Dairy Queen near there a few years before.

Between 1960 and 1970, Carmel's population would grow 364 percent to almost 7,000.

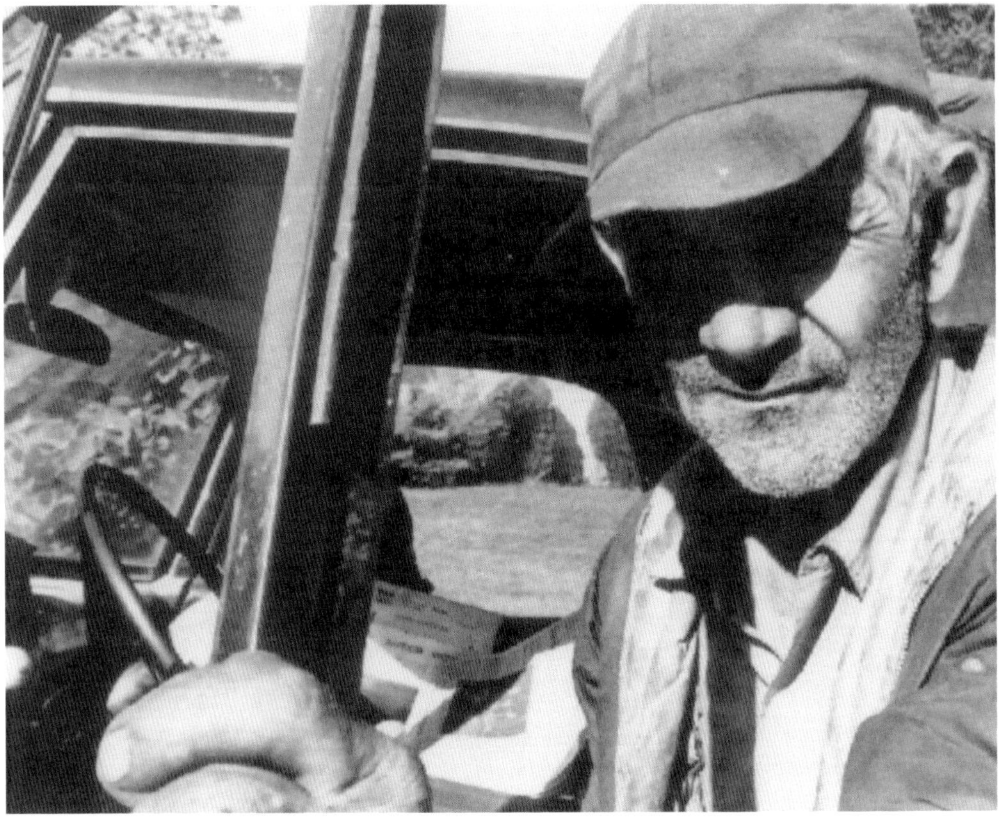

John W. "Two Gun" Brunson (1905–1984)

Many have written about diamonds in the rough, but none sum up John Brunson better than Roman poet Juvenal. Juvenal wrote, "Many individuals have, like uncut diamonds, shining qualities beneath a rough exterior." John was born on the outskirts of Indianapolis in 1905. Schooled only through the fifth grade and from a poor family, Brunson did not have many career options. John struck out on his own at an early age. Whether by choice or circumstance, it is not known, but he took advantage of a necessity of others and turned it into his livelihood. Throughout the 1950s, 1960s, and 1970s for a few dollars a month, John would come to people's houses in a beat-up pickup truck with wooden side gates and quietly haul their trash away. He would haul anything too—from paper grocery bags full of trash to a broken water heater. And somehow, this slight-in-stature man got it all into his truck by himself. The cab of the truck was crammed full with items tossed out by customers that John felt still had purpose or value. Most mornings before his route, John could be found hanging out at the downtown drugstore having coffee with the other regulars. If one ever needed to get a hold of him to haul something, he or she did so by dropping in there or calling and asking for him. There is more than one story in the lore of Carmel as to how John became Two Gun, but the nickname, for whatever reason behind it, stuck and stayed forever in the hearts and memories of Carmelites. Never married and no children of his own, Two Gun was rumored to have gifted children in need everything from an ice cream cone to college tuition. These were pretty generous deeds for an uneducated man doing a job no one else wanted. Never sell those rough, uncut diamonds short. They have more value than one might think when polished with the unconditional love of the impartial and innocent. (Courtesy of the Carmel Clay Historical Society.)

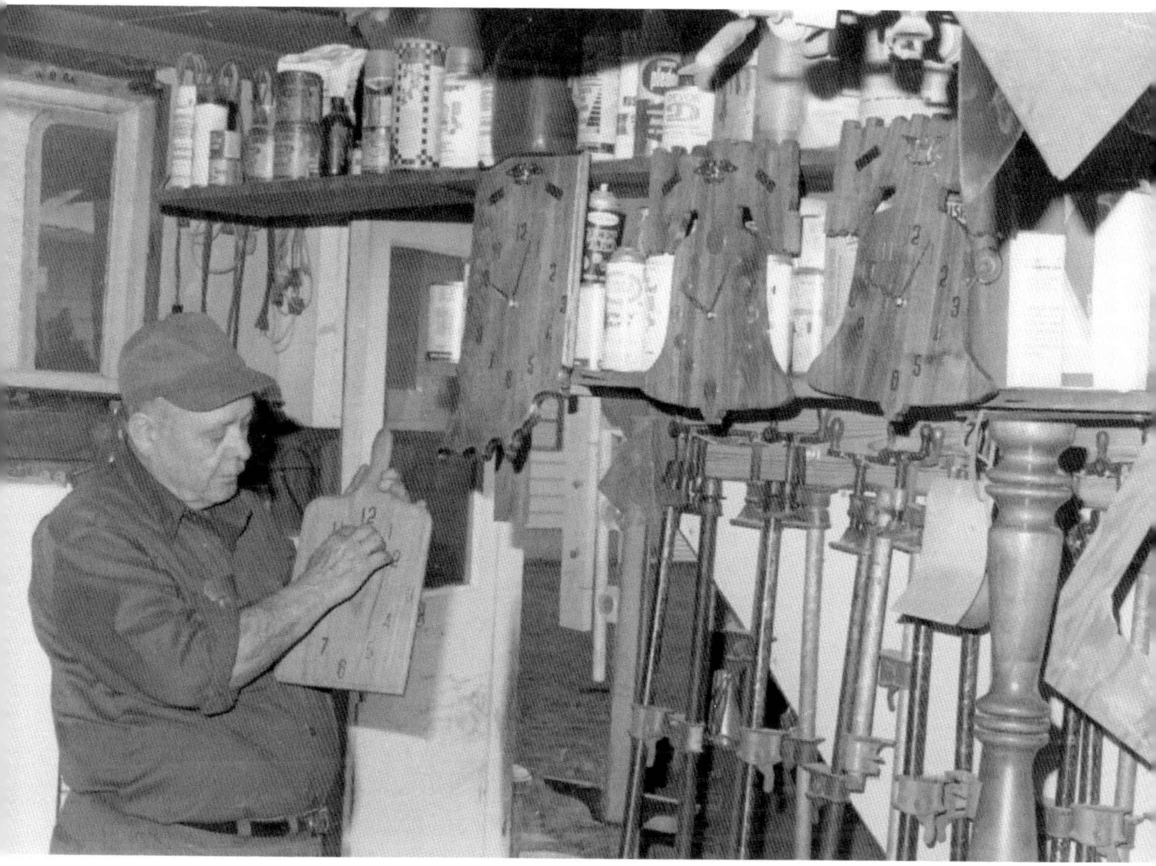

John M. Christy (1903–1991)
Born in Tipton County shortly after the turn of the century, John Milton Christy, Carmel's justice of the peace, was a carpenter and volunteer fireman for Carmel. (He also helped—again, as a volunteer—to build the first fire station.) Carmel benefitted from his readiness, and from 1939 to 1942, John was the superintendent of the water and street departments. Once retired, John could be found most days in his workshop in an old barn on property he owned near his home. Friends and family knew to find him there and would often stop by for a history lesson and a story or two. John was a skilled woodworker, and in and around 1976, America's bicentennial, he produced numerous clocks shaped like Indiana and the Liberty Bell. (Both, courtesy of Dale Christy.)

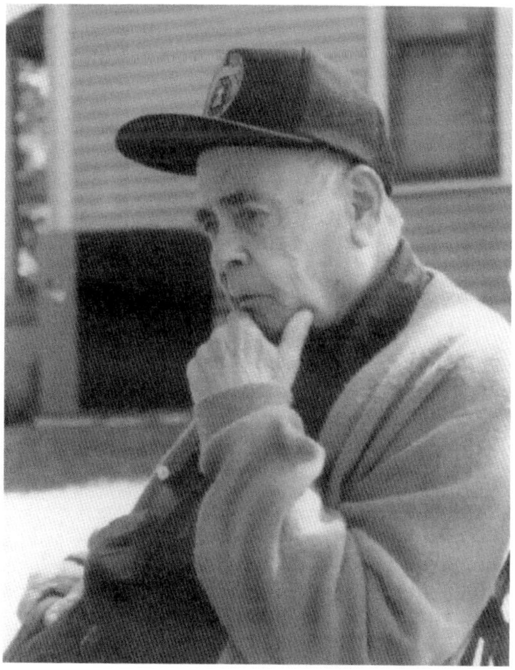

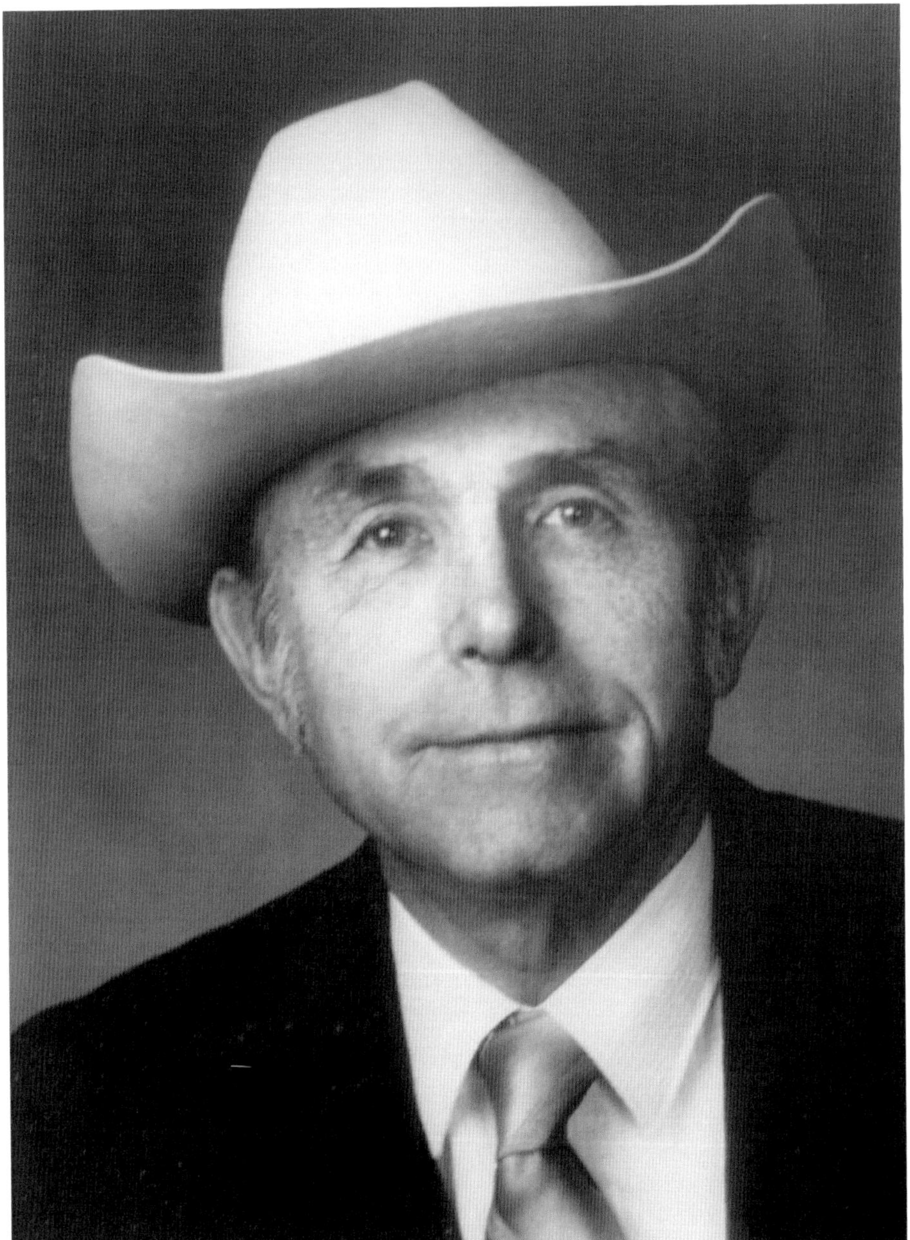

Robert C. Peterson (1923–)
In the mid-1960s, Lynnwood Farm, a Purdue University research facility, was in need of a good man to manage its 623-acre operation, located where Northview Church and Plum Creek subdivisions and golf course sit today. Bob Peterson, a Ball State graduate and holder of a master's degree in animal science from Purdue, would become the farm's superintendent. This was no small feat with the acreage and the number of buildings there were, but Bob handled it with great skill and organization. Raising five children on the farm, he and his wife, Trudy, would remain there until 1988, when he retired and the farm was sold to developers. Bob is most proud of being inducted into the Indiana Livestock Breeders Hall of Fame by his peers. (Courtesy of Ann Peterson Day.)

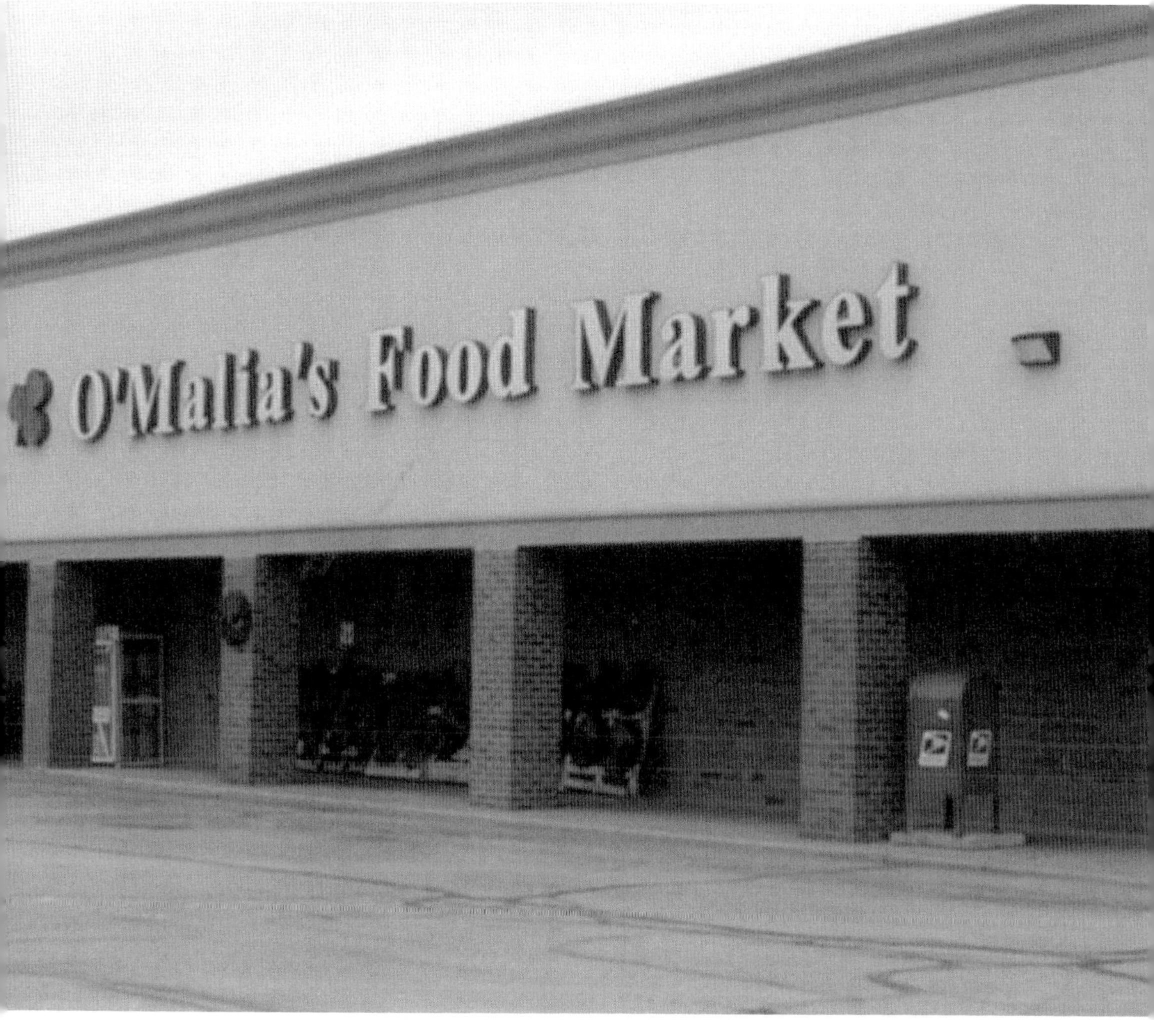

George J. "Joe" O'Malia (1920–1996)
In the late 1960s, Joe O'Malia had the foresight to know what Carmel would soon become with the extension of Keystone Avenue north from 86th Street. In 1970, when Carmel's population was a mere 6,600, Joe opened his first of many grocery stores at 126th Street and Gray Road. Carmel's population would explode, and he would go on to own and operate three more stores in the Carmel area and then branch out into Hamilton and eventually Marion County. O'Malia's stores held a comfortable, small-town feel not like the bigger chain stores in the area. In 2001, Marsh Supermarkets purchased the group and eventually renamed the stores; however, the original store still carries the original O'Malia name.

Loren W. "Lefty" Haskett (1920–2008)

As a young man of 23, Carmel native Loren Haskett went up Easy Red Sector of Omaha Beach on D-Day and survived. Loren, who picked up the nickname "Lefty" in the Army, settled into a quiet life of farming with his wife and young family after his medical discharge from the US Army in 1945. He was a skilled mechanic always working on someone's car, truck, tractor, or mower—but never for money. In 1961, when farming was no longer lucrative, he became a letter carrier with the Carmel Post Office. After a walking route in the city, he became Carmel's first rural route carrier and delivered mail on the east side of Keystone until his retirement in 1986.

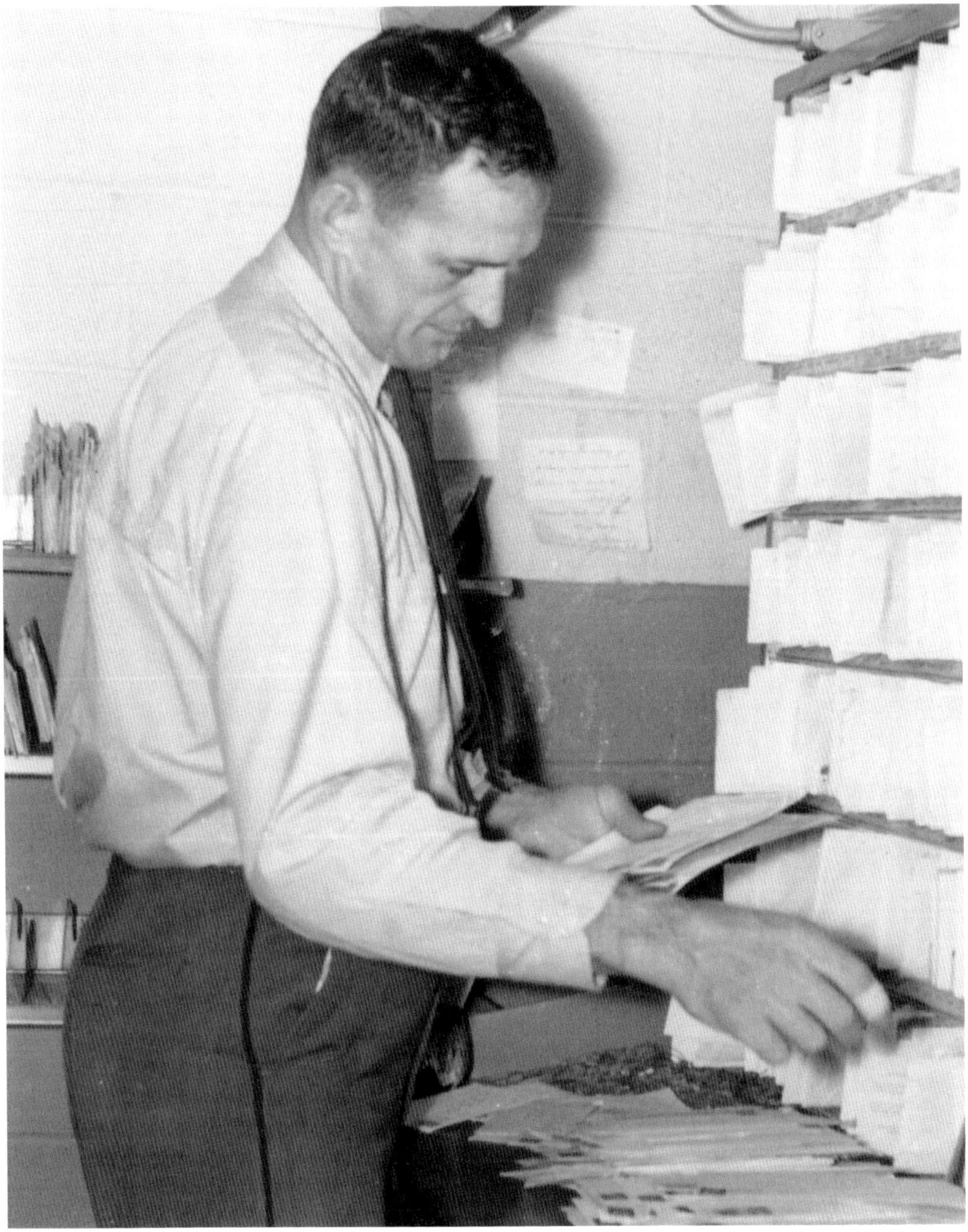

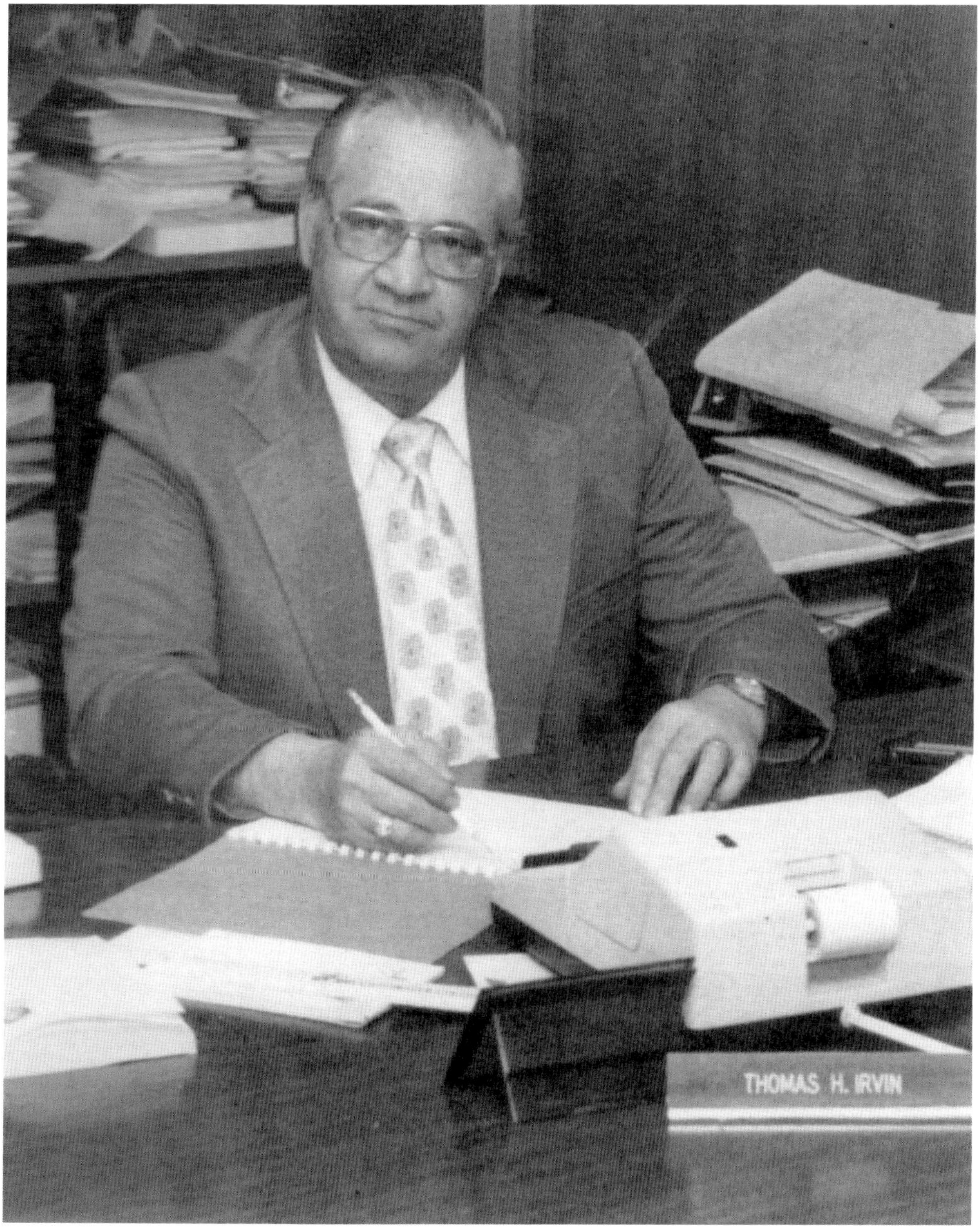

Dr. Thomas H. Irvin (1923–2003)
Virginia native Tom Irvin arrived in Carmel in the late 1950s after serving during World War II with the US Army. He began teaching and coaching the varsity basketball team at Carmel High School. In 1961, when Carmel Elementary School was opened, he was the inaugural principal. He soon took a job in administration with Carmel Clay Schools and served as curriculum director and then assistant superintendent for 16 years. Dr. Irvin was instrumental in the development of a public pool for the community, which was eventually constructed to the north of Carmel Junior High School on Guilford Road. He also served as a police commissioner for Carmel and was the Hamilton County Veterans Affairs officer. (Courtesy of the 1976 Carmel High School yearbook, *Pinnacle*.)

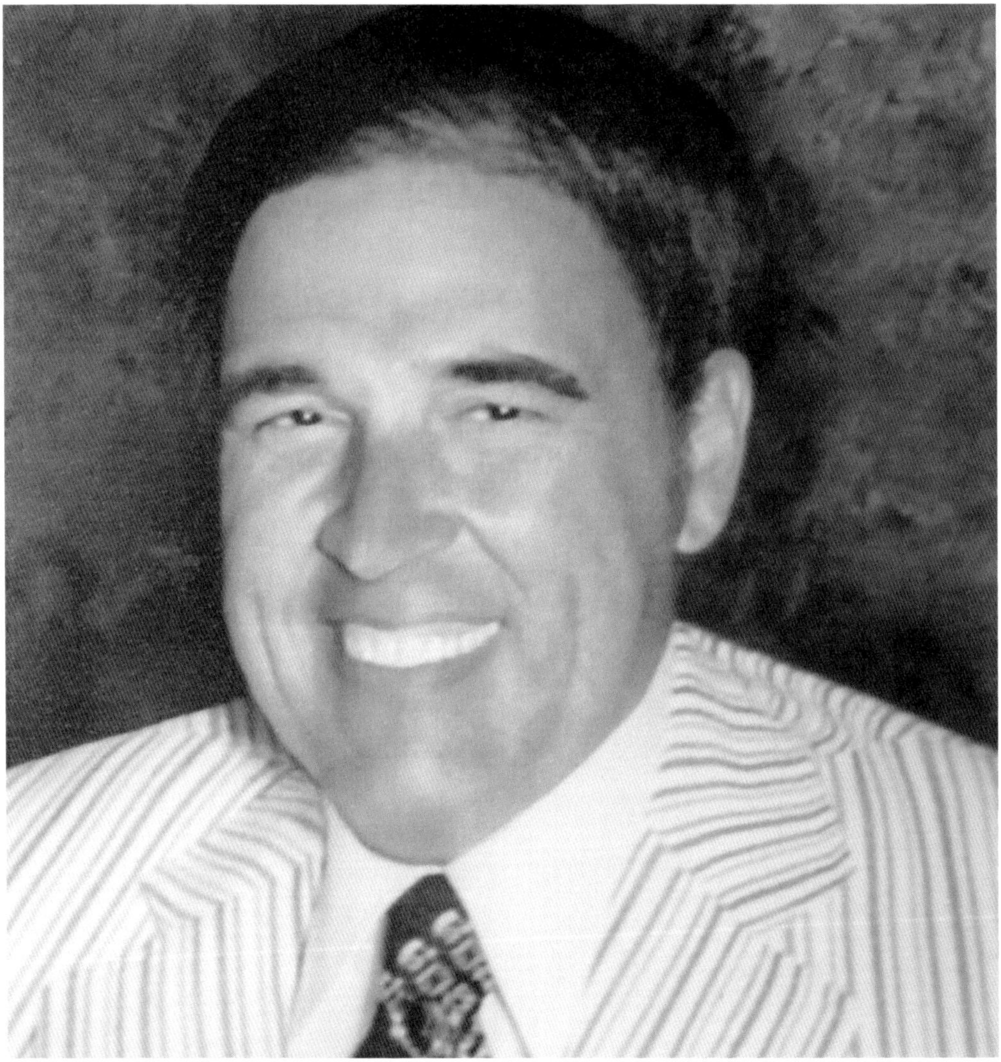

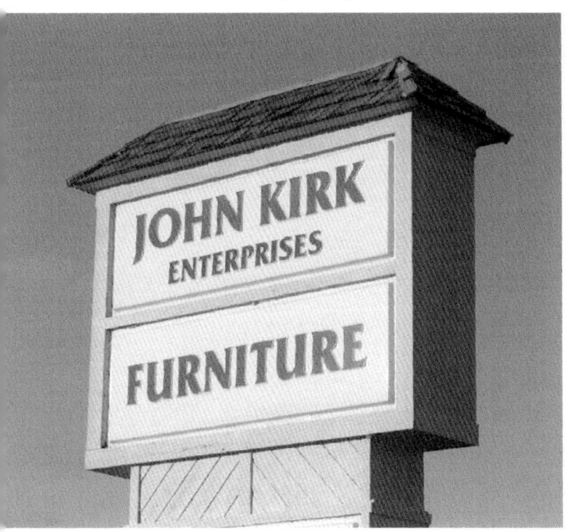

John T. Kirk (1929–2015)

While its only neighbor used to be a trailer park, John Kirk Furniture Galleries now sits among luxury hotels, a grocery superstore, and office buildings. John Kirk was born in Carmel and was a 1947 graduate of Carmel High School. In 1952, he opened John Kirk Furniture Galleries, located exactly where it is today. Not many businesses can boast about that history and esteem. Able to sell anything and banking on growth in Carmel, John expanded to boats and real estate. He and his wife, Edith, raised their family on the family's farm in western Clay Township. John was a recipient of the State of Indiana's Sagamore of the Wabash and was named honorary lieutenant governor as well. (Above, courtesy of the *Indianapolis Star*; left, author's collection.)

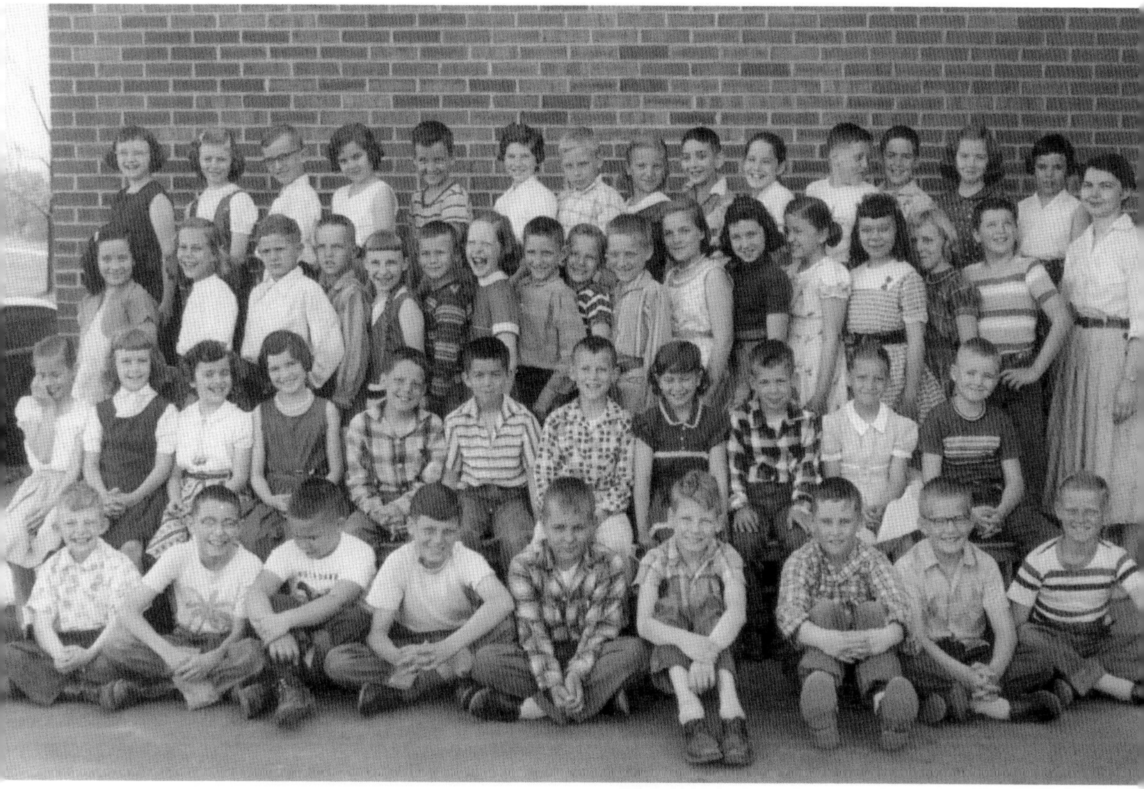

Phyllis E. (Horton) Rockhill (1924–)
The daughter of Carmel merchant Oakley Horton, Phyllis was born in Noblesville but moved to Carmel when her father opened his butcher shop/meat market in 1926. A Carmel High School graduate of 1942, she attended Butler University and soon secured a job as a teacher with Carmel Clay Schools. She is pictured above (third row on the right) with her first class at Orchard Park Elementary. These students would go on to make up a part of the class of 1965. Phyllis moved to Carmel Elementary, where she taught fourth grade until her retirement. It is impressive that she can still recall students' names by their pictures. She received the Heritage Award from the Carmel Clay Historical Society in 2014. (Above, courtesy of Phyllis Rockhill; right, photograph by Jennifer D. Hershberger.)

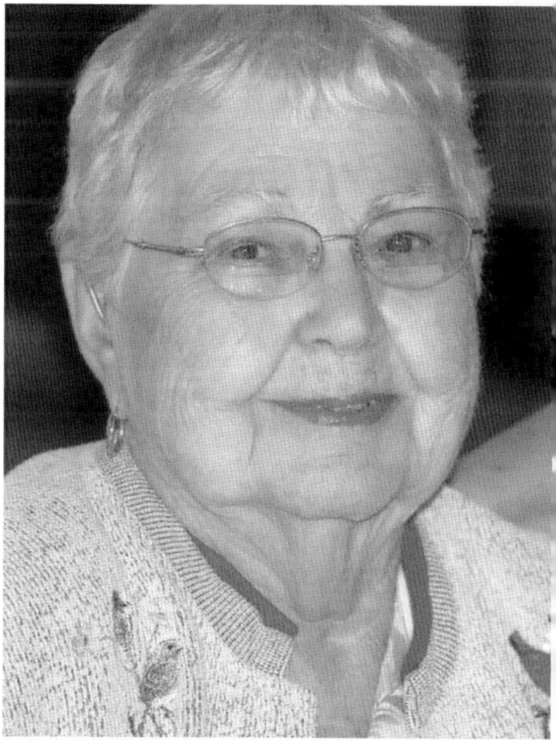

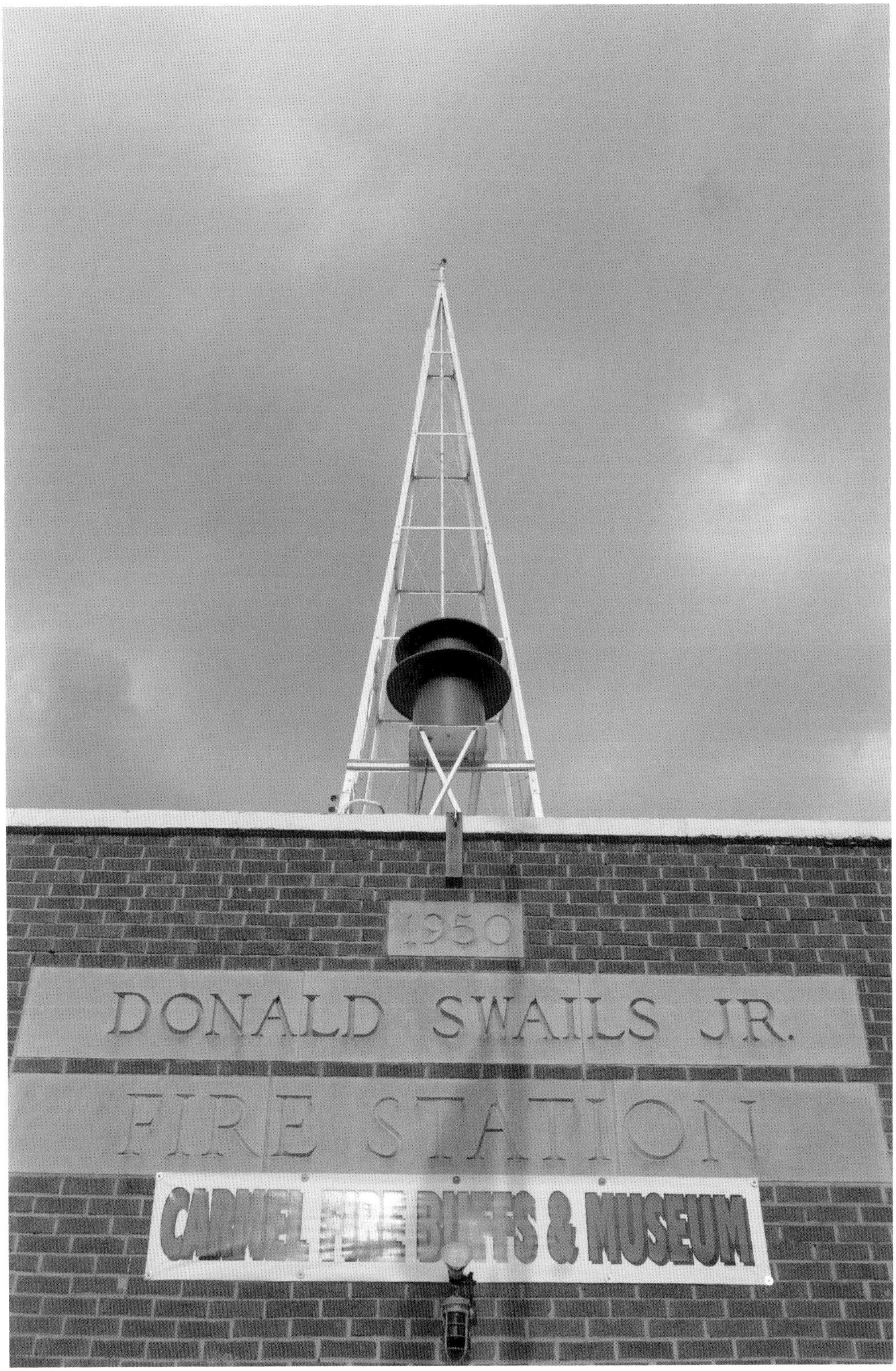
1950
DONALD SWAILS JR.
FIRE STATION
CARMEL FIRE BUFFS & MUSEUM

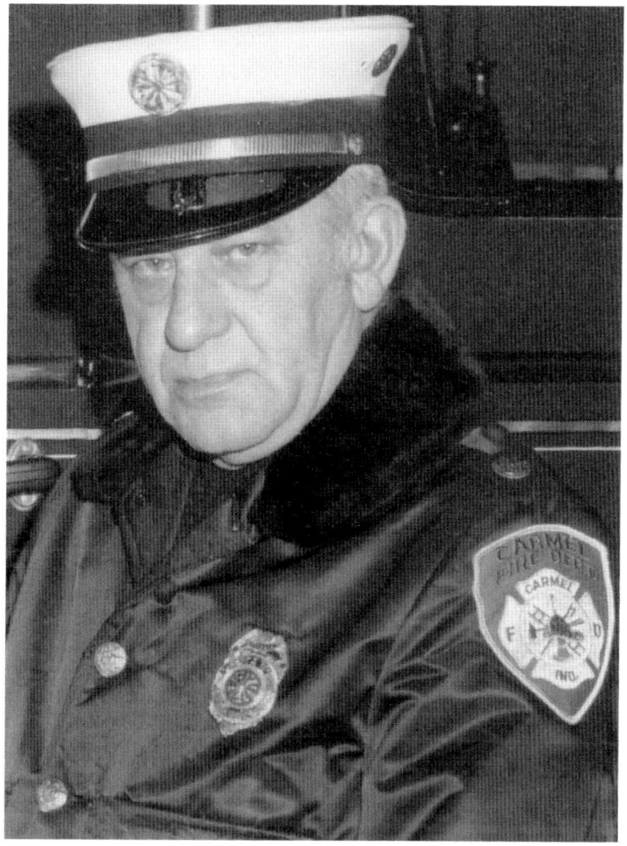

Donald Swails Jr. (1917–1982)
Below, Donald Swails, Carmel's fire chief, receives a monetary donation raised by Carmel's Boy Scout Pack 131 in 1973. Swails, a Lebanon, Indiana, native, made a significant impact on the Carmel Fire Department. After working for a telephone company and pitching in semiprofessional baseball for extra cash, he landed in Carmel to foster an interest that he claimed every young boy has. He wanted to be a fireman. As fire chief, he was Carmel's first-paid municipal employee in 1952 and held the position for 30-plus years. Upon his death, Swails was the only fire chief Carmel had ever had. (Clockwise from top left, photograph by Jennifer D. Hershberger; courtesy of Deborah Swails Collins; courtesy of Deborah Swails Collins.)

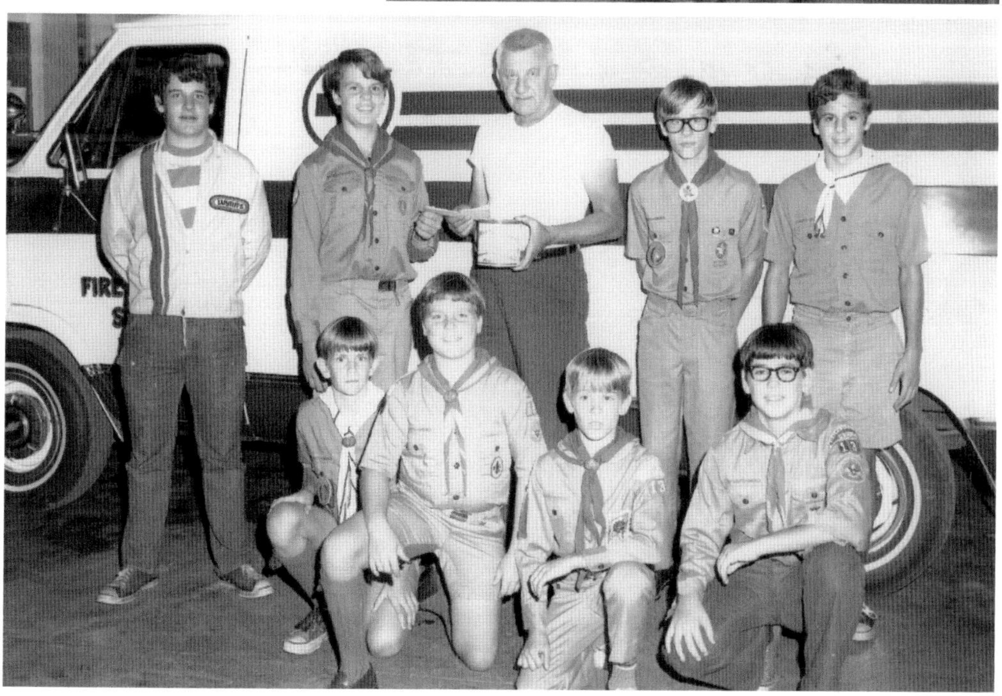

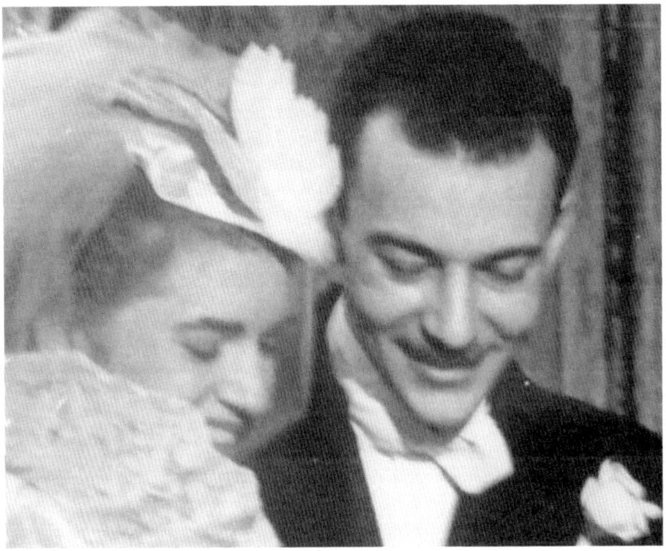

Avriel J. (Christie) Shull (1931—1976)

Thornhurst Addition on West Main Street in Carmel has been listed in the National Register of Historic Places since 2010. After graduating from Carmel High School in 1948, Avriel Christie attended Butler University and Herron Art School in Indianapolis. She started her own art business, got married, and shifted her focus to architectural design and construction, all within a span of three years. Her husband, Richard K. Shull, was a columnist for an Indianapolis newspaper. Their 1951 wedding was featured in *LIFE* magazine. Avriel went on to design numerous housing additions, homes, apartment complexes, country clubs, and shopping centers across the United States. She was doing it all in a time when most post–World War II women were keeping house. (Left, courtesy of Bambi Shull Stonebraker; below, photograph by Jennifer D. Hershberger.)

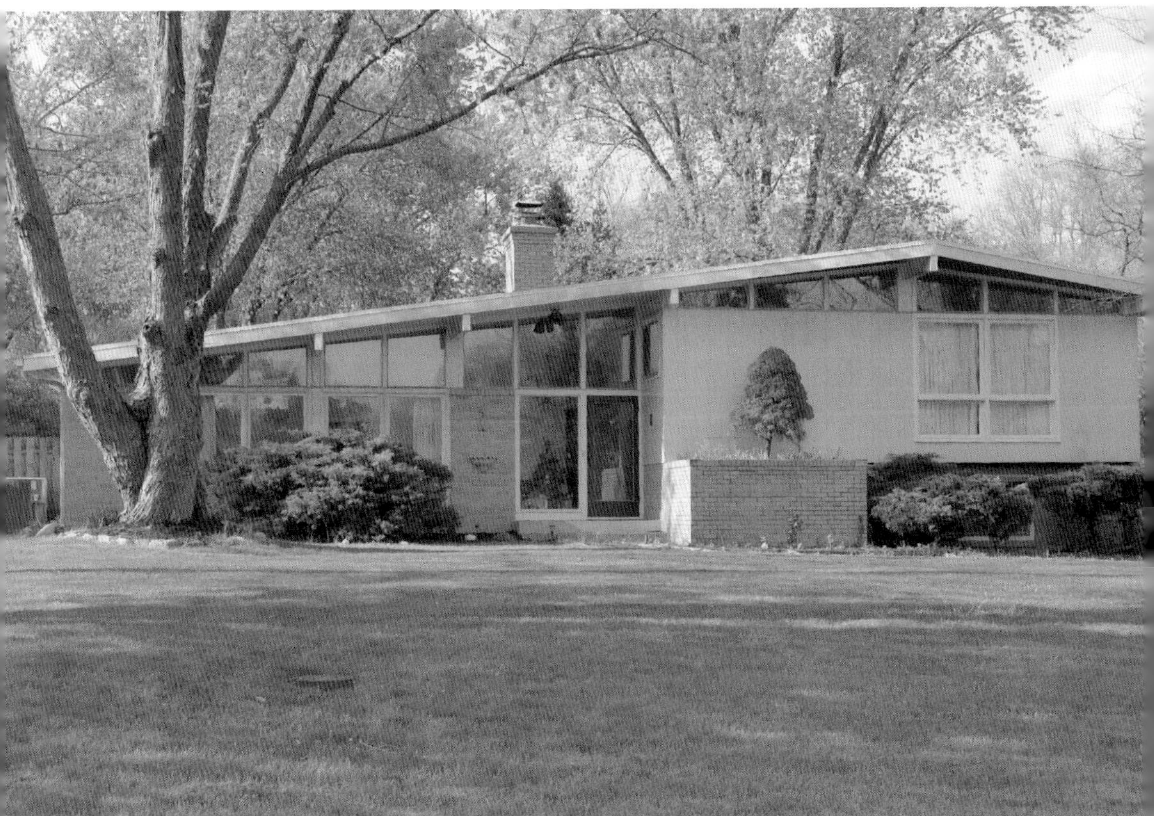

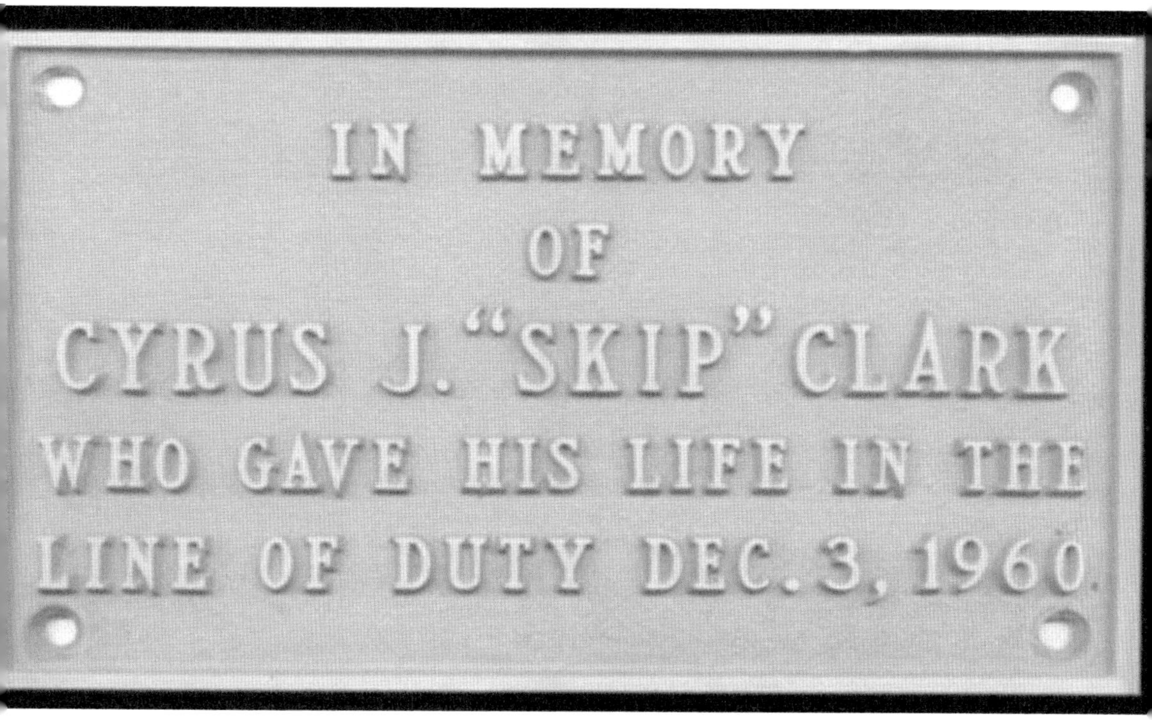

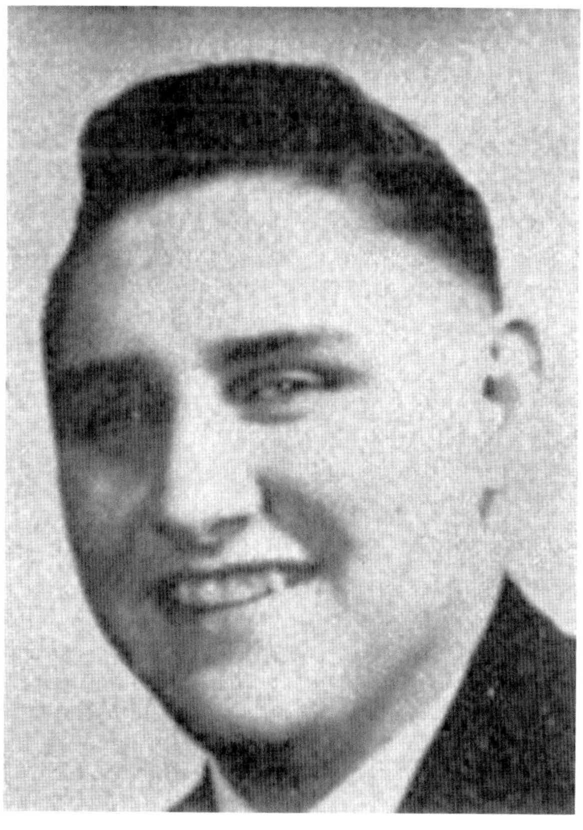

Cyrus J. "Skip" Clark Jr. (1933–1960)

Carmel has lost only one firefighter in the line of duty during its years as a volunteer and paid department. That firefighter was assistant chief Skip Clark. During the early days of the month of December 1960, temperatures were unseasonably warm reaching the 50-degree mark for several days in a row. Responding to a grass fire, Skip Clark and another firefighter left the station in the department's modified Jeep that was able to maneuver through fields to reach such fires. On the way, they encountered a car that they had to swerve to avoid and that sent them into a ditch. Upon attempting to get out of the ditch, the Jeep overturned, and Skip Clark perished. He was only 27 years old and left behind a wife and four young children. (Above, courtesy of the OMNI Centre for Public Media, Inc.; right, courtesy of the 1951 Carmel High School yearbook, *Pinnacle*.)

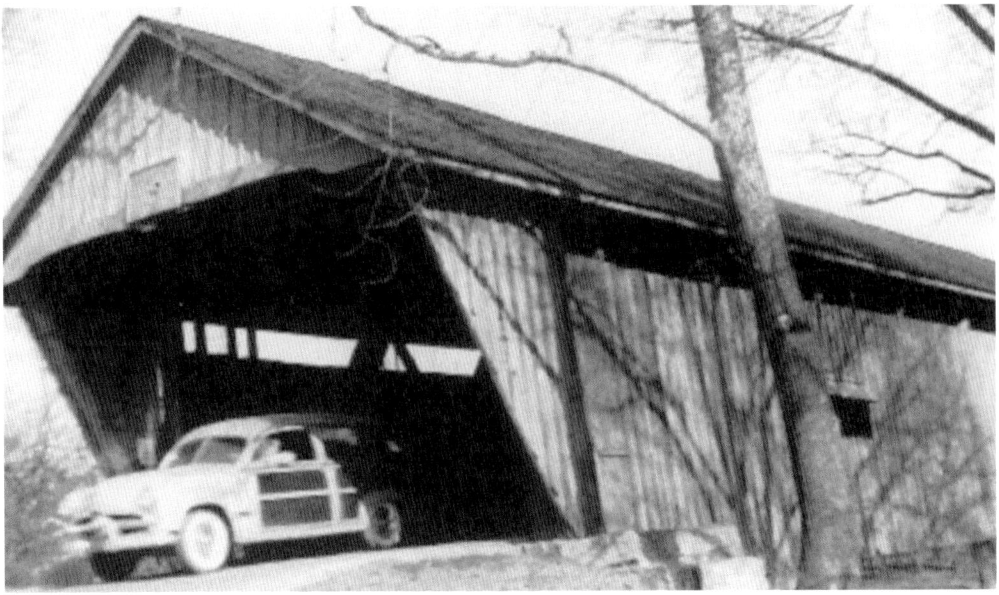

Eller-Heady Bridge Arsonists (1957)

One of Carmel's great unsolved mysteries is that of who set the fire that destroyed the Eller-Heady covered bridge. Built in 1869, the bridge spanned White River on what is now 116th Street. In 1957, it connected Carmel in Clay Township to Fishers in Delaware Township. The Clay Township border had been moved in 1954 from Rangeline Road to the river. On the night of October 6, 1957, the arsonist(s) doused the historic wooden bridge with an accelerant, likely gasoline, and set fire to it. In minutes, the bridge was at the bottom of White River. The loss of the bridge was devastating and a disadvantage for the county as it was on a major east–west thoroughfare. A new bridge would not replace it until 1959. (Above, courtesy of Carmel Clay Historical Society; below, courtesy of the *Noblesville Daily Ledger*, 1957.)

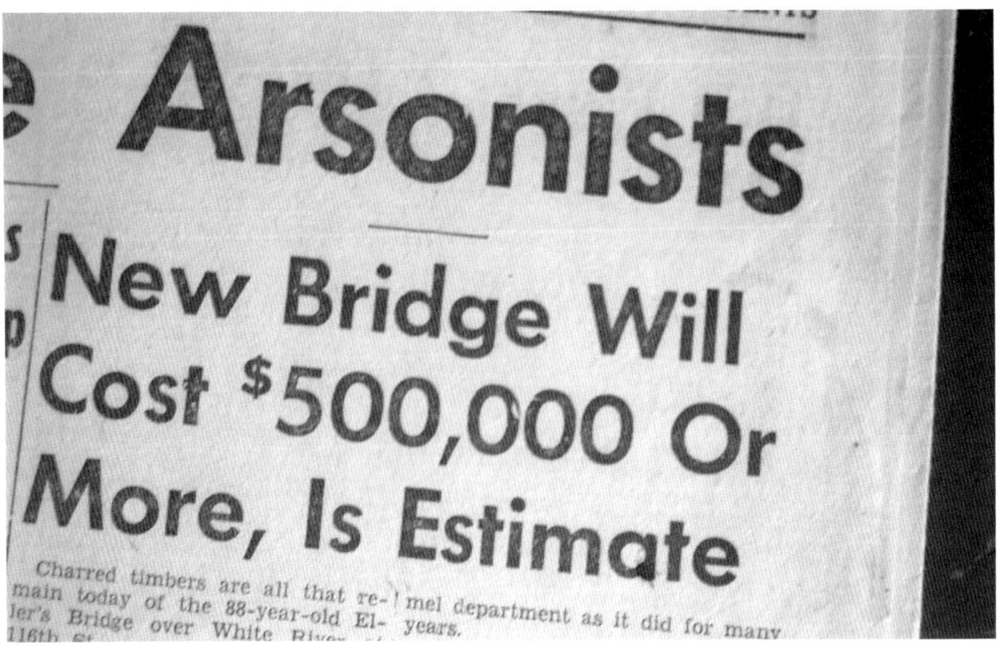

Arsonists

New Bridge Will Cost $500,000 Or More, Is Estimate

Charred timbers are all that re-
main today of the 88-year-old El-
ler's Bridge over White River

mel department as it did for many
years.

David F. Causey (1930–2014)

A grandson of Vice Pres. Charles Fairbanks, David Causey resided on the family property east of Carmel situated on Cool Creek. David married Barbara Hinkle, daughter of Butler University's renowned basketball coach Tony Hinkle. David was an avid car-racing enthusiast, and he and his twin brother, Dean, built a dirt track on the farm. David would win his first major race at the Road America 500 in 1960. Cricklewood Farm was founded by the twins and was a large Holstein dairy farm. The brothers were always trying innovative procedures and used hydroponics on site. The large property where the Causeys resided straddles Cool Creek, and a housing addition bears the Cricklewood name today. (Courtesy of the *Indianapolis Star*, 2014.)

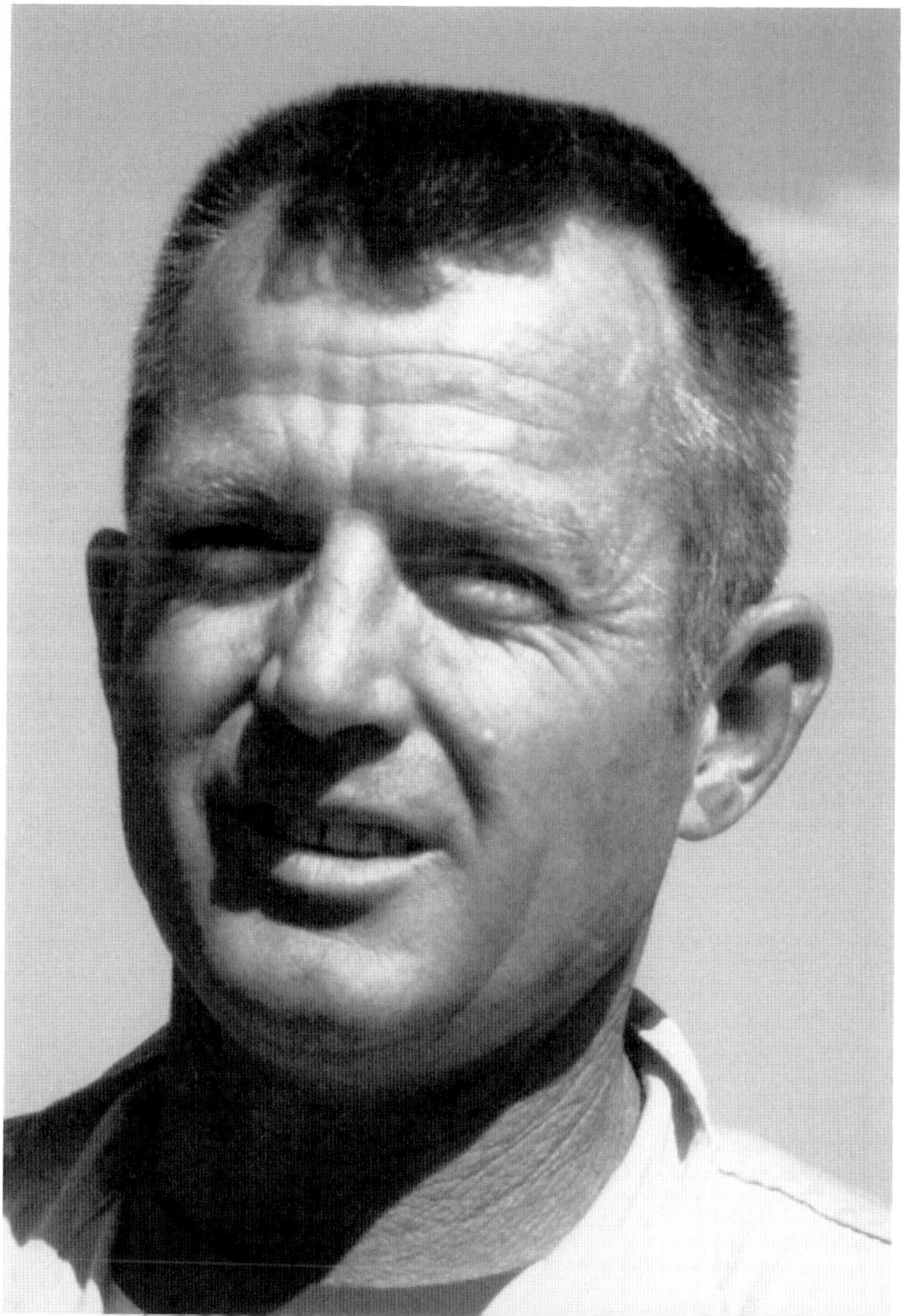

Gerald L. Adams (1927–2002)

In Carmel's growing years, the community was fortunate to have a deep pool of qualified volunteers who eventually became paid employees as Carmel prospered. Born in 1927 in Marshall, Indiana, Gerald Adams and his family moved to Carmel in 1929. A Carmel High School class of 1945 graduate, he attended Butler University. He became a volunteer fireman for Carmel in 1941 at the age of 14. Gerald became Carmel's assistant fire chief (a paid position) and served for two years. He and his wife, Mildred, lived directly across the street from the fire station to make it more convenient for him to respond to any call that might come in. (Courtesy of Luanne Hodgin.)

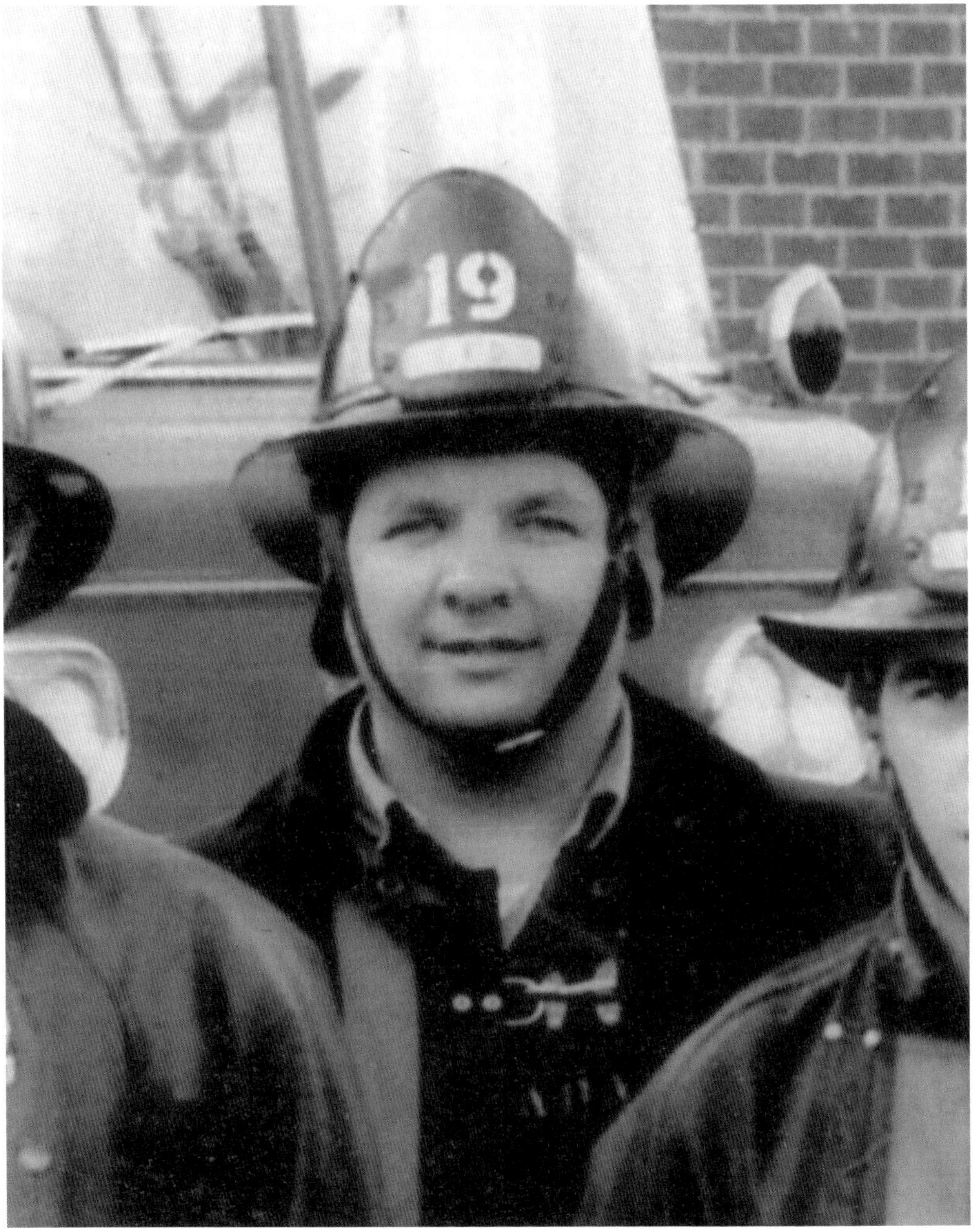

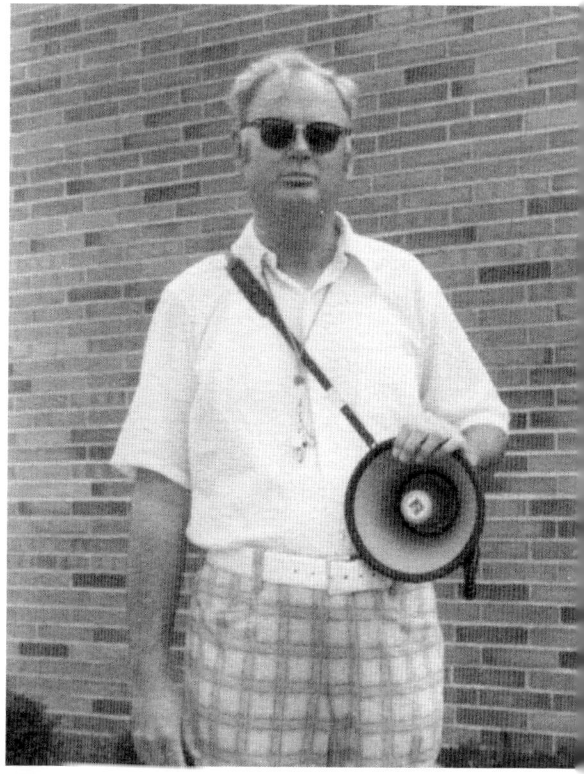

Benjamin E. Loveall (1926–2008)
The son of an accomplished musician, as well as a musician himself from age nine, Ben Loveall landed at Carmel High School in 1960 as the band department head. After high school, the Jasper, Indiana, native joined the US Army, where he played in several dance bands, entertaining the troops. After graduation from Butler's Jordan School of Music, he taught 23 years at Carmel, retiring in 1982. Marching band students will always remember him with his trusty bullhorn on his shoulder. His most favorite musical event at CHS was the spring production of *Allegro*. He would write the entire program, which involved the concert bands and the dance group, the Coquettes. *Allegro* always concluded with a big finish, like a Las Vegas show, and had elaborate costumes and pageantry. (Both, courtesy of the 1976 Carmel High School yearbook, *Pinnacle*.)

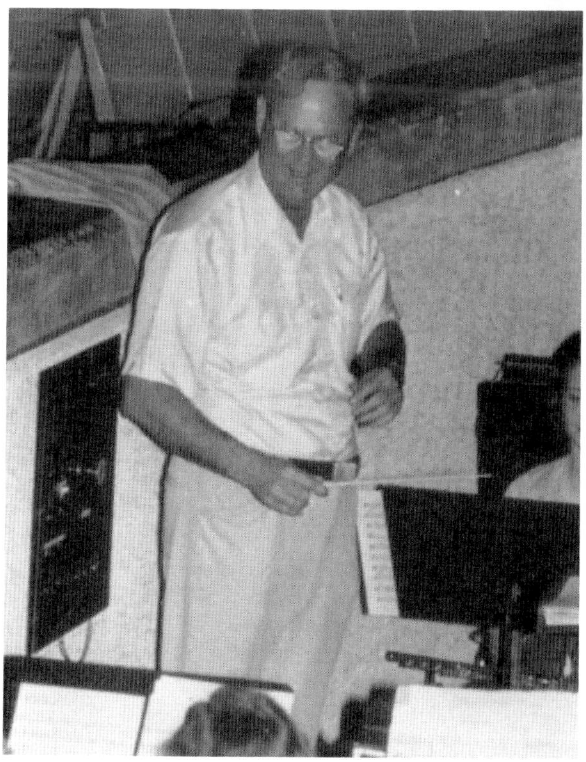

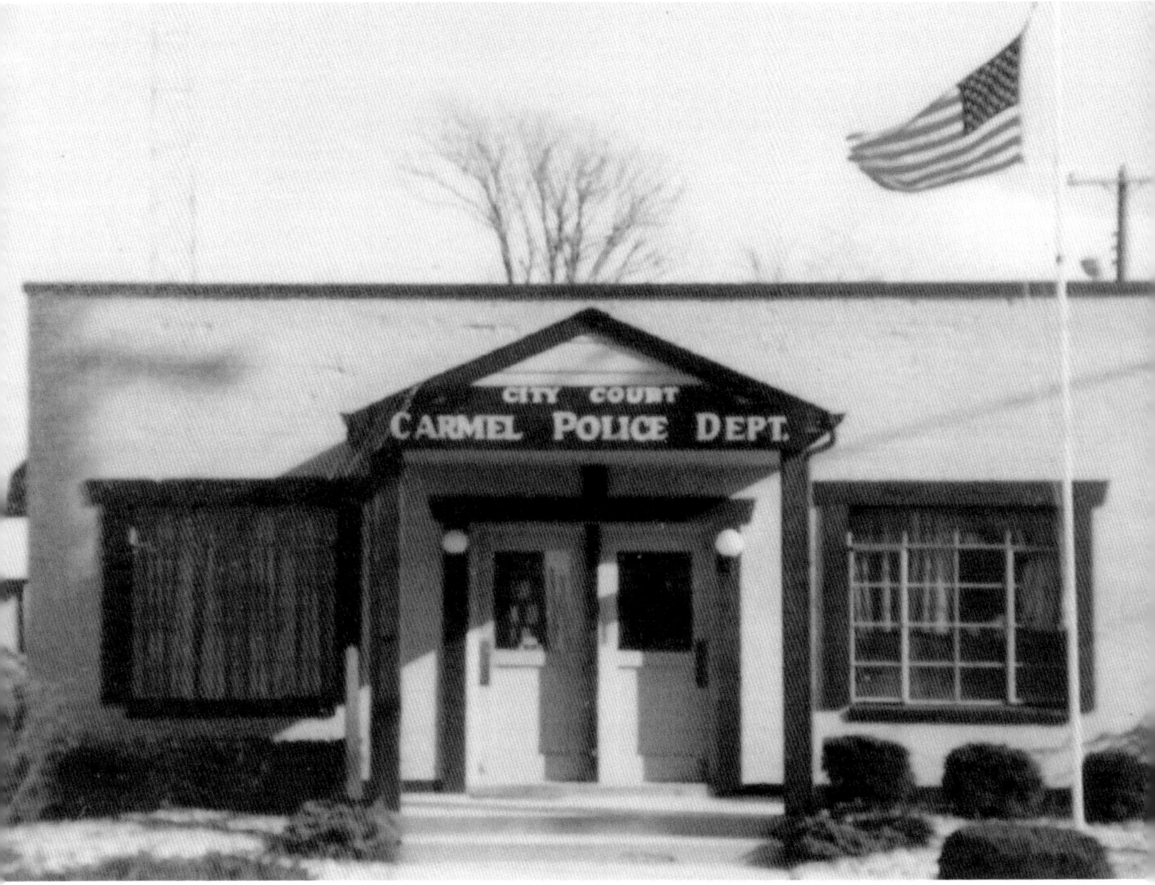

Mary E. (Lowe) Davis (1925–2014)

Before one could download an app for smartphones, police and fire runs, weather warnings, and civil defense drills were broadcast on Bearcat and Uniden radio scanners that could be purchased for the home. Different departments used different frequencies that could be secured by scanner owners in the form of a crystal placed inside the unit to receive that department's radio transmissions. For decades, a familiar voice on Carmel's police frequency was that of dispatcher Mary Davis. Mary landed in Carmel to live and raise a family after meeting her future husband, Richard, at a USO dance in Greenville, South Carolina, while he was serving in the Army Air Corps during World War II. Richard was from the Indianapolis area, and that is where they chose to raise their family. Mary filled her free time working for the City of Carmel in the capacity of an assistant to the clerk-treasurer and building commissioner. Mary and Richard were charter members of Our Lady of Mount Carmel Catholic Church (OLMC). Mary was a founding member of the Carmel Fire Department Ladies Auxiliary and was named Woman of the Year by the Business and Professional Women's Club. She volunteered for OLMC Women's Club, the Carmel Clay School Board, Carmel Clay Historical Society, and the Home Place Area Lions Club. (Above, courtesy of Carmel Clay Historical Society; opposite, courtesy of Dick Davis.)

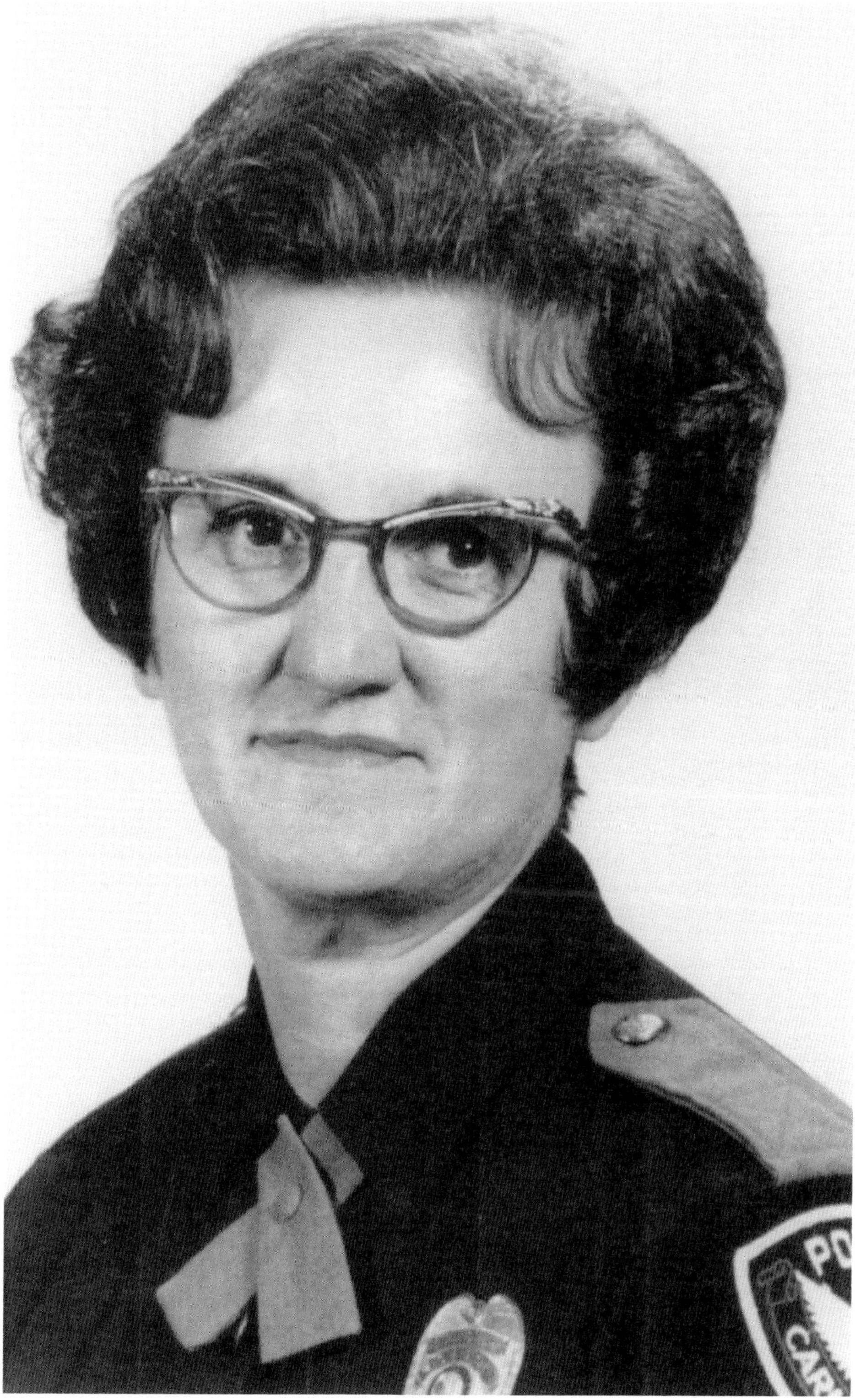

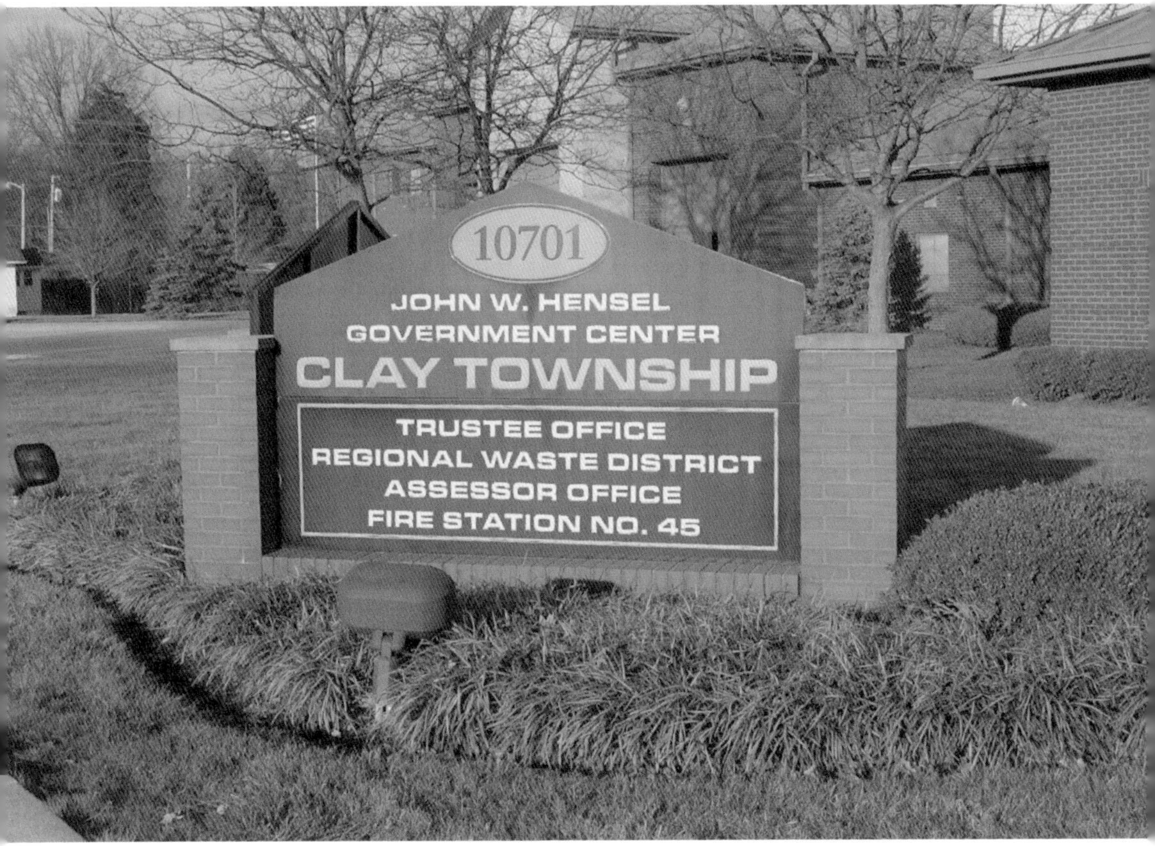

John W. Hensel (1930–1997)
Born and raised in Carmel, John graduated from Carmel High School in 1948. After graduation, he joined the US Army and served in Korea. John's family farm on 106th Street was purchased in 1969 for a school. Forest Dale Elementary, which opened in 1974, carries the name of the Hensel farm. John went on to serve as Clay Township Trustee for many years, giving tirelessly to the government business of the township. The John W. Hensel Government Center, located just north of 106th Street on College Avenue, handles the daily business today. John and his wife, Rosemary, were both township advocates for many years. (Author's collection.)

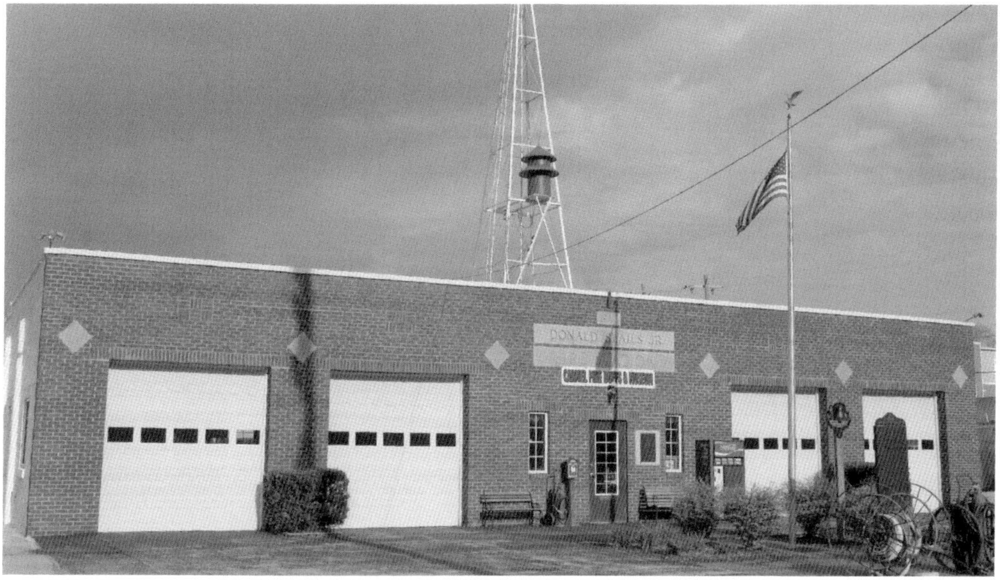

James K. Martin (1942–)

Jim Martin is a retired career firefighter. A Carmel native and Carmel High School graduate of 1960, he began his career with Carmel Fire Department and worked there as assistant fire chief until his retirement. Once retired, Jim founded the Carmel Fire Buffs & Fire Department Museum, which is housed in the old main fire station. The museum is a nonprofit organization and houses former Carmel fire vehicles as well as some acquired from the area and department memorabilia. It is a regular stop on the Carmel Clay Historical Society's elementary school walking tours of downtown Carmel. Jim gives endless hours working on engines, washing and waxing vehicles, and sometimes taking vehicles to shows across the state. (Both photographs by Jennifer D. Hershberger.)

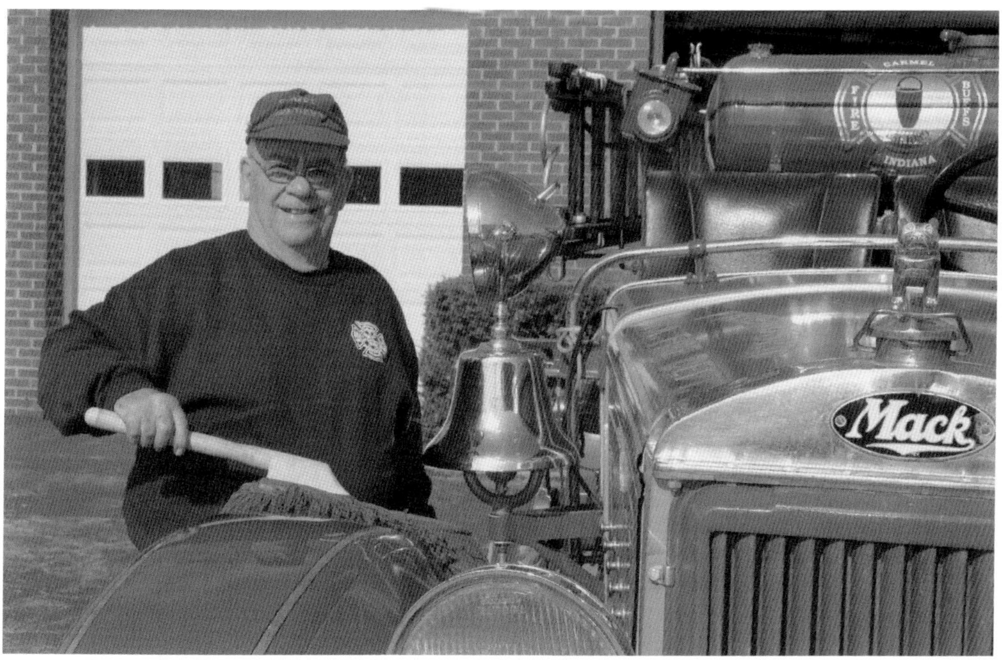

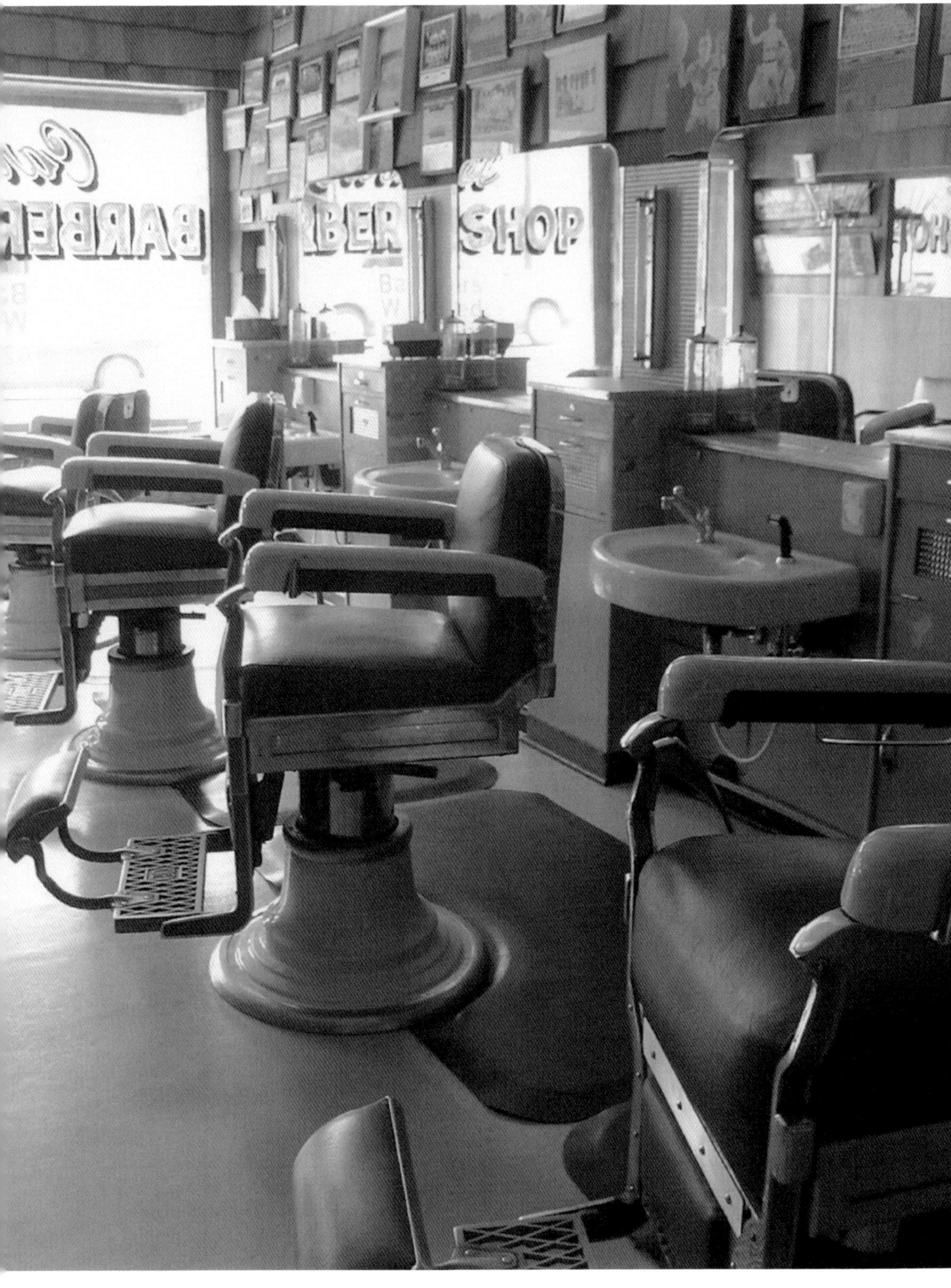

Richard P. "Dick" Ramsey (1931–2009)

Most high school athletes in the 1940s were required to keep their hair cut short and clean. Dick and his brother always patronized Bill Beard's barbershop on West Main Street. Dick graduated from Carmel High School in 1949 and joined the US Army in 1952. Coming to the decision that he wanted to become a barber and having been in touch with Bill over the years, he enrolled in barber school in the fall of 1959. The following year, he began barbering in Bill's barbershop. In the early 1970s, he purchased half of the barbershop from Buck Buckles. Barber Joe Rogers purchased the other half from Bill Beard. Dick bought the shop outright from Joe in 1983 and managed it until his retirement. At left, the Carmel Barber Shop sits clean and silent just before Dick Ramsey and his wife, Janice, lock the door for the final time. (Both, courtesy of Janice Ramsey.)

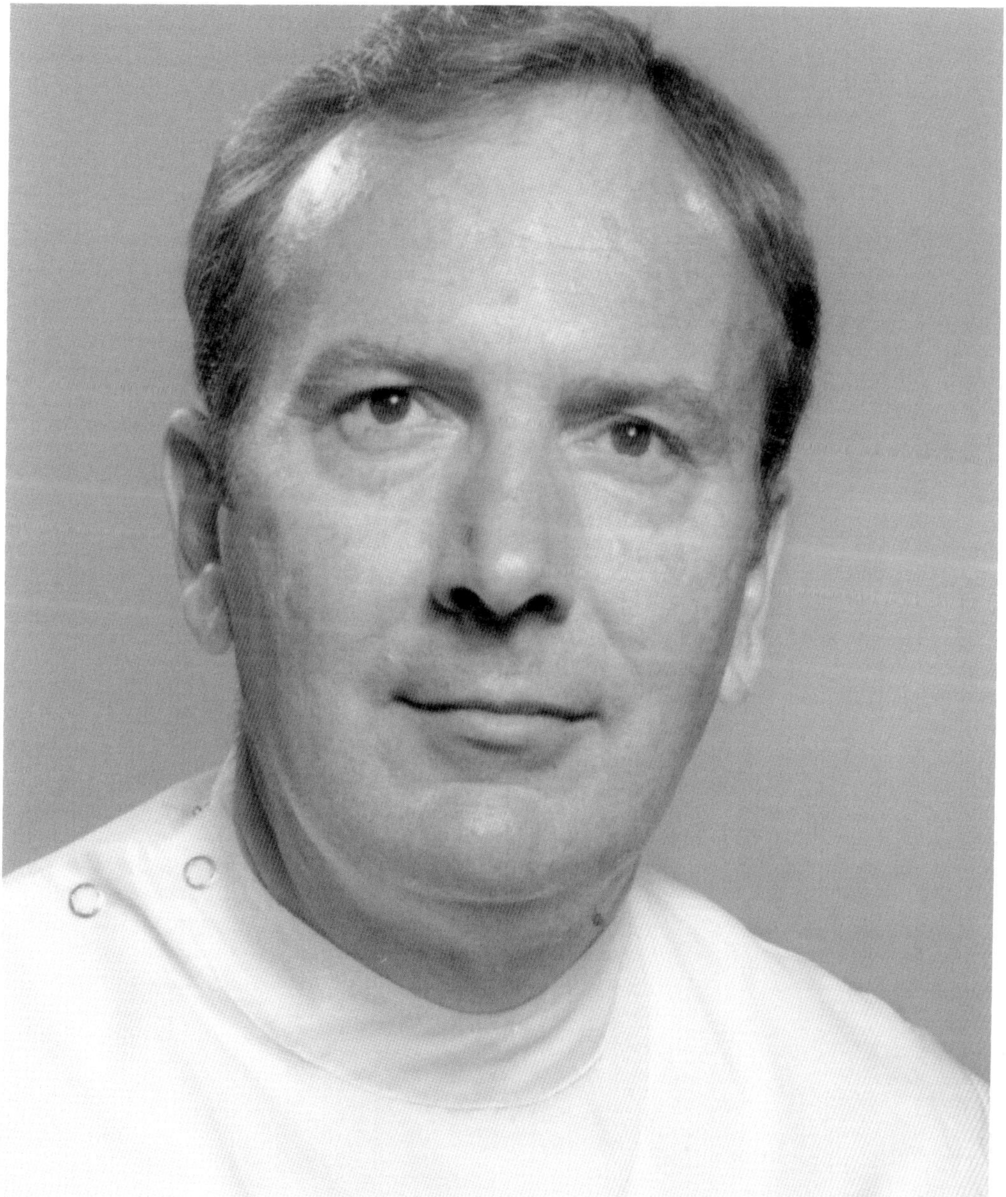

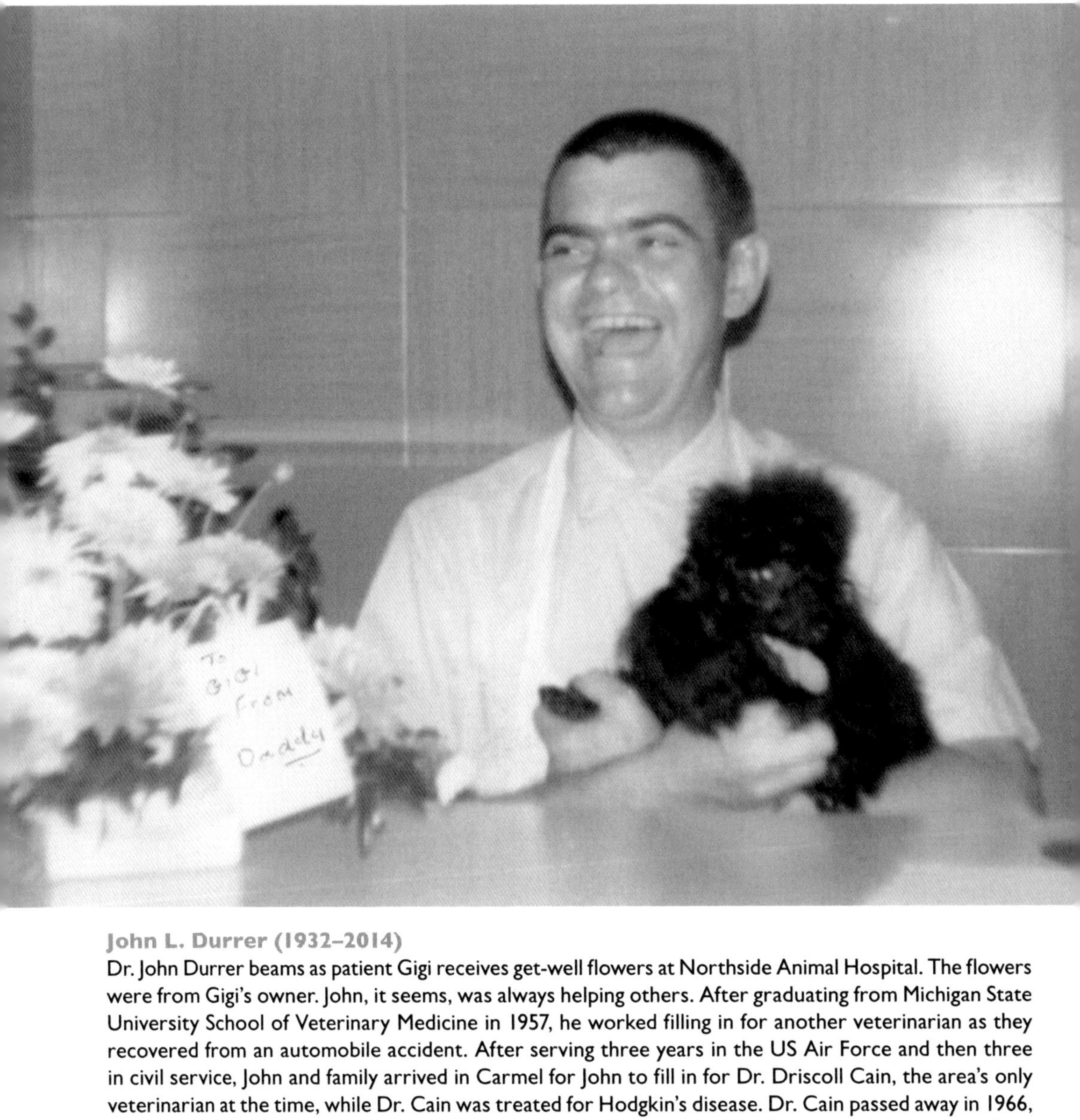

John L. Durrer (1932–2014)

Dr. John Durrer beams as patient Gigi receives get-well flowers at Northside Animal Hospital. The flowers were from Gigi's owner. John, it seems, was always helping others. After graduating from Michigan State University School of Veterinary Medicine in 1957, he worked filling in for another veterinarian as they recovered from an automobile accident. After serving three years in the US Air Force and then three in civil service, John and family arrived in Carmel for John to fill in for Dr. Driscoll Cain, the area's only veterinarian at the time, while Dr. Cain was treated for Hodgkin's disease. Dr. Cain passed away in 1966, and John bought the practice. The clinic was the only small animal clinic in Carmel, and clients came from Indianapolis for his care of their beloved pets. John sold his practice in 1985 but filled in when needed at various clinics throughout the state until 1999. Northside Animal Hospital was accredited with the American Animal Hospital Association while under his management. (Courtesy of Peg Durrer.)

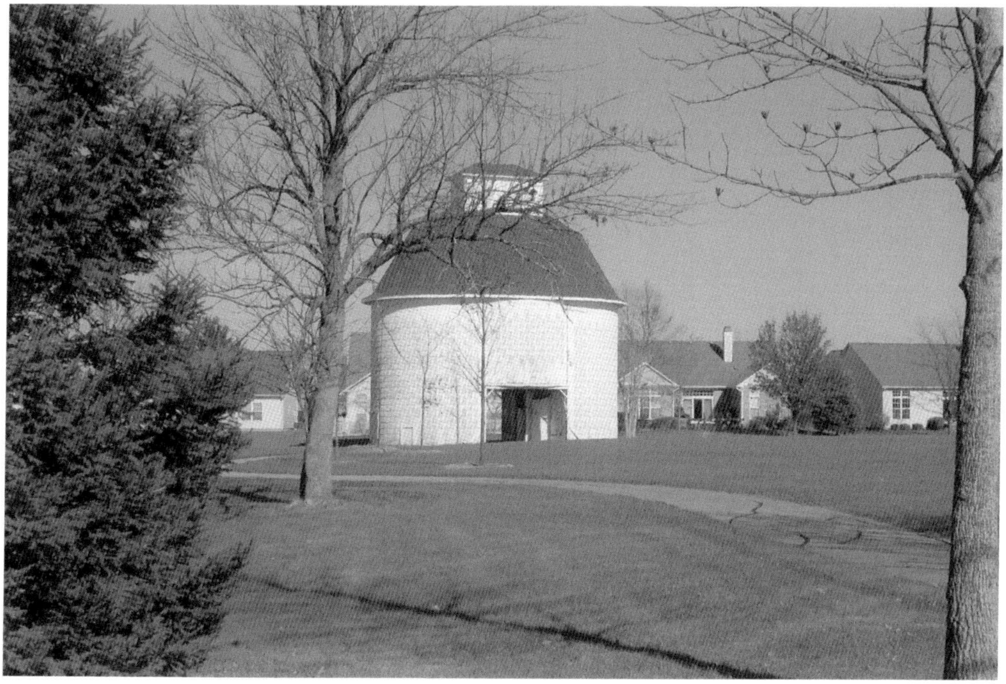

Charles J. Lynn (1874–1958)
Vice president and general manager of Eli Lilly and philanthropist Charles Lynn established Lynnwood Farm on 623 acres in eastern Carmel in 1934. He had an interest in livestock and Percheron horses. He lost his first wife in an automobile accident. The second Mrs. Lynn was not interested in the farm, so in 1942, Charles deeded the farm to Purdue University for animal-breeding research. There were several farms that made up the main farm, and they were all numbered. The buildings were state-of-the-art for the time with heated floors in the barns for winter and air-conditioning for summer. The farm was sold to developers in 1988. A few of the original buildings still stand, one of which is the grain silo on Plum Creek Golf Course. (Above, author's collection; below, courtesy of Carmel Clay Historical Society.)

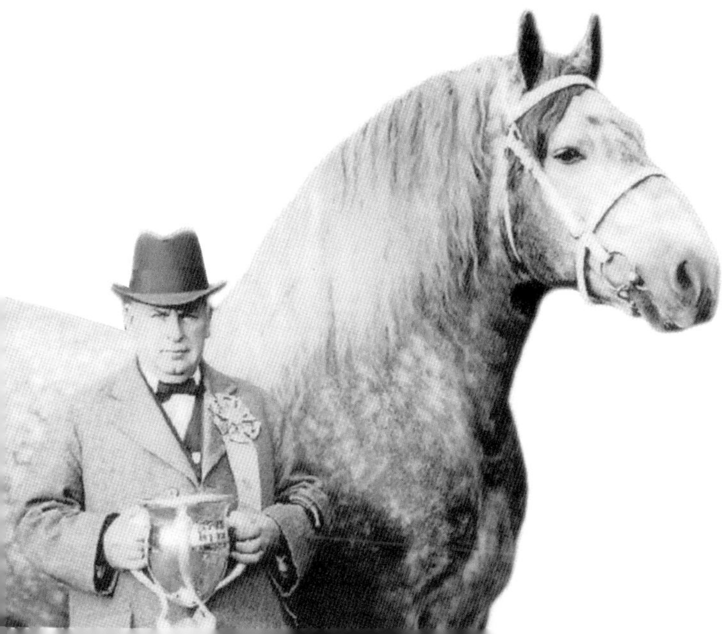

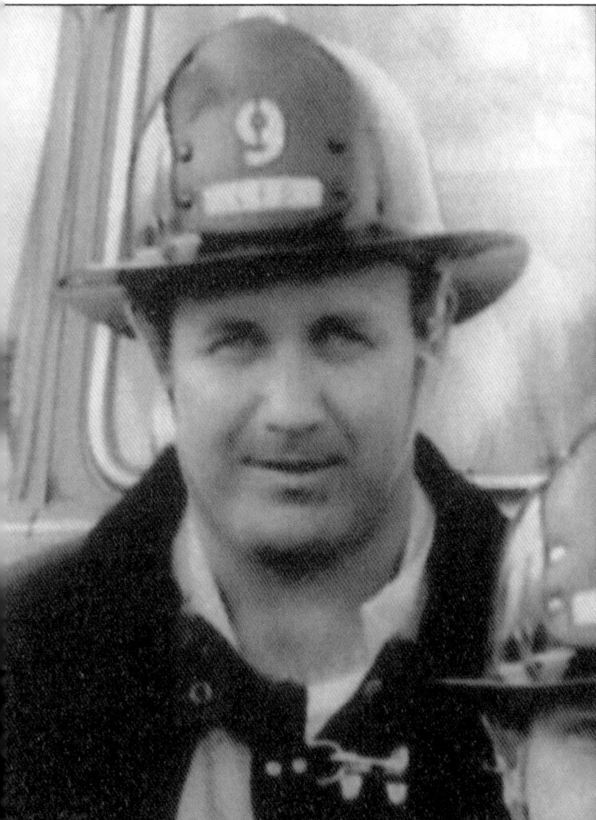

Robert T. "Speed" Hodgin (1928–2000)

Smokey the Bear (Robert "Speed" Hodgin) escorts an arsonist (Steve Couts) to jail and is assisted by faithful sidekick Sparky (Mike Callahan) to show those along the CHS homecoming parade route that the Carmel Fire Department will not tolerate this kind of crime. Carmel native Speed graduated from Carmel High School in 1946. Drafted by the US Army, he began working for Standard Oil, and upon his discharge, he purchased the bulk plant, delivering home-heating oil and gasoline to area farmers through Hodgin Oil for the Marathon Oil Company. In the 1970s, he and another friend began a business delivering cubed ice to various local events such as the Indianapolis 500 and to gas stations and liquor stores for retail purchase. The company was aptly named Speed-ee Ice. (Both, courtesy of Luanne Hodgin.)

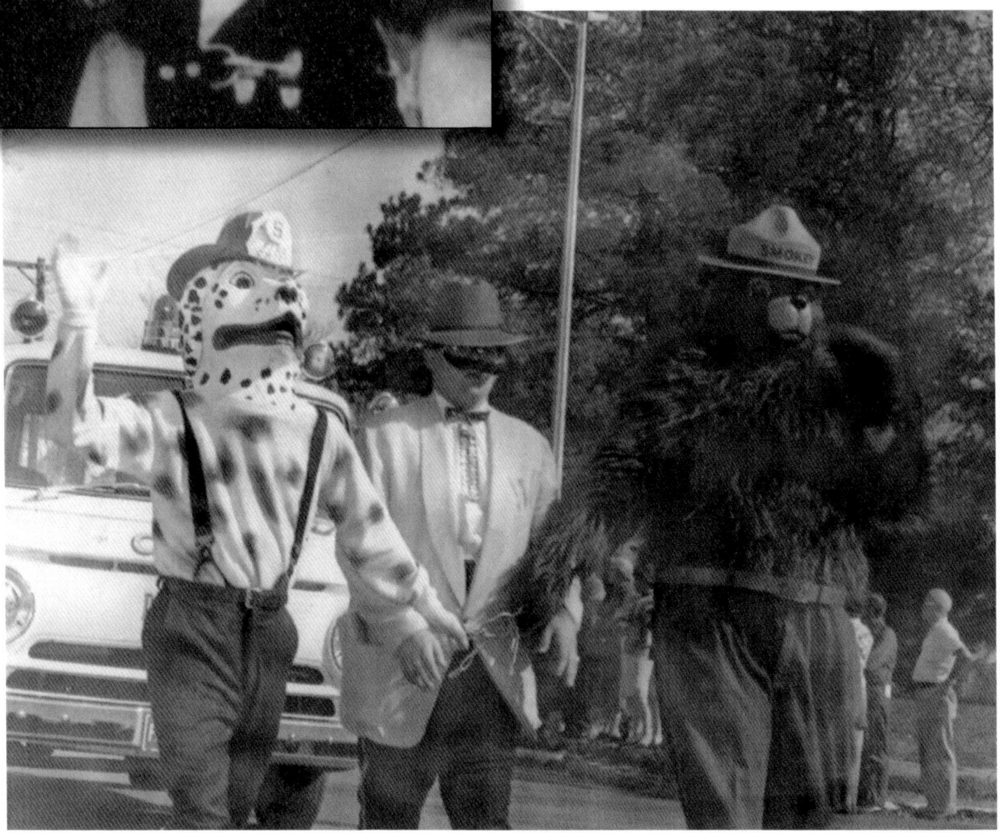

Jack L. Edwards (1929–2005)

Home Place's longtime resident and advocate Jack Edwards repairs a broken headstone in historic Farley Cemetery, where his parents are buried. Jack oversaw the effort to restore the cemetery, which was founded in 1838. Jack's decades of journaling and collecting are compiled in his 1992 book *A View of Home Place, Indiana.* A comprehensive resource for all wanting historical information of the southern portion of Clay Township, the 250-page tome consists of excerpts from local newspapers, Jack's journals, maps, historical books, church and cemetery records, and many photographs taken by Jack and his wife, Janet. Jack and good friend Marvin Pike are responsible for establishing the Home Place–Clay Township Military Museum & Library on College Avenue. (Courtesy of *A View of Home Place, Indiana.*)

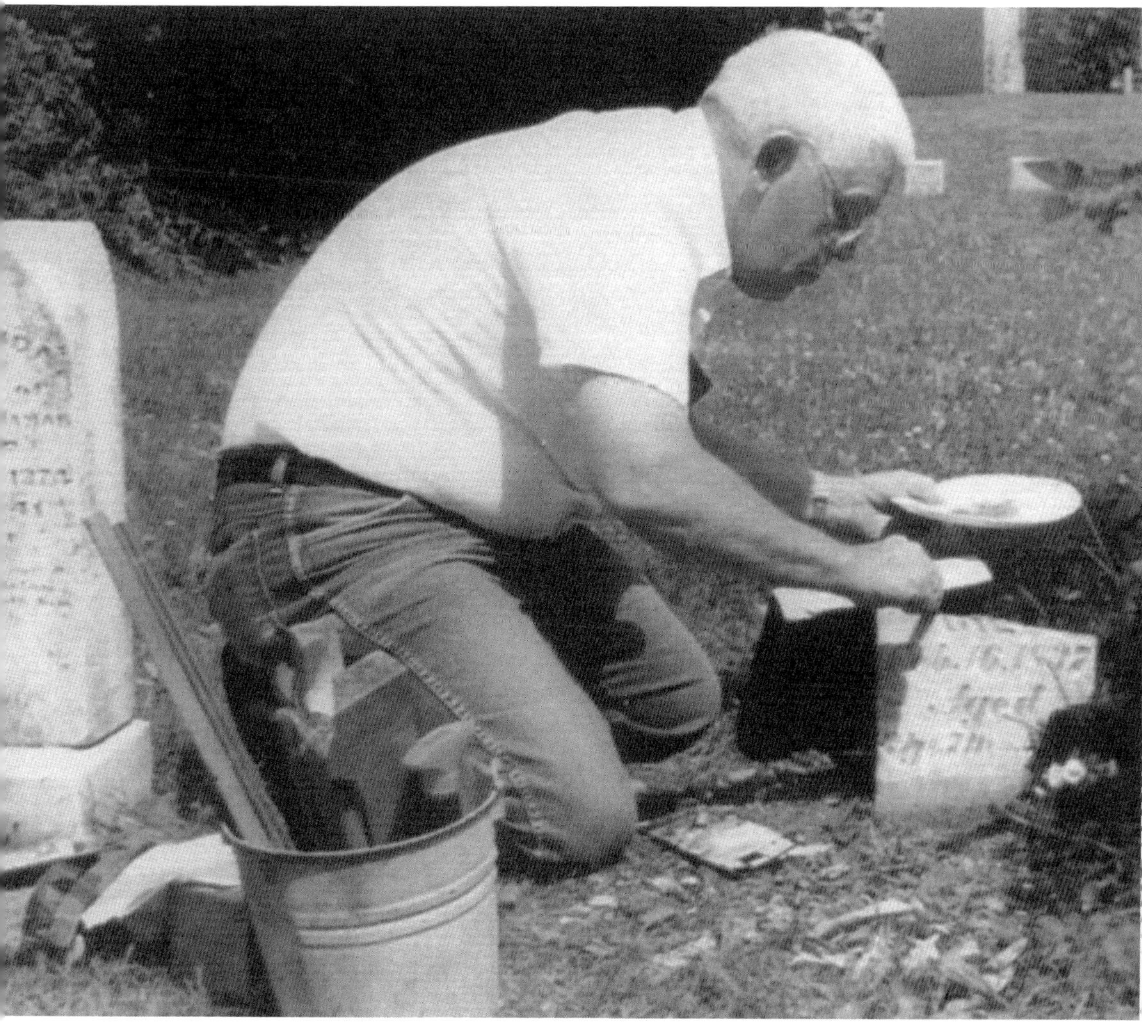

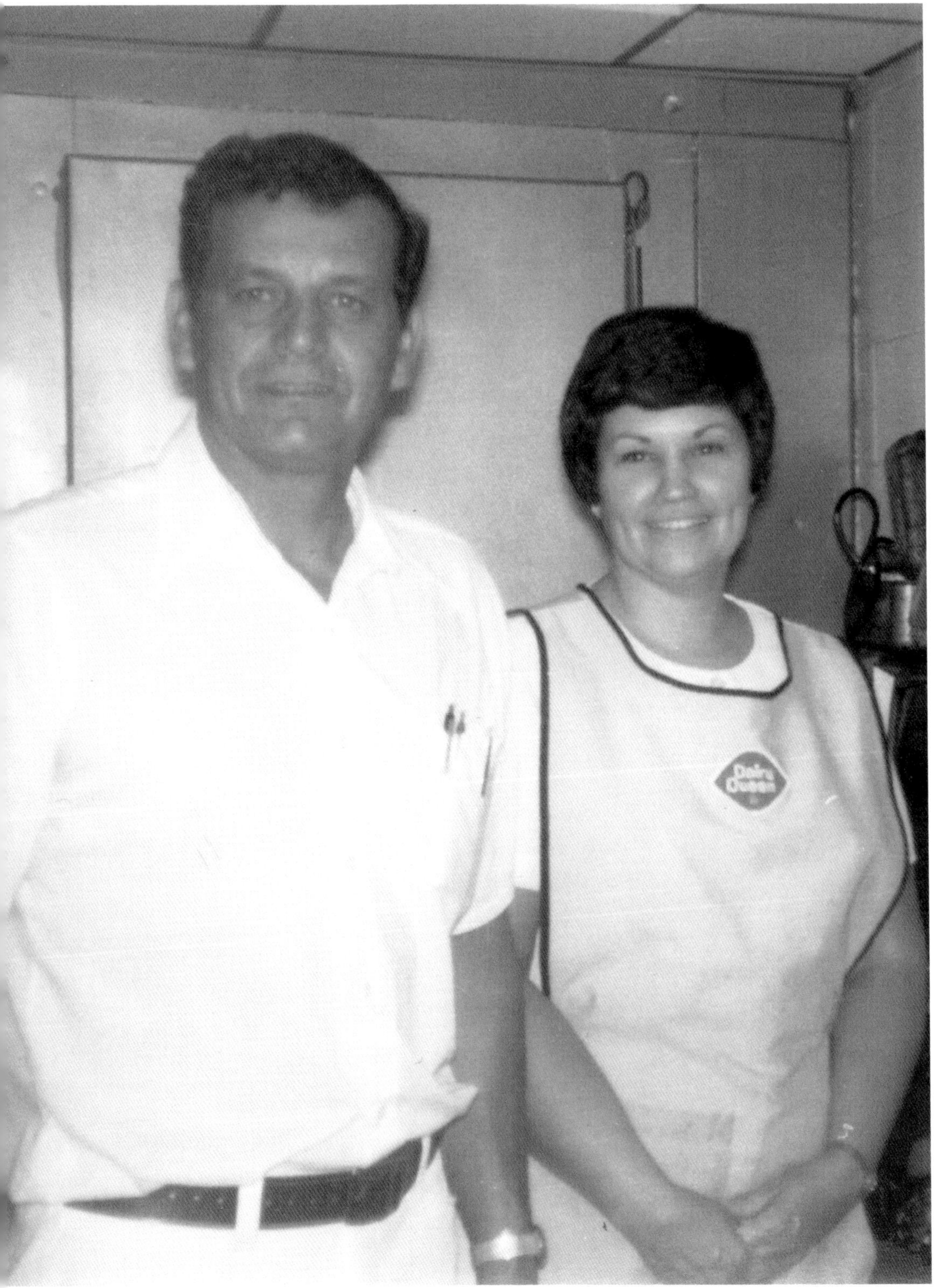

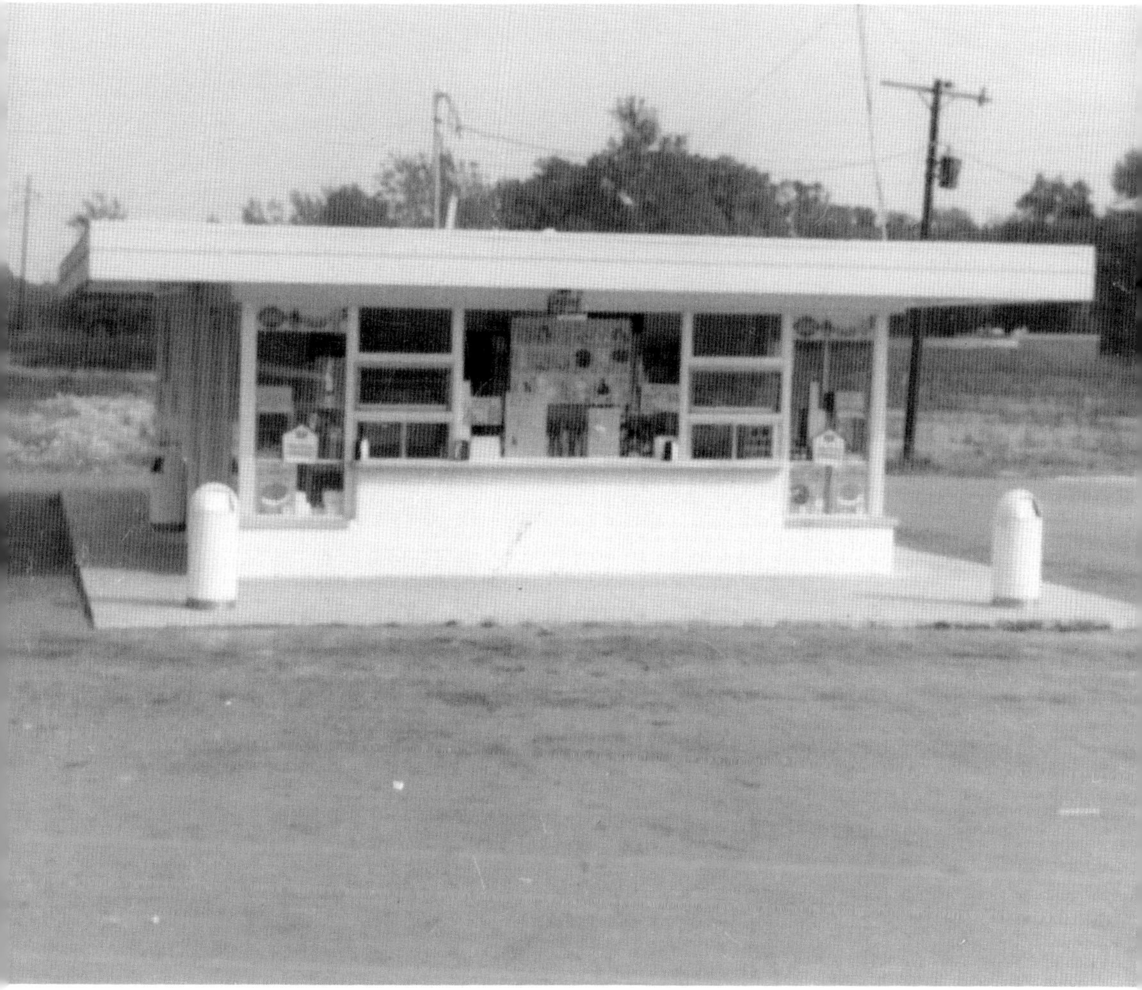

Donald M. Dunkerly (1935–2007)

About 55 years ago, a beloved Carmel icon opened its doors. The Carmel Dairy Queen is still open for business in its original location, a rare phenomenon these days in any city or town. Don Dunkerly was born in Bicknell, Indiana, in Knox County. In 1953, he joined the US Army and served his country for three years. Upon his discharge, Don was Carmel's first mail carrier with a walking route. With two partners, Dunkerly drew up the plans for the Carmel DQ in 1957. Construction began almost immediately. Don eventually bought out his partners, and he and his wife, Waneta, owned and operated the DQ for 16 years, teaching numerous teens the etiquette of a service position. He obtained his pilot's license and became a staple of the Carmelfest Fourth of July Parade, during which he could be seen "driving" his patriotically decorated airplane. Carmel has no landing strip or airport, so in order for Don to be in the parade, Keystone Avenue was shut down for Don to land and take off. (Both, courtesy of Waneta Dunkerly.)

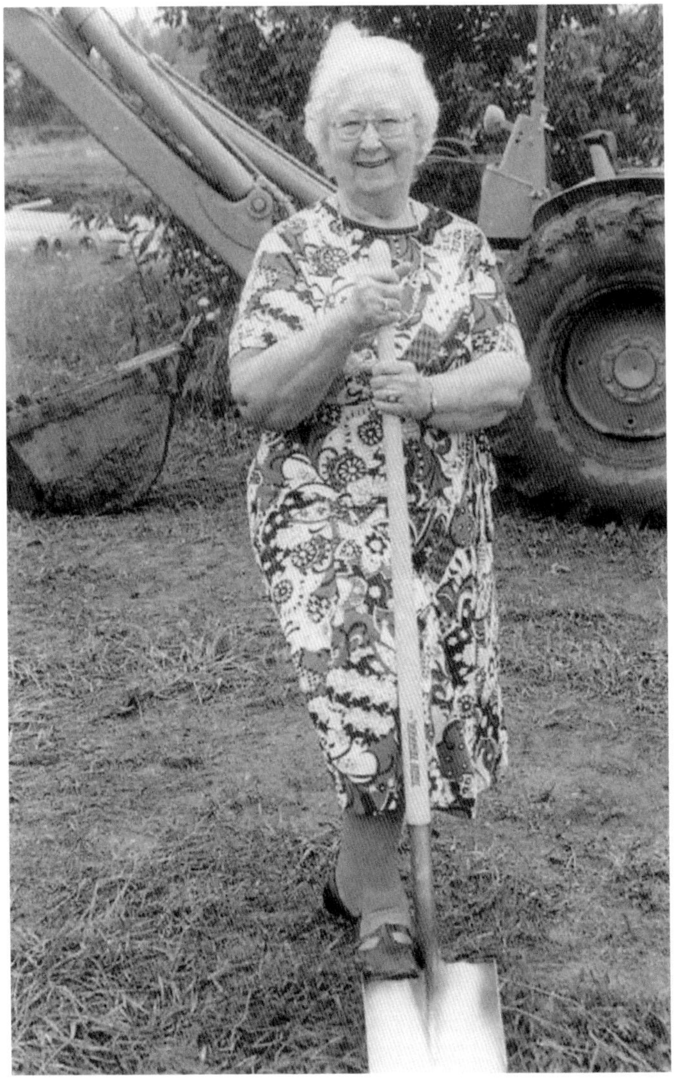

Minnie M. Doane (1910–1992)
Anyone who has been to a concert at the common area of Carmel City Center knows the gazebo that doubles as a stage is named in recognition of Minnie Doane. But who is Minnie? A 1928 graduate of Carmel High School, Minnie went to work in a local bank as a teller. Then, it was off to the local telephone company. Before there were rotary phones, she was the local operator whose voice a person heard when requesting a call be connected. She was a member of the Women's Army Corps (WACs) during World War II and served in Australia, New Guinea, and the Philippines. It is known that she was the first American woman to set foot on foreign land during wartime. Minnie returned home to her job at the telephone company, reaching the position of supervisor. Devoted to her community, she was a member of countless organizations and almost always reached a position of leadership within them. She ran for and was elected to Carmel's city council and served from 1976 to 1980. She served a second term at a later date. She was the first veteran elected president of the American Legion Auxiliary. Listed in the 1982 edition of *The World Who's Who of Women,* her accomplishments are esteemed and numerous. She received a Sagamore of the Wabash from Gov. Robert Orr in 1983. (Courtesy of Carmel Clay Historical Society.)

CHAPTER FOUR

Growing, No Pains

With the completion of Keystone Avenue, the sleepy farm town was sleepy no more. Soon, executives and white-collar workers from Indianapolis were migrating north to live in the suburbs. There was virtually no crime.

Businesses were seeing the advantage of being out of the constricted confines of Indianapolis. Businesses from out of state wishing to relocate to the area found the growing suburb a good place to be. With these businesses and potential development, the town believed it was time to be more organized and develop a means of governing with structure. A town board was elected, a city court created, and a plan commission formed. Fred Swift and Phil Hinshaw would both serve dutifully on the board. In 1976—the year of the country's bicentennial celebration—the town of Carmel grew up and became a city. Carmel's first mayor, Albert Pickett, was a visionary who started in motion the momentum that is still going strong today.

The city outgrew the Carnegie library, and in 1972, a new facility on East Main Street directly across from the high school would open. The town would purchase the old library and set up its office and administration there.

Carmel's growing reputation of quality schools drew residents from all over to make their homes there. With this influx of people, Carmel was rapidly outgrowing its schools. By 1974, Carmel now had four elementary schools. Clay Junior High School was opened that year and caused great discussion and concern about the split. It ultimately would only affect those students presently at Carmel Junior High School, as incoming students would not know any different. It was decided by the school corporation that any ninth graders (then junior high was grades seven, eight, and nine) who wished to remain at Carmel Junior for that year could do so. Superintendent Robert Hartman was sympathetic, as his own children attended school in the system. A great leader, Hartman encouraged new ideas and led Carmel Clay Schools through this period of tremendous growth. Carmel was also on the map for its sports programs from the Carmel Dads' Club, the idea of football coach Dick Nyers, to Carmel High School.

In 1980, Jane Reiman was elected as Carmel's second mayor. She would serve two terms with energy and integrity. Through her administration, Carmel saw even greater change with an increase in churches, schools, and businesses. St. Vincent Hospital in Indianapolis made the decision to build an additional hospital in Carmel. Robert Book would be instrumental in making it happen.

The city's multiyear plan for government buildings would continue with the construction of city hall, a new police headquarters, and a common area to be used for events in the future. Carmel's parks were on the rise and would grow due to the efforts of many. Today, they range from a park along White River, to a "spray" water park, and to Central Park with its state-of-the-art Monon Community Center.

By the year 2000, Carmel would have 37,700 permanent residents.

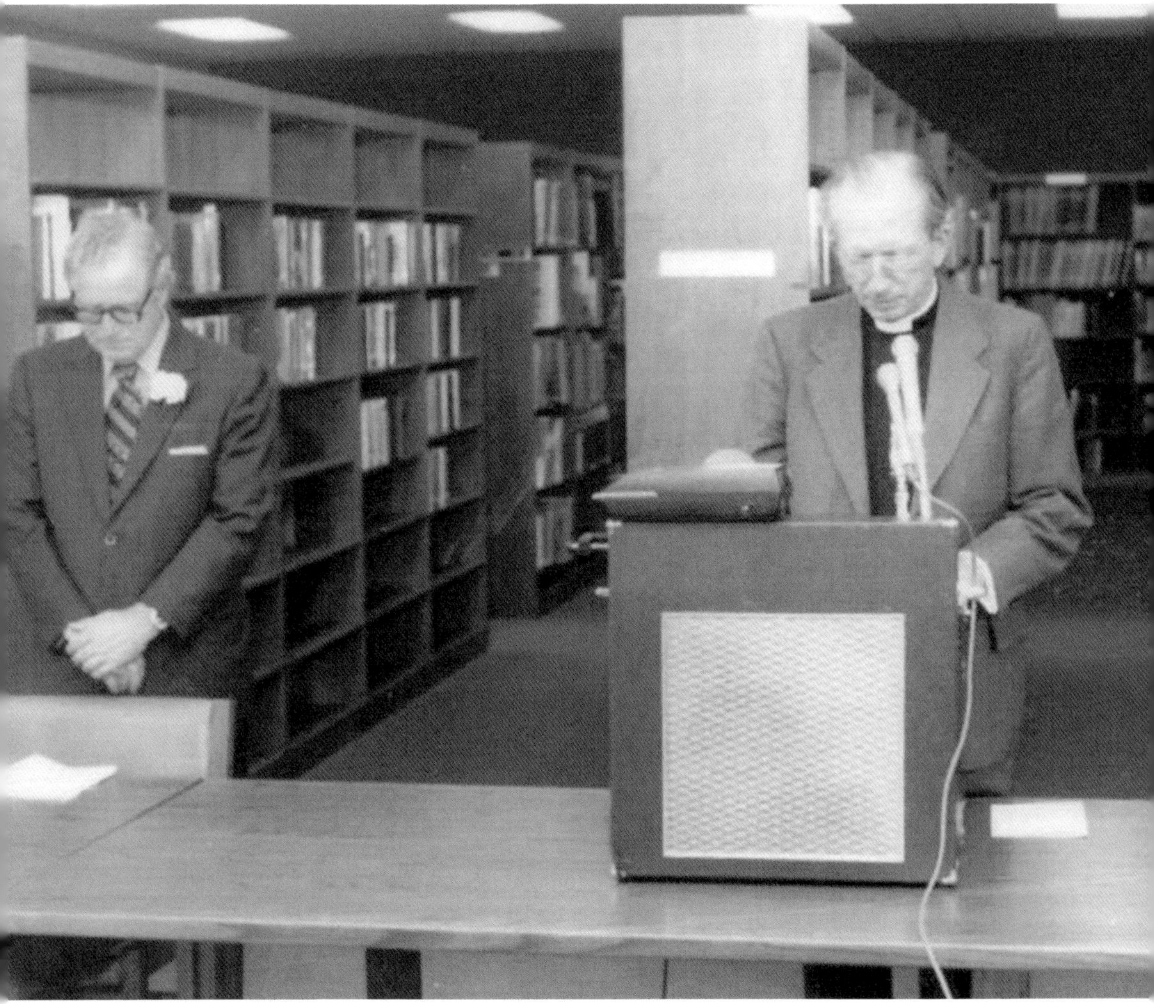

Rev. Warren S. Saunders (1913–2003)

Rev. Warren Saunders, pastor of Carmel United Methodist Church, gives the invocation at the swearing in ceremony of Carmel's first elected city government officials in 1976. The ceremony took place in the old library located across from Carmel High School. Gov. Otis Bowen stands to his right. Warren Saunders grew up on a celery and tomato farm in Oneco, Florida. Enlisting in the US Army in 1942, he was an officer manning antiaircraft batteries in Iceland. After World War II, Warren enlisted at Emory University in Atlanta and earned two degrees, one in economics and the other theology. He came to Carmel in 1964 via churches in Richmond, Leesburg, and Goshen to lead the congregation of Carmel United Methodist Church. He saw great growth in the church that was likely proportionate to the growth of the community. He was active in many civic organizations before and after his retirement. A founder of the Carmel Chamber of Commerce, he also served on its board of directors and numerous other boards. He made a bid for city council but was unsuccessful. He has been awarded the Sagamore of the Wabash, the ROSA Award (Rotary Outstanding Service Award), and many others. (Courtesy of Carmel Clay Historical Society.)

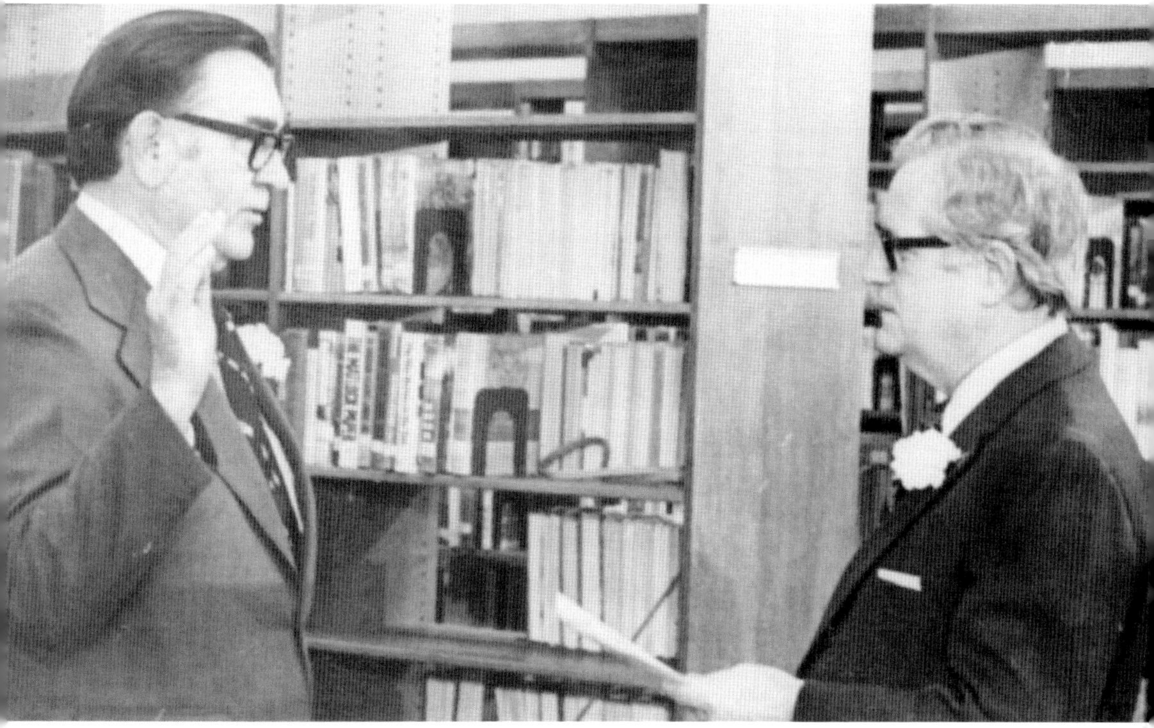

Albert B. Pickett (1918–2009)
Gov. Otis Bowen swears in Albert Pickett as Carmel's first mayor when it became a city with a governing seven-person council in 1976. The ceremony took place at the old library across the street from the high school. Born in Carmel in 1918, Albert went on to graduate from Carmel High School in 1936. He worked in the construction trade, eventually ending up in the aerospace industry with jobs, likely contract, with Aerojet General, Hughes Aircraft Company, and Lockheed Propulsion Company. With his experience, he served as Carmel's Building Commissioner for two years leading up to his campaign and subsequent election to the office of mayor. A quiet, reserved man, he was often misunderstood. Carmel's population grew 178 percent during the four years that Al Pickett was mayor. Numerous issues regarding infrastructure, utilities, and the police and fire departments were addressed and dealt with when he was mayor. Plans were initiated for a city service center with an office to house the mayor and council. (Courtesy of the 1976 Carmel High School yearbook, *Pinnacle*.)

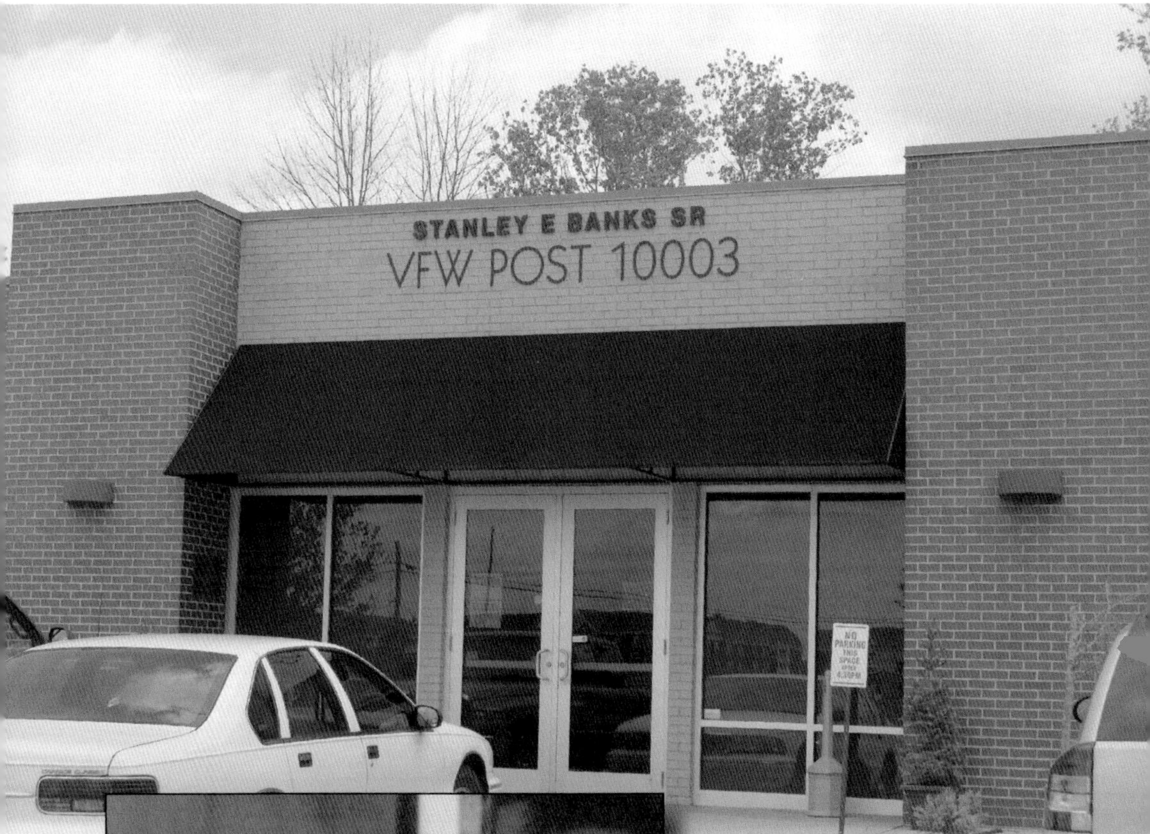

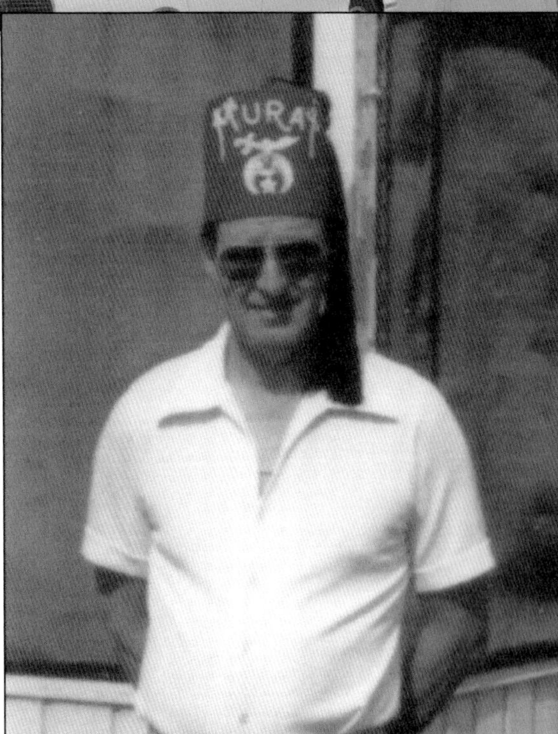

Stanley E. Banks Sr. (1929–2010)
During the 1960s and early 1970s, the grapevine of information for all things Carmel ran directly through the small café area of the Carmel Drugstore on North Rangeline Road. While who knows what kinds of deals were sealed there, the ones Stanley Banks sealed were always to help those in need. If there was a request or need, there would be Stanley Banks with no warning and no hesitation. In 1966, Stanley helped charter Carmel's Veterans of Foreign Wars (VFW) post located on Main Street above the barbershop. He held the position of post commander five times and district commander once. In 2012, then in its third and present location, the VFW Post No. 10003 on Old Meridian Street was named to honor him. (Above, photograph by Jennifer D. Hershberger; left, courtesy of the Banks family.)

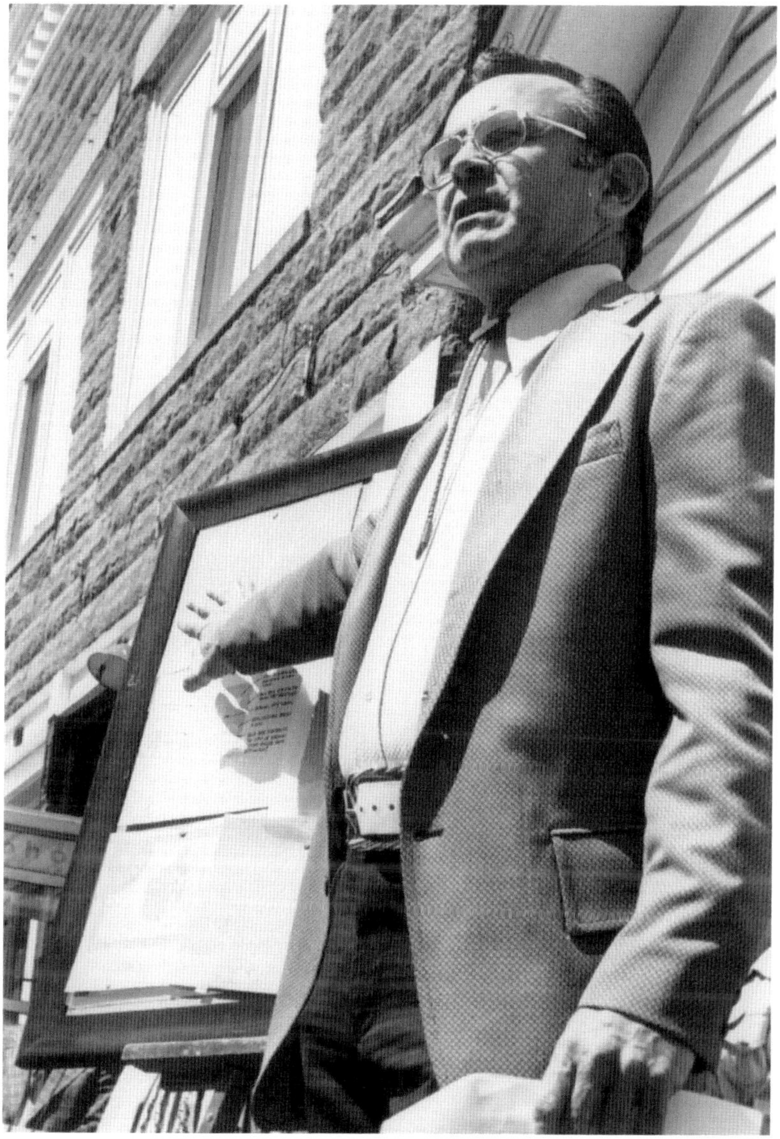

Frederick Philip "Phil" Hinshaw (1925–2011)
Lifelong Carmel resident Phil Hinshaw stands in front of the Bicentennial House (future Carmel Arts Council Building) and addresses the crowd during the Founders Day Celebration in April 1976. Phil was dedicated to the Carmel community his entire life, but his greatest legacy left to all is the book he wrote in 1987 titled *The Heritage of Carmel*. It is compiled of photographs, memoirs, and newspapers clippings spanning Carmel's then 150-year history. Phil Hinshaw graduated from Carmel High School in 1943 and attended Wabash College, Butler University, and Michigan State. He served in both the US Army and the US Air Force. And then, it was Carmel's turn. Phil was a volunteer fireman and on Carmel's town board. Numerous organizations and committees benefited from his participation and valued input. Phil and his wife, Nancy, operated an antique and floral business located on West Main Street for 25 years. The shop was aptly named The Heritage of Carmel Antique and Flower Shop. A family man to the core, he never slighted them with his community spirit of volunteerism. He managed quite nicely to give 100 percent to everything to which he committed. (Courtesy of the Carmel Clay Historical Society.)

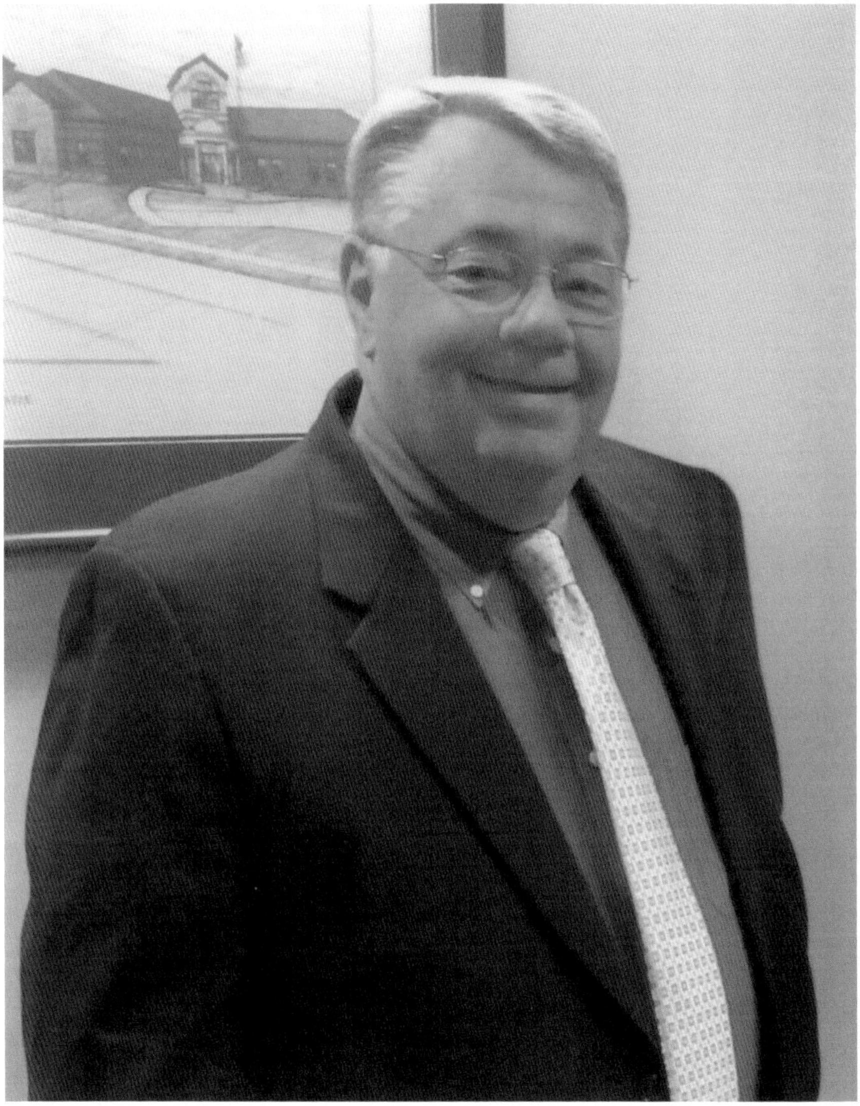

Douglas Callahan (1953–)
Former fire chief Doug Callahan is the ninth of Charles and Elizabeth (Bracken) Callahan's 15 children. A Pike High School graduate, Doug began his career with the Carmel Fire Department in 1973 joining two of his brothers. During his 34 years with the department, he was involved in creating the emergency medical technician program that staffed the department with combination paramedics/firefighters. He served almost 11 years as fire chief. Those years saw great growth for the department in the hiring of 23 new firemen, opening of two new fire stations, and the rebuilding of one. In that time period, the Carmel Fire Department doubled in size. In his retirement from CFD, Doug is currently serving his third term as Clay Township trustee. His daily responsibilities include providing township assistance for needy families. He also is on the PrimeLife Enrichment's board of directors and instructs CPR classes for the American Heart Association. In 2015, Station No. 45 was named for Doug in recognition of his devoted service to the department and Carmel community. Mayor James Brainard bestowed the city's highest award on Doug in the Range Line Pioneer Award. A true, caring community servant, Doug always has the safety of others in mind. (Photograph by Donna Hansen.)

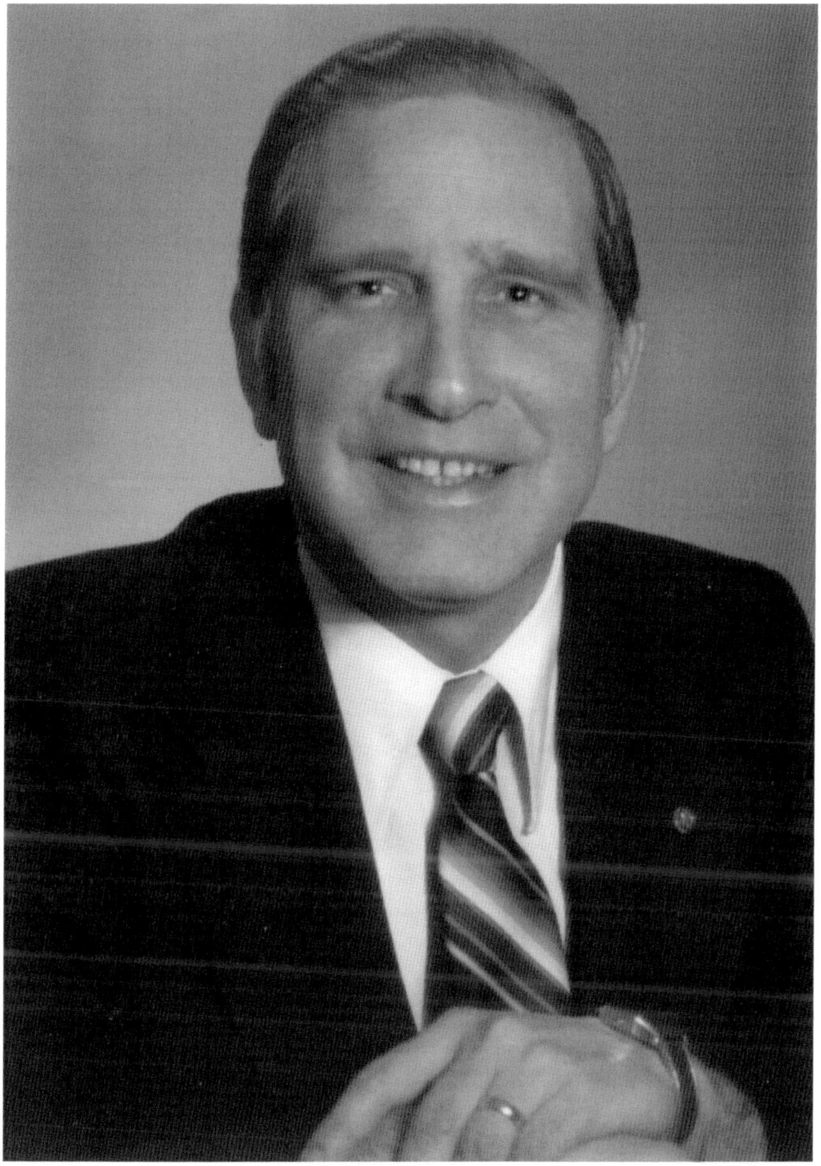

Theodore E. Johnson (1934–1998)
Carmel's fourth mayor, who served from 1992 to 1995, was Ted Johnson. A native of Columbus, Ohio, he grew up in a neighborhood there that instilled in him his honesty and respect for community. After serving on Carmel's city council for 11 years, Ted was elected to the office of mayor in 1991 and served one term. Ted and his wife, Nyla, arrived in Carmel in 1971 when Carmel's population was just 6,700. A mere 24 years after the end of his term, it would be nearly 30,000. Ted's unique vision was an asset to a growing city. Many of his proposals helped to ease Carmel into its present identity. Ted proposed a bridge over White River at 96th Street, but it would not come to fruition until after his death. He was a strong proponent of increasing the number of parks of which the community reaps the rewards today. Ted was a family man who cared deeply for his loved ones. That devotion in his character did not diminish outside the Johnson home. He sought reelection in 1995 but lost to current mayor James Brainard. (Courtesy of Jenny Johnson Rundle.)

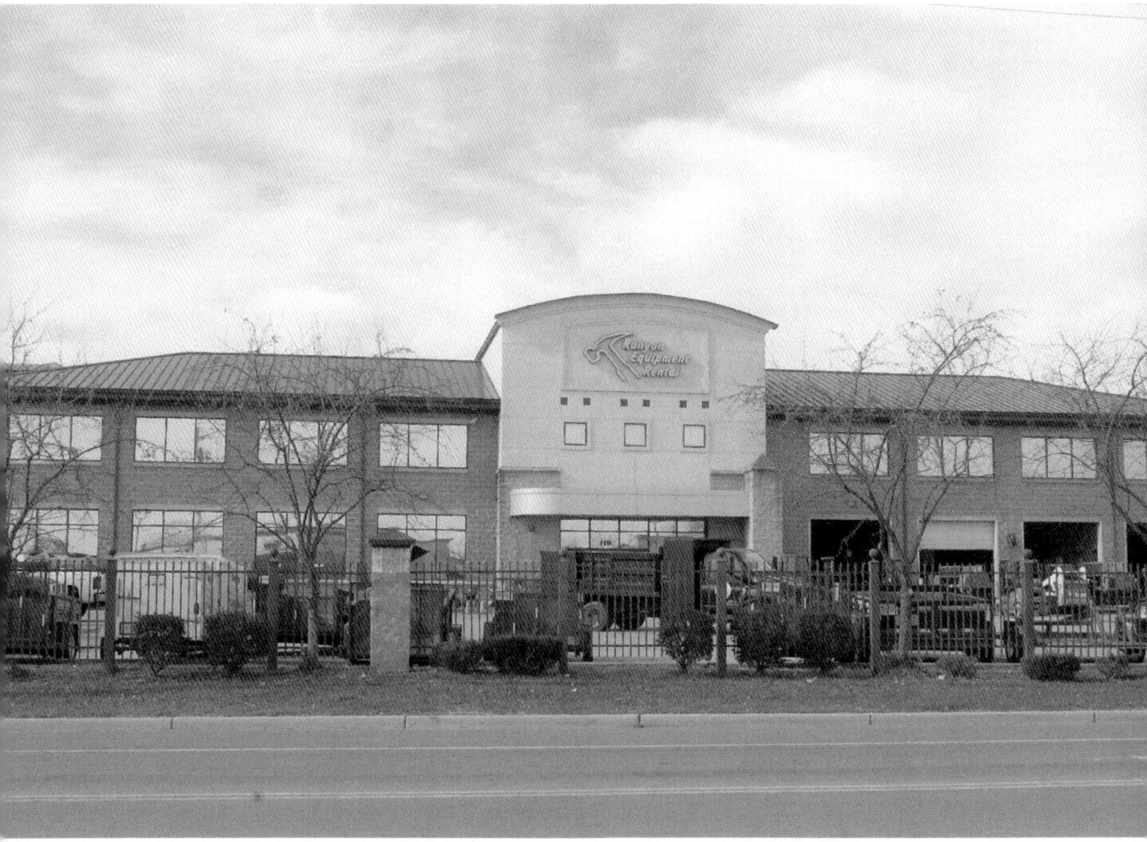

Jack P. Runyon (1922–1978)
Carmel resident Jack Runyon had the foresight in the 1950s to see what Carmel would likely become. He and his wife, Mildred, began a business that would be synonymous with Carmel for many years. Jack opened Jack's Tool Rental on 146th Street, which later moved to North Rangeline Road. Jack's customers would come from surrounding counties to rent equipment too expensive to buy especially for some as a one-time use. Throughout the years, when someone would need a particular piece of equipment, he or she could hear them say, "Let's see what Jack has." The company was turned over to son Gary to manage in 1978, and he eventually sold out to a large, national corporation. But today, Jack's is back with Gary and Jack's namesake grandson at the helm. The business is now called Runyon Equipment Rental and is larger than ever. Jack Runyon made his mark on Carmel and is still on the lips of residents when there is a job to be done.

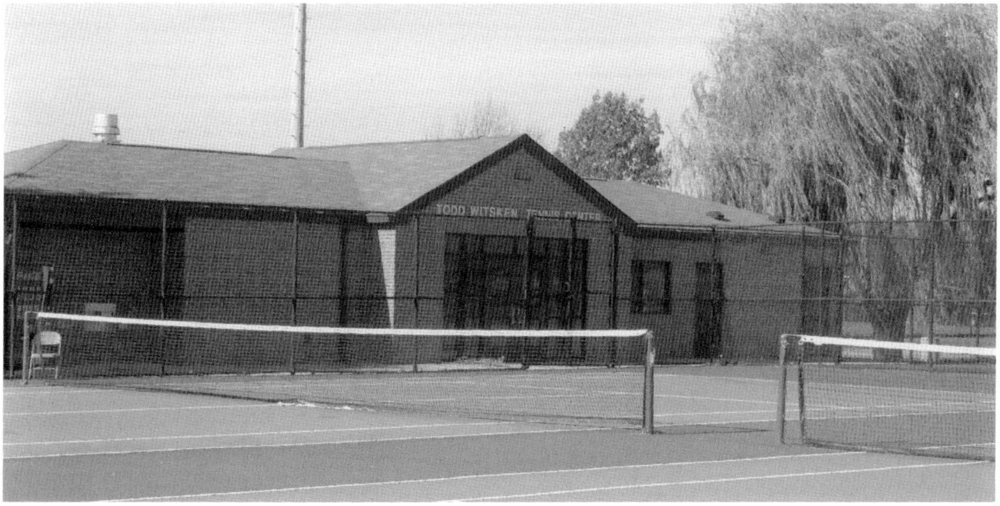

Todd M. Witsken (1963–1998)

Born in Indianapolis in 1963 to a family with eight children, Todd Witsken was not bashful and had a great work ethic and a positive attitude. All benefited him in his pursuit of a career as a professional tennis player. After graduating from Carmel High School with All-State honors in 1982, he attended the University of Southern California, where he was an All-Time American. He competed on the professional circuit, being most known for his success as a doubles player and played at Wimbledon in 1986 and 1989. Todd beat Jimmy Connors in the third round of the 1986 Open and went on to have a winning record before retiring from the pros in 1993 to focus more on home and family. He opened and operated tennis camps for children before he was diagnosed with brain cancer in 1996. Carmel High School's tennis center bears his name.

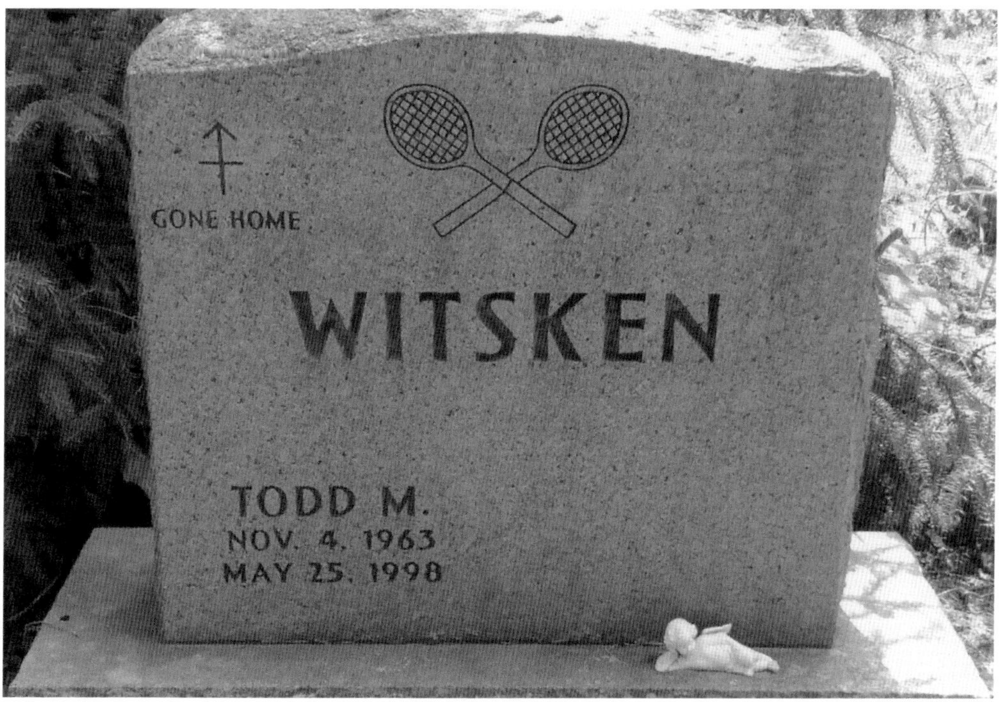

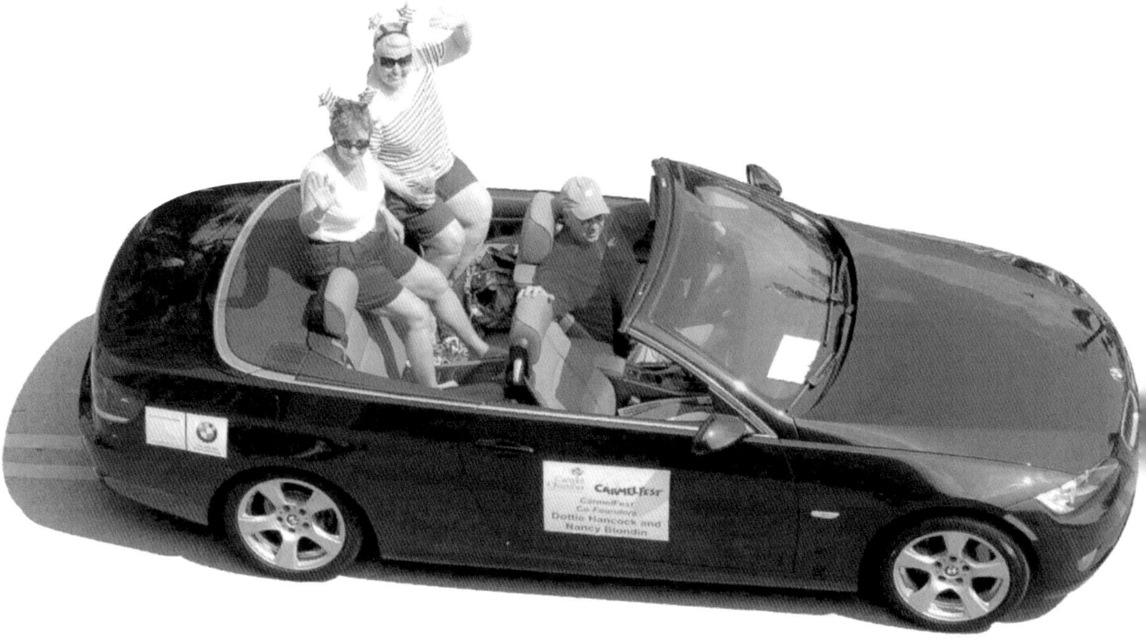

Nancy L. (Kealing) Blondin (1942–2015)
Former Carmel mayor Dottie Hancock and former executive director of the Carmel Clay Chamber of Commerce Nancy Blondin wave to the crowd along the route of the 2015 Carmelfest Fourth of July Parade. A lover of people with a great sense of humor, Nancy Blondin, a Fort Wayne native, served the Carmel community in many ways but will be most remembered for her 14 years leading the Carmel Chamber of Commerce during a period of Carmel making a name for itself. Nancy aided all Indiana chambers by filling the role of president of the Indiana Chamber Executives Association (ICEA) in 1992. She served on the Carmelfest committee when it was still an entity of the chamber of commerce. In 2000, Nancy received a Sagamore of the Wabash Award, Indiana's highest honor bestowed by the governor, for her significant contribution to the state. She was a stout supporter of education, and a scholarship in her name was established. She was a true mentor to all who asked anything of her. (Courtesy of One Zone.)

Otto N. "Nick" Frenzel III (1930–2010) (OPPOSITE)
A career banker spending his entire career with Merchants National Bank & Trust Company beginning in 1956, Nick Frenzel was not one to ever be idle. Born in Indianapolis and educated in the East, Nick served two years in the US Air Force being discharged as a first lieutenant. His banking career spanned four decades and included several presidencies and chairmanships with corporations such as Merchants National Corporation and National City Corporation. Smaller local banks that were subsidiaries of those in which he served were Union State Bank (Carmel, Westfield, and Noblesville), Mid-State Bank (Zionsville), and Danville State Bank (Danville). Countless charities were the recipient of Nick's time and expertise. The Frenzel family owned the 236-acre Hobby Horse Farm, located on Spring Mill Road north of Main Street. The Frenzels raised horses on a portion of the acreage and sublet farm space to others who lived on it and managed it. Today, Hobby Horse Farm has been sold to make way for a new housing community called Silvara. The barn will be saved to become a clubhouse for the development. (Photograph by Jennifer D. Hershberger.)

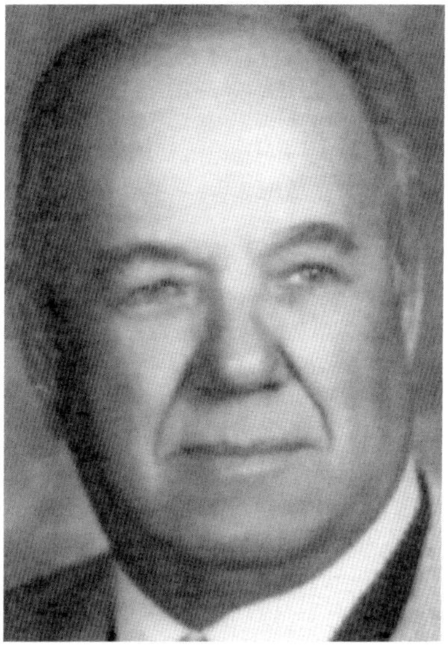

Ralph L. Wilfong (1918–1997)
In the late 1960s, developer Ralph Wilfong owned the land surrounding 116th Street and Keystone Avenue and had plans to build a shopping center. Born in Hancock County the sixth of ten children, Ralph had a keen interest in horse racing. He knew Leo McNamara, who owned Two Gaits Farm in Carmel located at 146th Street and Oak Ridge Road. McNamara had sold off some of his farm's acreage to begin development on the Village of Mount Carmel with hopes of it being a small, tight-knit community. Ralph purchased the remaining farm from McNamara in 1973 and would finish out building the project. The land north of 146th Street would become Village Farms. Today, Merchant's Square shopping center holds anchor stores like Marsh Supermarket, Tuesday Morning, Hancock Fabrics, and the brand new Flix Brewhouse. Wilfong planned and built Woodland Springs housing development too. An avid horseman, Ralph spent hours training, grooming, and racing Standardbred horses. He was instrumental in leading the quest to get pari-mutuel betting into Indiana. He felt if big purses were available, better horses would come. Today, Wilfong Land Companies is based out of Westfield and run by Ralph's son Beau. (Courtesy of "Hamilton County, Indiana, 175 Years & Counting," a supplement to the *The Noblesville Daily Ledger.*)

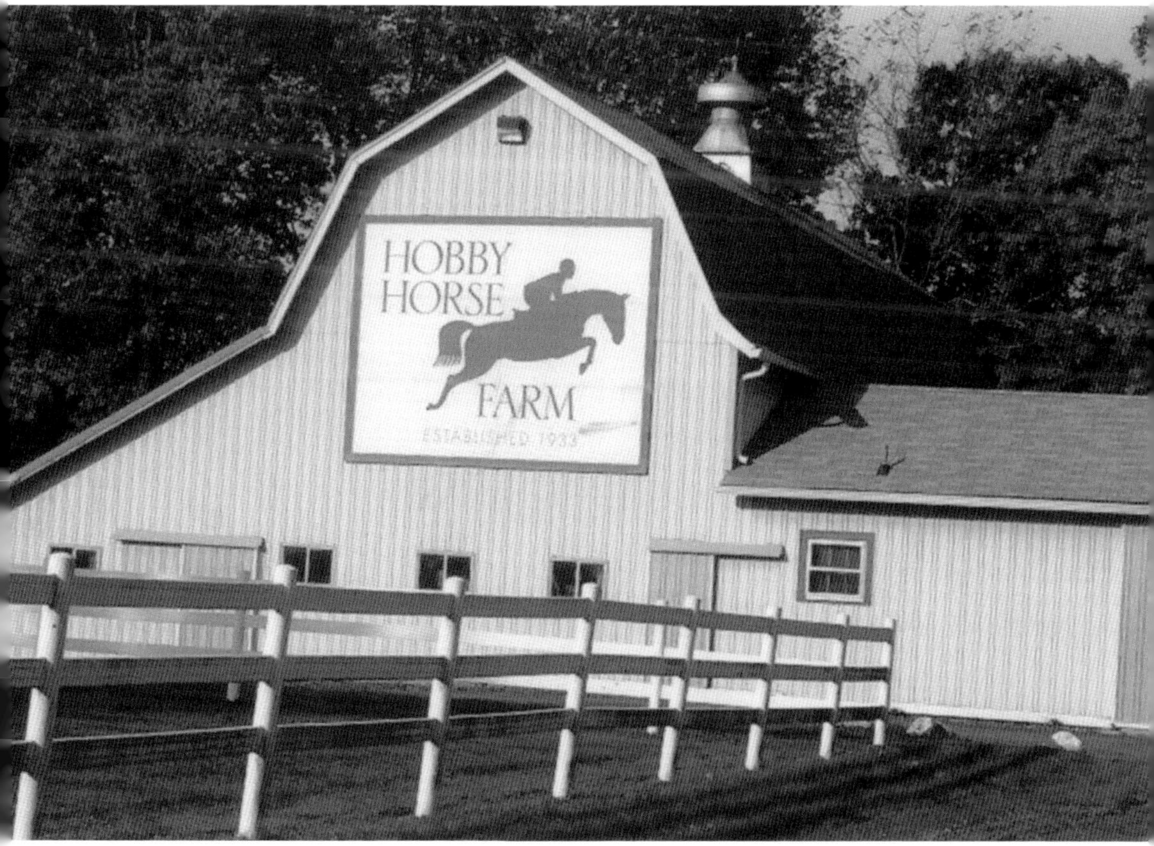

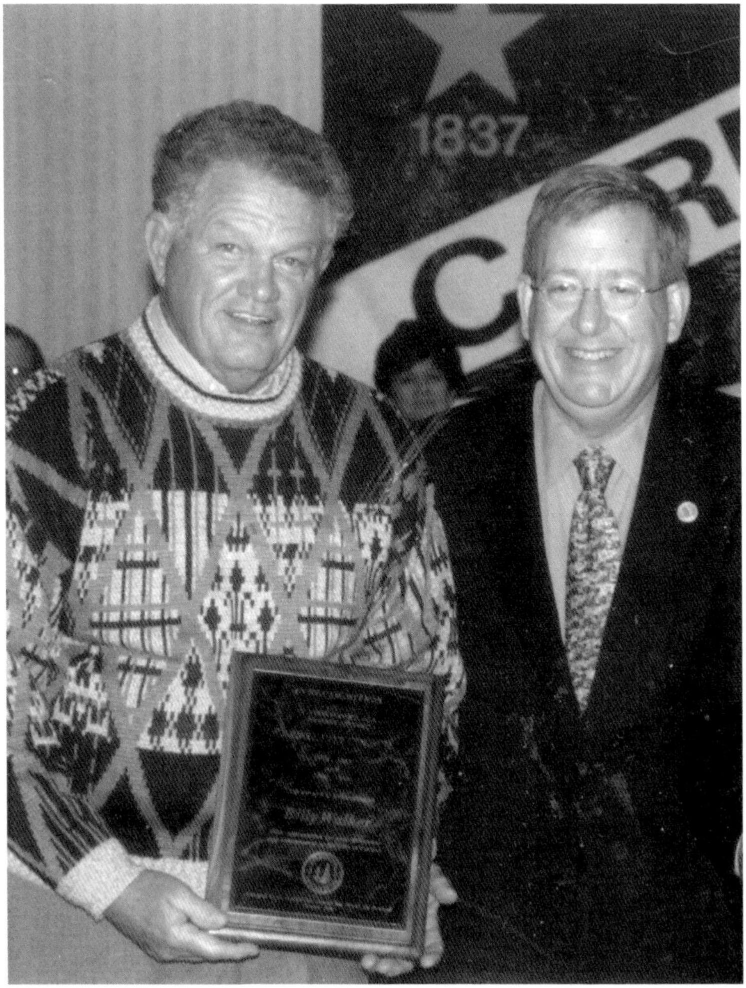

Billy L. Walker (1932–2002)

Former city councilmen Billy Walker receives a plaque recognizing his service to the City of Carmel from Mayor Jim Brainard. When North Central High School hired assistant principal Billy Walker in the mid-1960s, Carmel would reap the benefits. With Billy and his wife Evelyn's decision to make Carmel their home for their family, Carmel would receive years of public service from Billy. Born in Wolcott, Indiana, Billy graduated from Kentland High School and went on to attend the US Naval Academy, Indiana State Teacher's College (ISU), and Purdue University. A veteran of the US Marine Corps and Marine Corps Reserve, he learned discipline while serving his country, and it would come in handy when faced with the difficult challenges of helping to run a large, municipal high school, which he did for 27 years. Billy helped Carmel by serving on the board of public works and later on the city council. His love of young people would lead him to work with the National Drug Task Force. He also loved sports and was an official for football, basketball, and track. The 1984 Olympics named him an alternate official. Billy also was on the executive board of the Indiana High School Athletic Association, filling the capacity of vice chairman from 1976 to 1977. Some of the awards bestowed on him were Range Line Pioneer Award, Track and Field Hall of Fame, North Central Hall of Fame, National Drug Task Force Honors, and Sagamore of the Wabash. Spare time was a cherished commodity for Billy, and when he was not writing a book, teaching Sunday school, serving as a church elder, or running the Elks Boys' Camp, he could be found in his garden. (Both, courtesy of Evelyn Walker.)

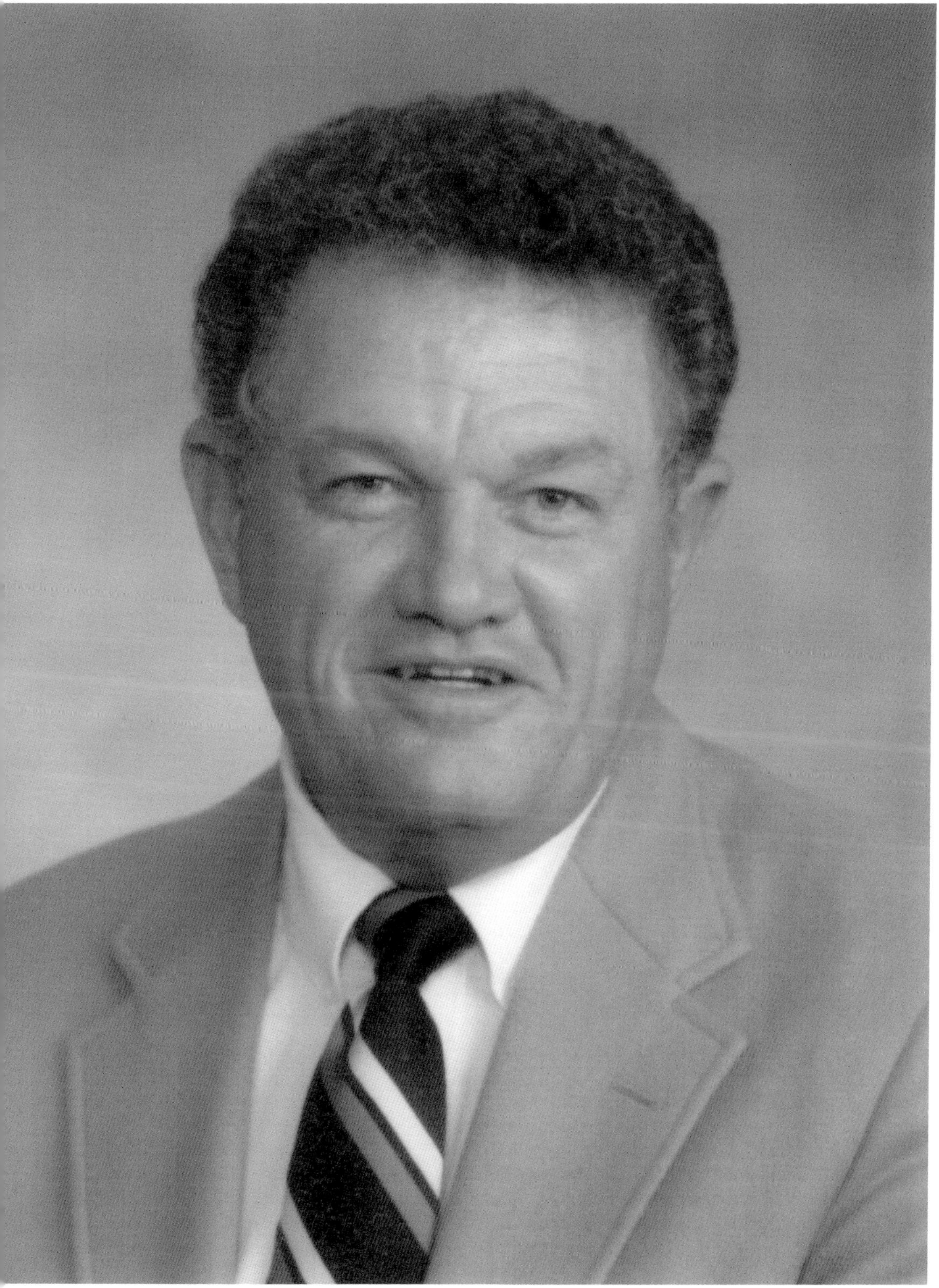

Dale E. Graham (1926–2007)

When Dale Graham arrived at Carmel High School in the early 1960s as a teacher and coach, he could not even begin to imagine where the next 30 years would take him. A 1944 graduate of Union Township High School in Columbia City, he graduated from Ball State and later received his master's degree from Butler University. He was a veteran of the US Army and the US Air Force. When he joined the staff at CHS as a history and government teacher, Carmel's population was 1,400. (Today, Carmel High School's enrollment is 4,900.) When Keystone Avenue opened the way north, Carmel was the place to live. In 10 years, the population would jump 364 percent. Becoming principal at CHS in 1964, Dale would lead CHS during years of extreme growth. He knew most every student by name and would often ask a student how his parents were by name. He was a friend to his staff and took his job as disciplinarian, personnel manager, and curriculum advocate with great seriousness, but found time to insert the fun things that students take away with them. No student or teacher can forget his Friday morning announcements and his booming "Good morning, all you T.G.I.F.ers!" Dale retired in 1989. The 1,500-seat auditorium in the performing arts wing of CHS proudly carries his name in remembrance of his time there. (Courtesy of the 1976 Carmel High School yearbook, *Pinnacle*.)

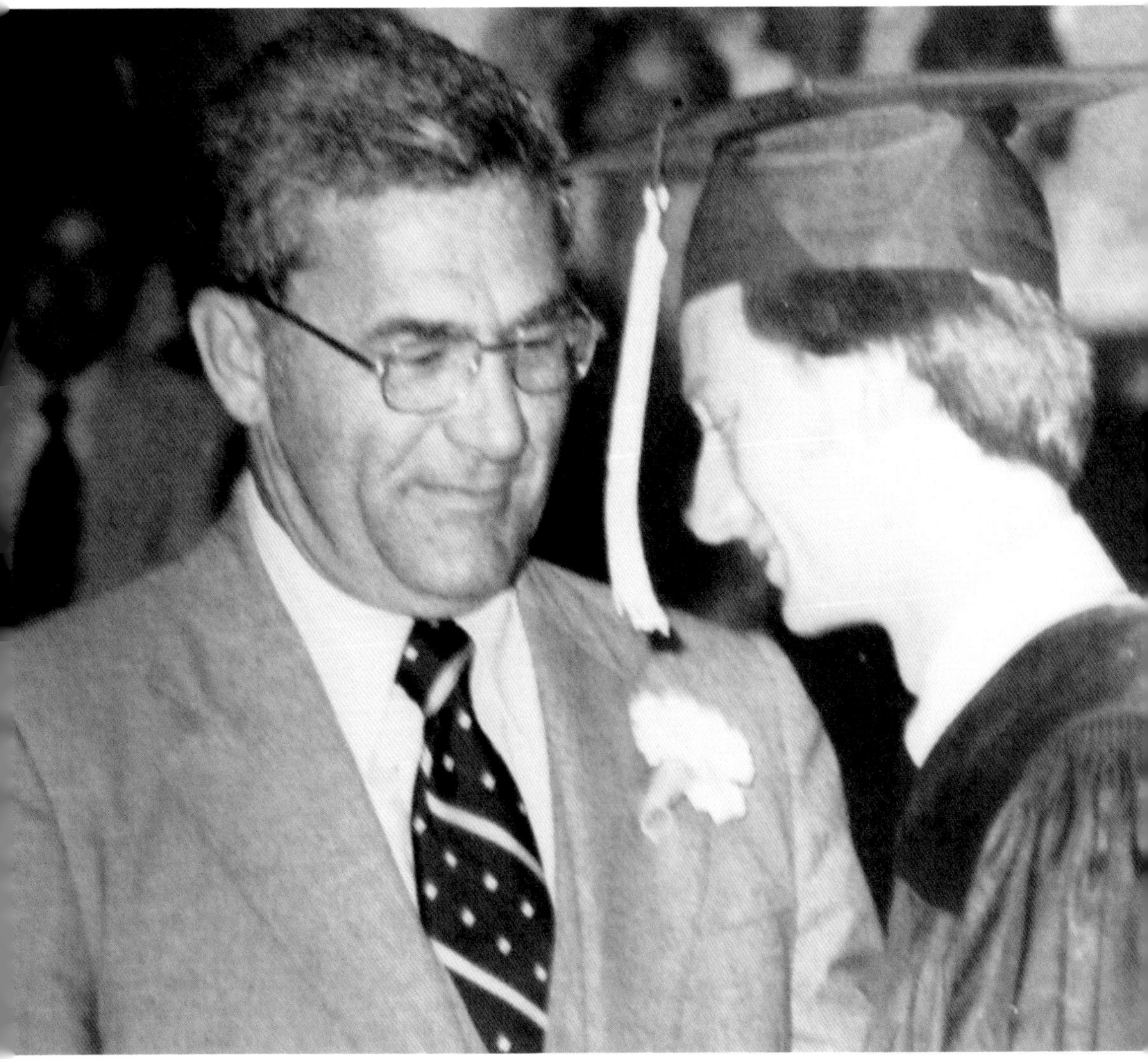

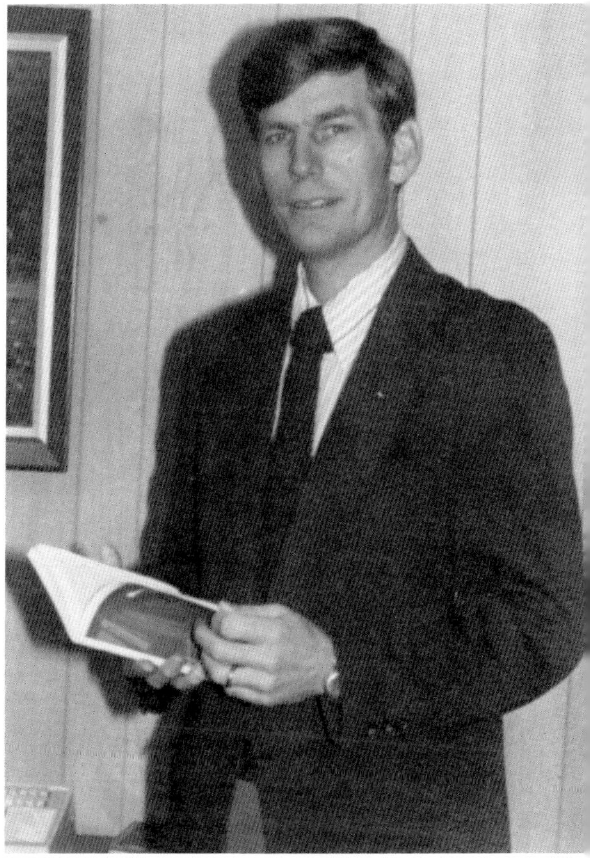

Dr. Robert D. Hartman (1930–2012)
When a school system is fortunate enough to lure an individual away from another for the purpose of employment that includes relocation, great consideration is given by the individual. The principal of Willard Elementary School in Evanston, Illinois, applied for, interviewed, and received the offer to be Superintendent Forrest Stoops's successor in 1968. At a young age, Robert Hartman already had an impressive resume, and while his years at the helm of Carmel Clay Schools would not lengthen his resume, they sure would enrich it. His 25-year term as superintendent was handled with great poise and self-assurance. Carmel's tremendous growth during his administration would bring unprecedented challenges. Dr. Hartman was the perfect choice for the job and spent 25 years leading the school corporation for the fastest-growing community in the state. (Right, courtesy of the 1976 Carmel High School yearbook, *Pinnacle*; below, author's collection.)

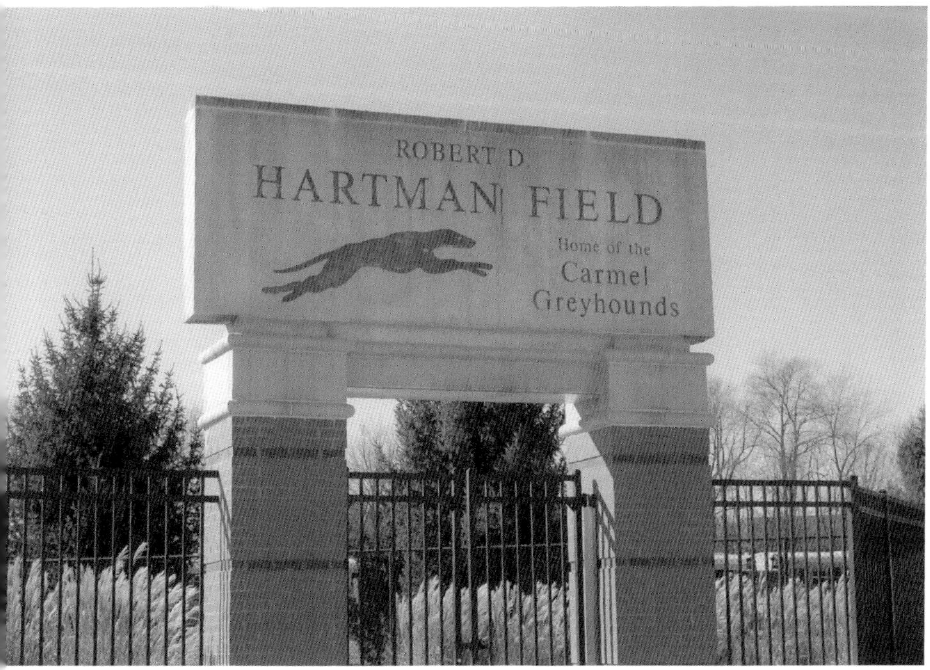

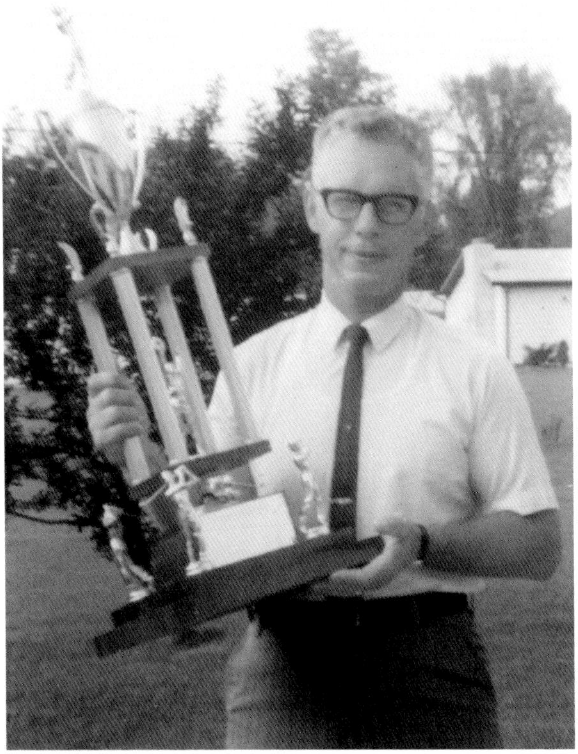

Donald L. Huffer (1933–)
In the "City of Champions," Don Huffer could well be called "the man who started it all." To date, Carmel High School has a cumulative, multisport total of 137 state championship titles, of which 127 are IHSAA sanctioned sports. It all began when Coach Huffer's boys' golf team won the first title in 1970. Born in Muncie and schooled in Anderson, Don graduated from Ball State and found himself on the staff of Carmel High School in 1957, but not until after serving the United States in Korea and receiving a Korean Ribbon, Bronze Star, and Purple Heart. CHS would open its new school the following year where Don would teach and coach for 36 years in five different sports. Don's golf teams brought home five state titles, and three individual state titles were earned by young men wrestling under Don's leadership. (Both, courtesy of Judy Huffer.)

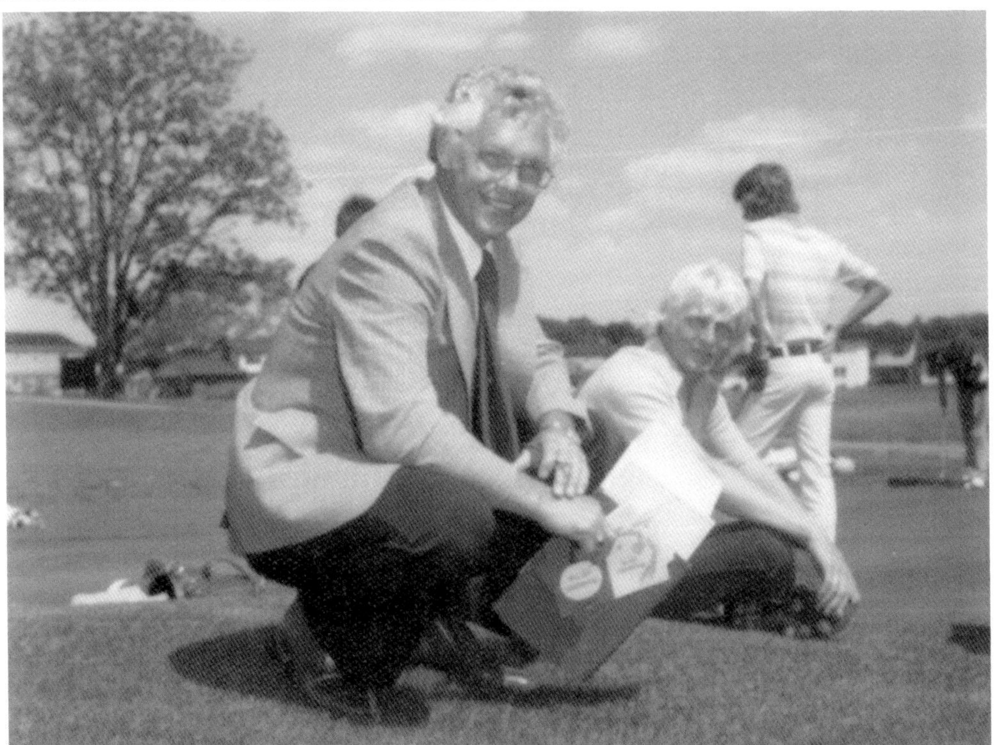

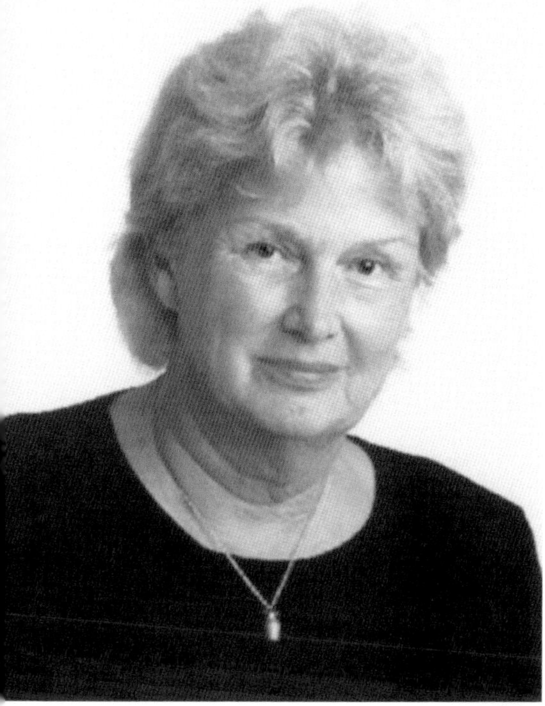

Peg Goldberg-Longstreth (1939–2012) Spencer, Indiana, native and Carmel art dealer Peg Goldberg found herself embroiled in an art deal scandal into which she innocently entered. In 1988, while on a buying trip for her studio in west Carmel, she came across a deal that was too good to be true. A Turkish art dealer offered her four 6th-century Greek mosaics for $1 million. In her mind, she did the math and knew they were worth much more. She arranged getting the money and returned home not knowing the mosaics had been taken from Cypress in a military invasion years before. Peg advertised the artwork as for sale, they were seen, and the authorities were notified. Peg was sued to return them to Cypress and was out the money. After her marriage, she moved to Naples, Florida, where she opened an art gallery. (Both, courtesy of the *Naples News*.)

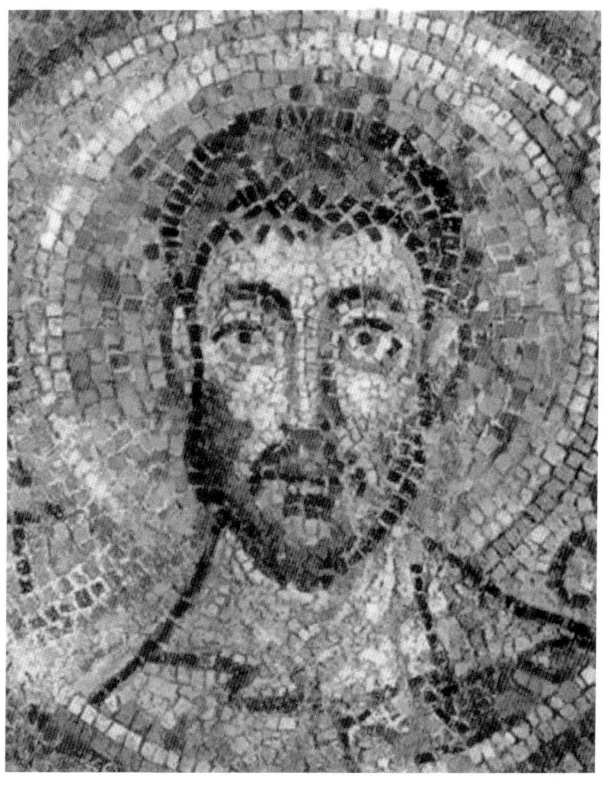

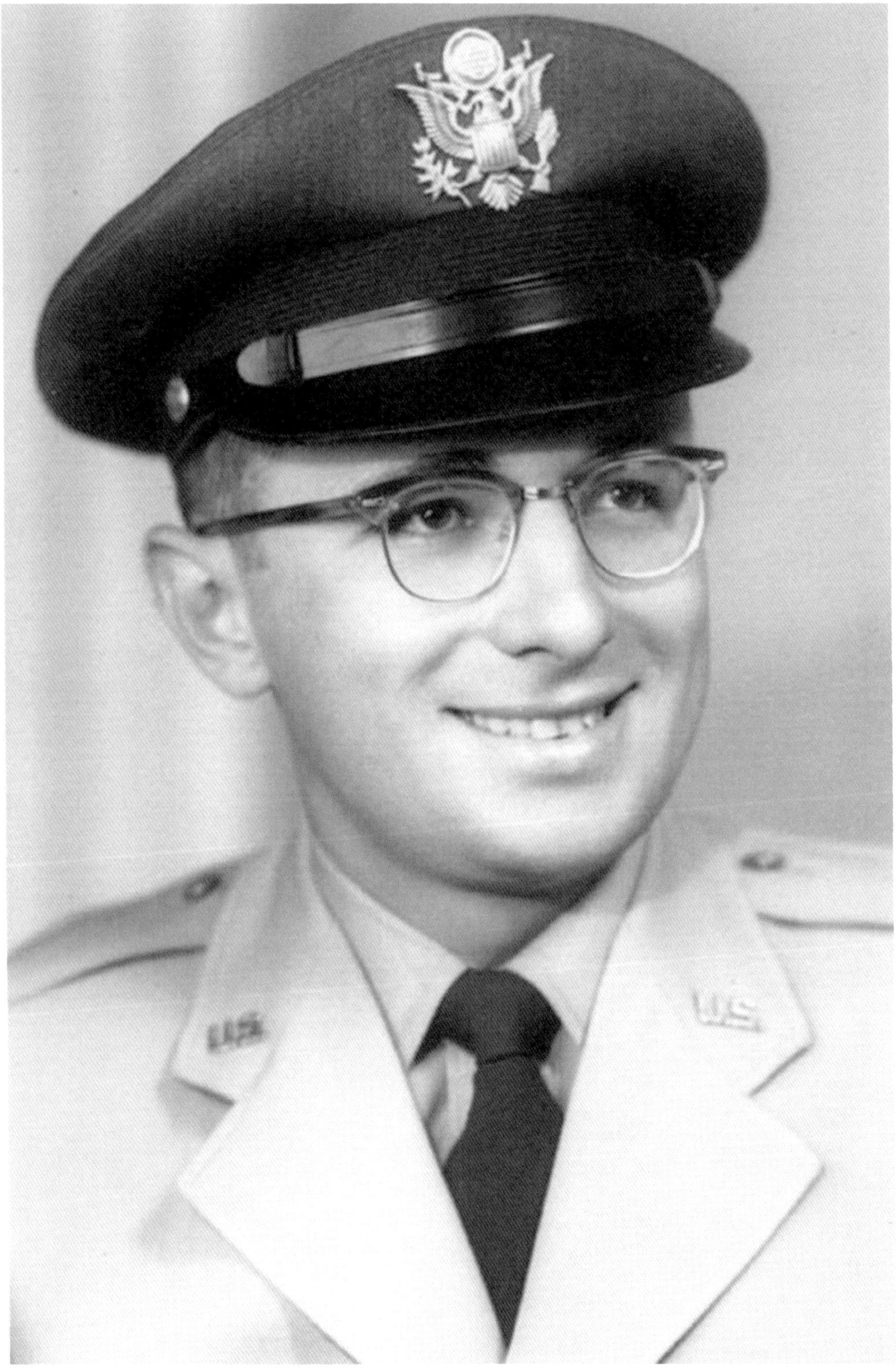

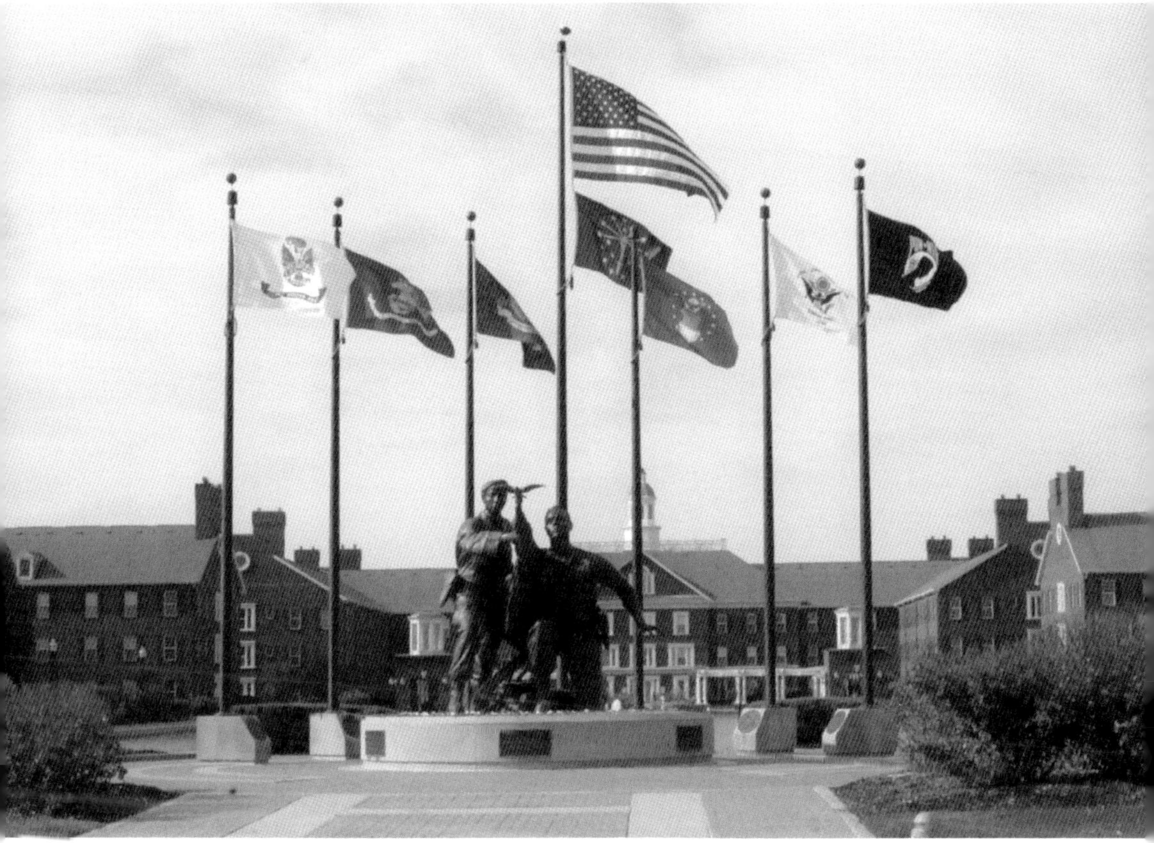

Lt. Col. Willis A. "Bill" Ensign Jr. (Ret.) (1932–)
Born in Buffalo, New York, and educated in Bowling Green, Ohio, Bill Ensign was commissioned to the US Air Force through the Reserve Officers' Training Corps (ROTC) on his college campus and went on to retire with the highest rank, lieutenant colonel. He and wife, Dorothy, ended up living in Carmel, where they raised their six children. Mayor Brainard, in his first term in 1996, decided Carmel needed a monument to honor those who have served in the armed forces. Bill volunteered and founded the Carmel Clay Veterans Memorial Committee, which was the principal fundraising entity. Citizens could purchase bricks that would be inlaid in the walkway leading up to the monument. They could request inscriptions honoring their family members who served. Money from the bricks would help fund the project. The monument was dedicated in 2006 and is an integral part of the City of Carmel's Veterans Day program each November. Bill received the Range Line Pioneer Award for his dedication to this project. (Opposite, courtesy of Cindy Ensign Baney; above, author's collection.)

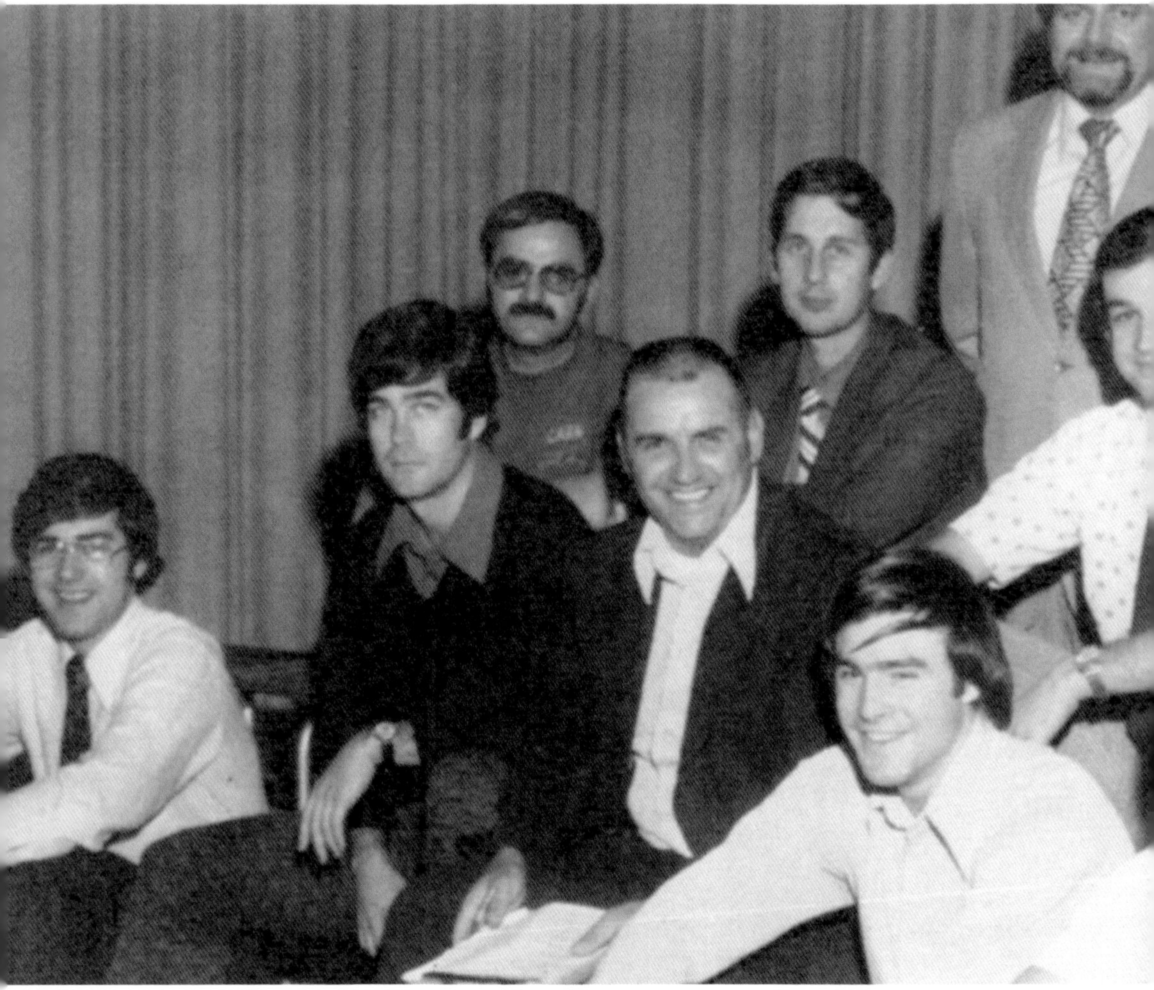

Robert D. Johnson (1934–2015)

Longtime Carmel Junior High School (now Carmel Middle School) educator, coach, and athletic director Bob Johnson sits amid his coaching staff. A Fishers High School graduate and an alumnus of Western New Mexico State and Butler University, Bob was hired by Carmel Clay Schools to develop a premier athletic program at Carmel Junior High School. The junior high programs were built with the hopes of sending accomplished athletes with good sportsmanship and skills to the high school programs. Anyone who lived in Carmel in the 1970s knew Bob as the manager of the Carmel Community Pool, located north of Carmel Junior High on Guilford Road. Bob always had a remarkable suntan and was affectionately known as "Cherokee Bob." He not only coached youth and made them better people, he taught youth business and social skills as employees of the pool. During his career, he received many Indiana Athletic Directors Association Awards, as well as national awards. (Courtesy of the 1974 Carmel Junior High School yearbook, *Vista*.)

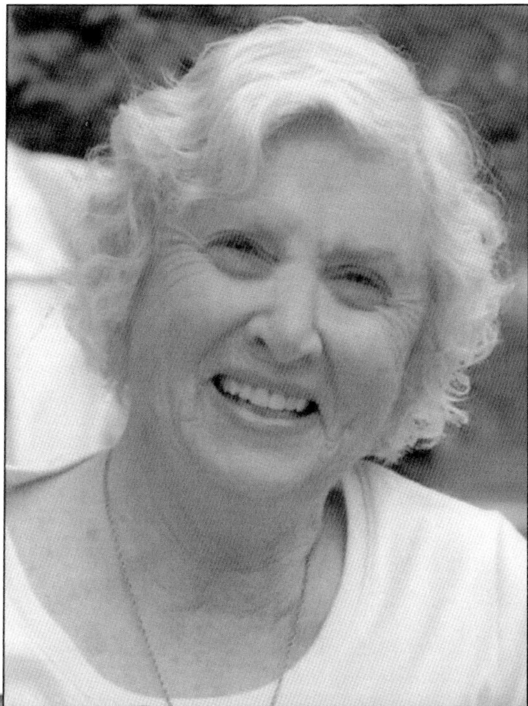

Jane C. (Applegath) Reiman (1933–)
Mayor Jane Reiman sits at a conference table preparing for a meeting in city hall in 1987. Born in Canada, Reiman served as mayor for a quickly growing city from 1980 to 1987. When she was elected, she was one of only a handful of females voted to serve. During her two terms, Carmel grew by 150 percent, which posed some great challenges for how to handle what a municipality is faced with when expanding at such a quick rate. Mayor Reiman had vision and follow-through, and the city succeeded with little or no growing pains. She did not seek a third term. In 2011, at age 78, she ran for city council but did not win the seat. Today, she can be found in city hall once again heading up the mayor's youth council. (Left, photograph by Jennifer D. Hershberger; below, courtesy of "Celebrate Carmel—A Welcome Home," an *Indianapolis Monthly* magazine supplement, 1987.)

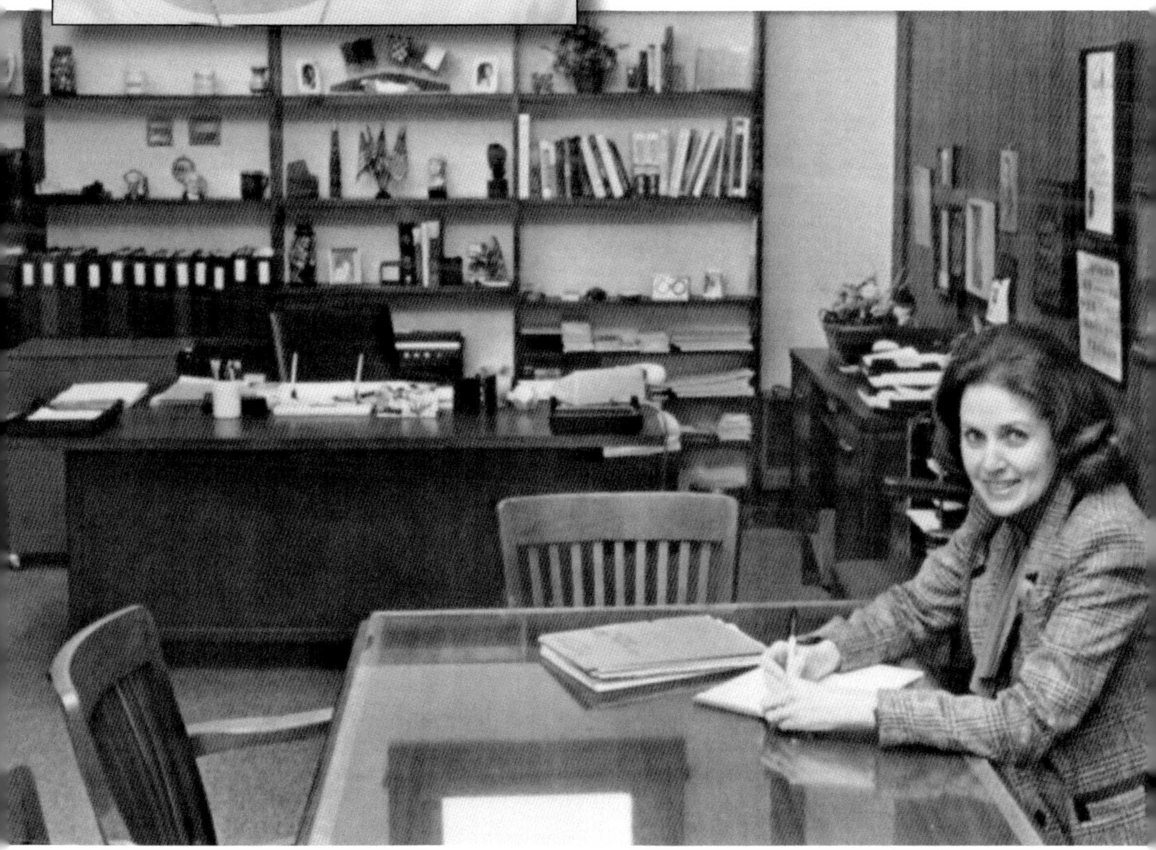

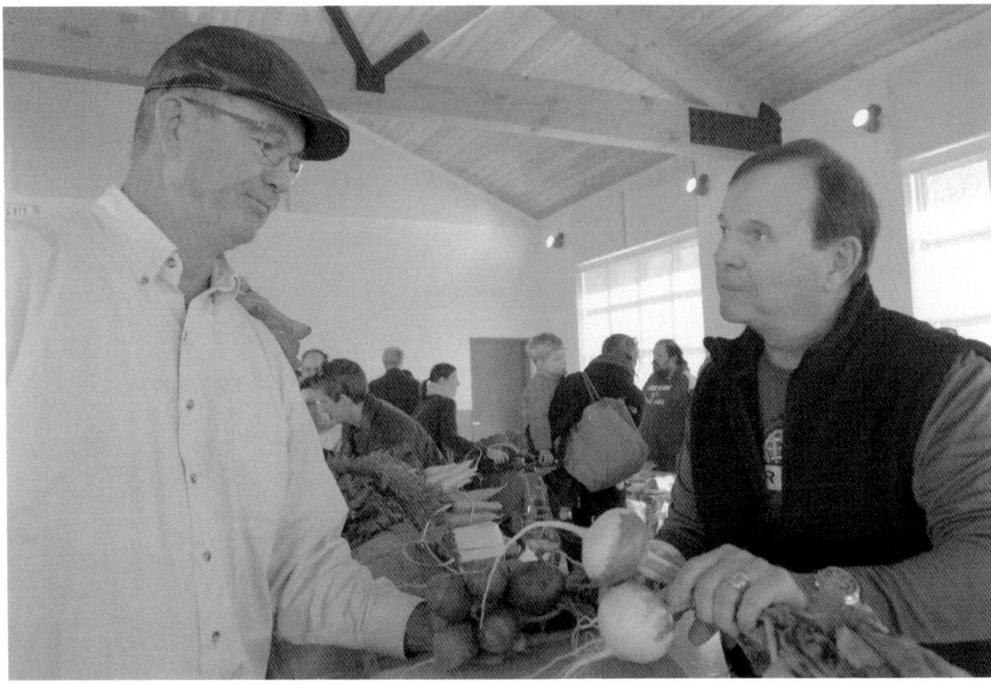

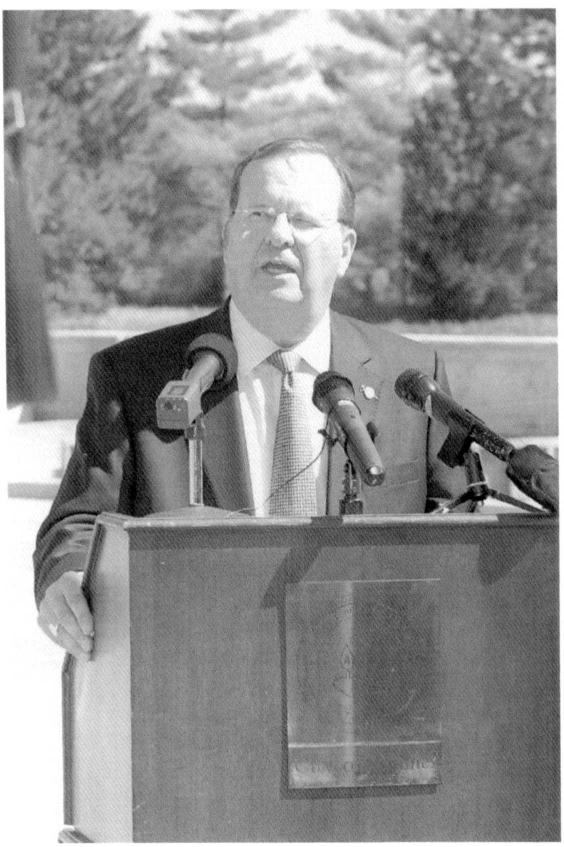

Ronald E. Carter (1943–)
Pictured above, Ron Carter is seen talking to a customer about turnips at the Winter Carmel Farmers Market; at left, he is speaking to an audience when Keystone Parkway was completed and dedicated in 2010. Indianapolis native Ron Carter served on the board of zoning appeals in the early 1990s and was instrumental in making the Monon Greenway a reality. He is president of the Carmel Farmers Market and Winter Carmel Farmers Market. (Photographs by Jennifer D. Hershberger.)

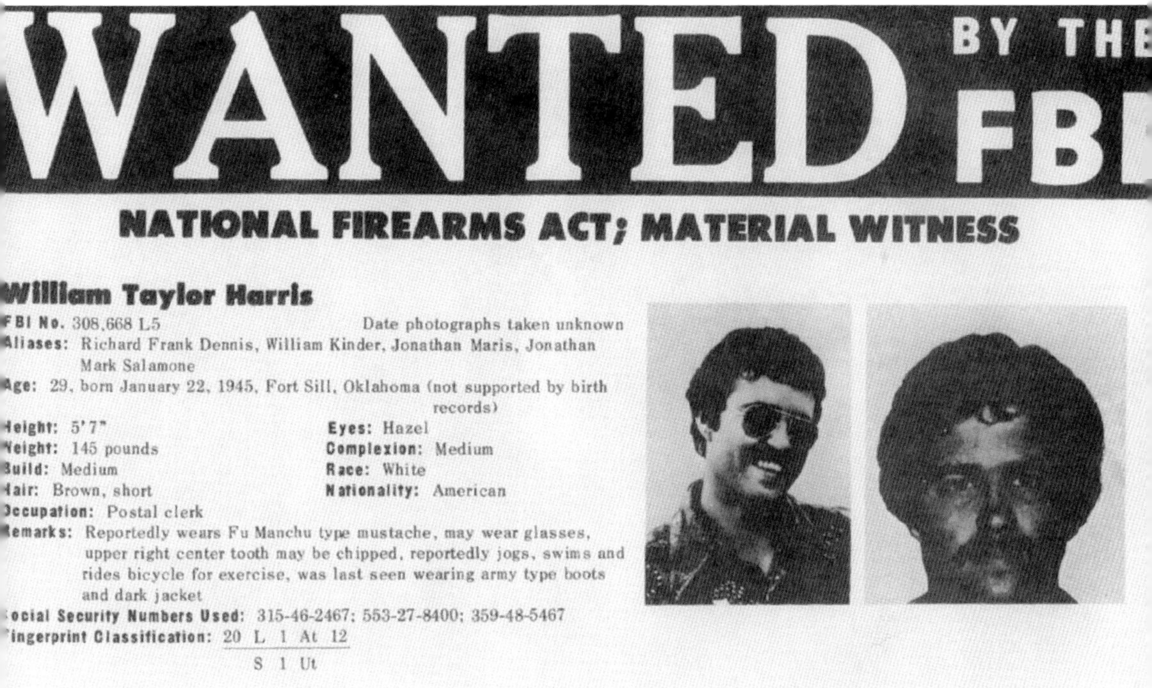

WANTED BY THE FBI

NATIONAL FIREARMS ACT; MATERIAL WITNESS

William Taylor Harris

FBI No. 308,668 L5 — Date photographs taken unknown

Aliases: Richard Frank Dennis, William Kinder, Jonathan Maris, Jonathan Mark Salamone

Age: 29, born January 22, 1945, Fort Sill, Oklahoma (not supported by birth records)

Height: 5' 7" — **Eyes:** Hazel

Weight: 145 pounds — **Complexion:** Medium

Build: Medium — **Race:** White

Hair: Brown, short — **Nationality:** American

Occupation: Postal clerk

Remarks: Reportedly wears Fu Manchu type mustache, may wear glasses, upper right center tooth may be chipped, reportedly jogs, swims and rides bicycle for exercise, was last seen wearing army type boots and dark jacket

Social Security Numbers Used: 315-46-2467; 553-27-8400; 359-48-5467

Fingerprint Classification: 20 L 1 At 12 / S 1 Ut

William T. Harris (1945–)

Bill Harris graduated from Carmel High School in 1963 and soon joined the US Marines. He later met and married Emily Montague while attaining his master's degree from Indiana University in Bloomington. There, the Harrises learned of the Symbionese Liberation Army (SLA), a left-wing domestic terrorist group. Moving to San Francisco to follow the group, the Harrises were deeply rooted in the organization with Bill using the moniker "General Teko." In February 1974, the group would make national headlines when they abducted newspaper magnate William Randolph Hearst's granddaughter Patty Hearst in Berkeley, California. The Harrises and SLA members were considered fugitives and wanted by the FBI. Soon after the kidnapping, an SLA propaganda video surfaced of Patty appearing to be a member. In May 1974, the Harrises were caught on surveillance video shoplifting ammunition in a gun store. In their attempt to escape, Patty was also caught on video shooting a machine gun to essentially distract law enforcement and aid the Harrises to freedom. They were finally arrested in 1975. Bill served a seven-and-a-half-year sentence for the kidnapping. Bill and Emily both would be tried and sentenced again in 1999 for their connection to a bank robbery that resulted in a death in 1975. Bill was paroled in 2006. (Courtesy of the National Archives.)

Robert M. "Bobby" Cox (1956–)
Sports lover and accomplished athlete Bobby Cox graduated from Carmel High School in 1975 and went on to attain his bachelor's and master's degrees from Butler University. After a 21-year career with Carmel Clay Schools teaching, coaching, and serving as athletic director at Carmel Junior High and Carmel High School, he was appointed as the eighth commissioner of the Indiana High School Athletic Association. (Courtesy of Bobby Cox.)

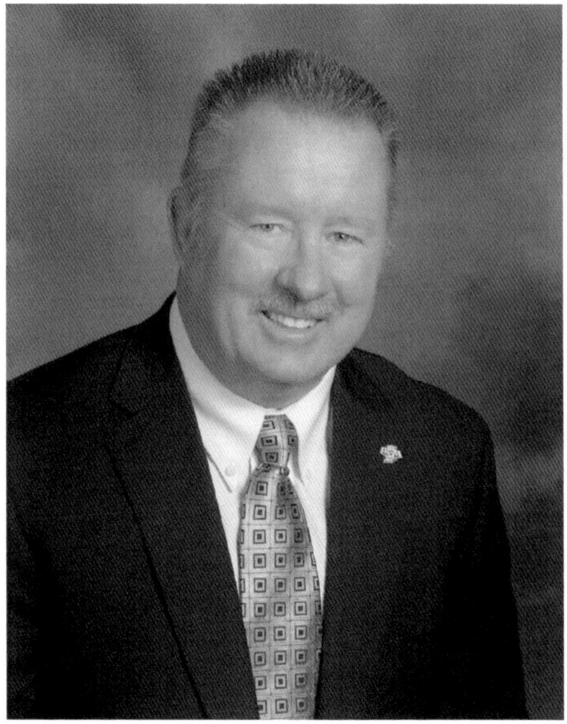

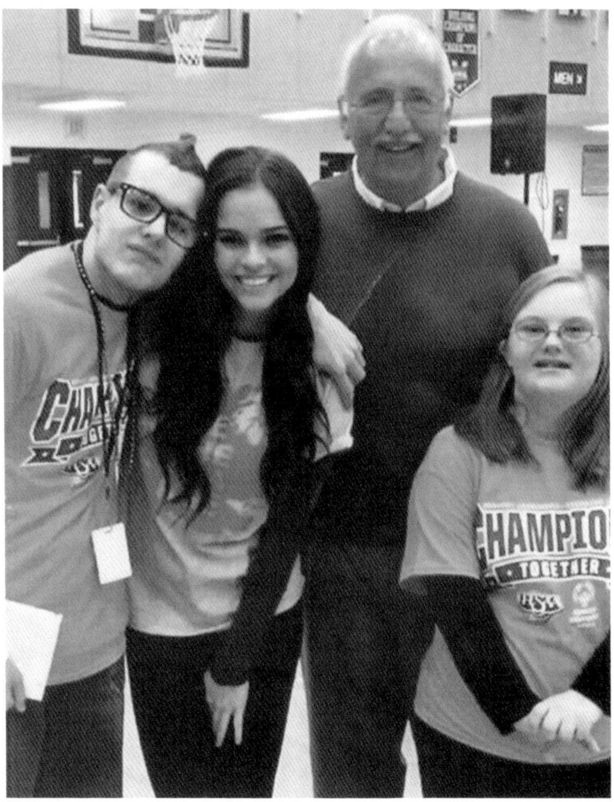

Lee R. Lonzo (1951–)
Michigan City native Lee Lonzo poses with Champions Together participants at Mooresville High School in 2014. Former teacher, city council member, and city attorney Lee mentors high school students in a program he established to provide orientation for incoming high school freshmen across the nation. He also works in the partnership of the Special Olympics and the Indiana High School Athletic Association, called Champions Together. (Courtesy of Lee Lonzo.)

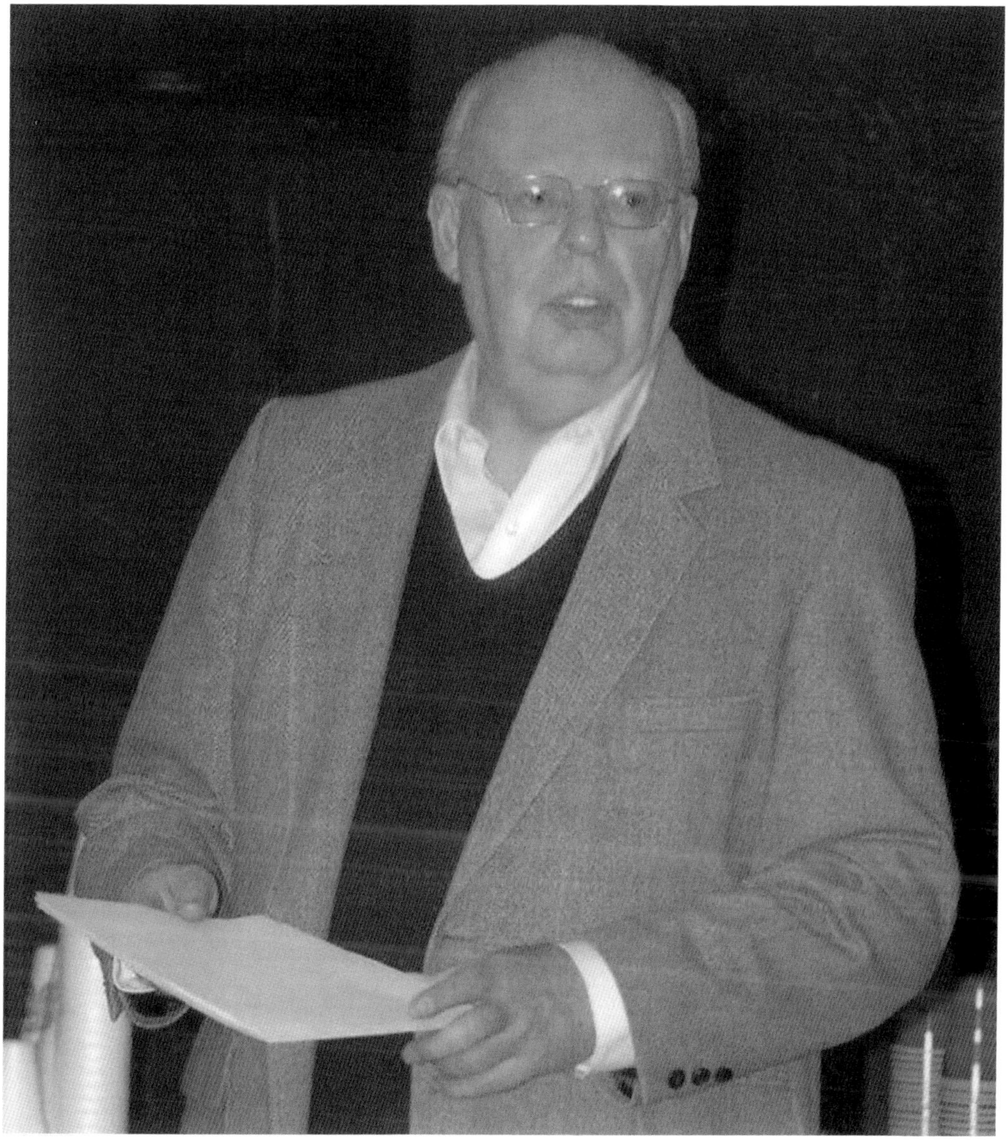

Fred T. Swift (1942–)
Former president of the Carmel Clay Historical Society Fred Swift addresses those in attendance at the society's annual meeting, introducing the incoming board members for the following year. Fred graduated from Carmel High School in 1960 and attended Franklin College. Following his love for journalism that he discovered in high school, he went to work as a reporter for the *Noblesville Daily Ledger*, the former daily newspaper that covered Hamilton County. After 21 years, he left the position of editor to pursue his interest in county government and served another 21 years as assistant to the county commissioners. Fred is retired now but is hardly idle. He contributes a column to another newspaper, *Hamilton County Reporter*. He is active in his church, the historical society, Meals on Wheels, and the Carmel Clay Republican Club. He was a town board member before Carmel became a city in 1976 and went on to serve on the city council. He was honored for his work on the Indiana Law Enforcement Training Board with a Sagamore of the Wabash Award. The now defunct Carmel Jaycees recognized him with their Distinguished Service Award for his time with Carmel's city government. (Photograph by Jennifer D. Hershberger.)

Dick Nyers (1934–)

Dick Nyers is pictured in 2014 at a book signing for Dan Chapman and Pam Shepherd Otten's newly released book *A Town of Champions: A History of the Carmel Dads' Club*. The name Dick Nyers and football are synonymous in Carmel—from his 10 years as head coach at Carmel High School to his part in the formation of the Carmel Dads' Club. Dick played football for Manual High School in Indianapolis and later for Indiana Central College, now the University of Indianapolis. He had a two-year career with the Baltimore Colts and is credited for receiving a pass from quarterback Johnny Unitas. What is so special about that pass? It was the first touchdown pass thrown in the National Football League (NFL). Dick is also currently the oldest living, former NFL player. When Coach Nyers left Carmel High School in 1967, he went to Ball State to serve as an assistant, and later as head coach at Indiana Central, now Indiana State University, in Terre Haute. While coaching at Carmel High School, he saw a need for an organized football program for younger children, and in 1959, the Carmel Dads' Club was born. The traveling football team for fourth-through-sixth graders was called the Carmel Pups, a play off of the CHS mascot, the greyhound. Today, the Carmel Dads' Club is a multi-facility, 750-team, 11-sport organization with 5,500 members that touts that its success stems from parent volunteers who coach, keep score, referee, run concession stands, and do field maintenance. (Author's collection.)

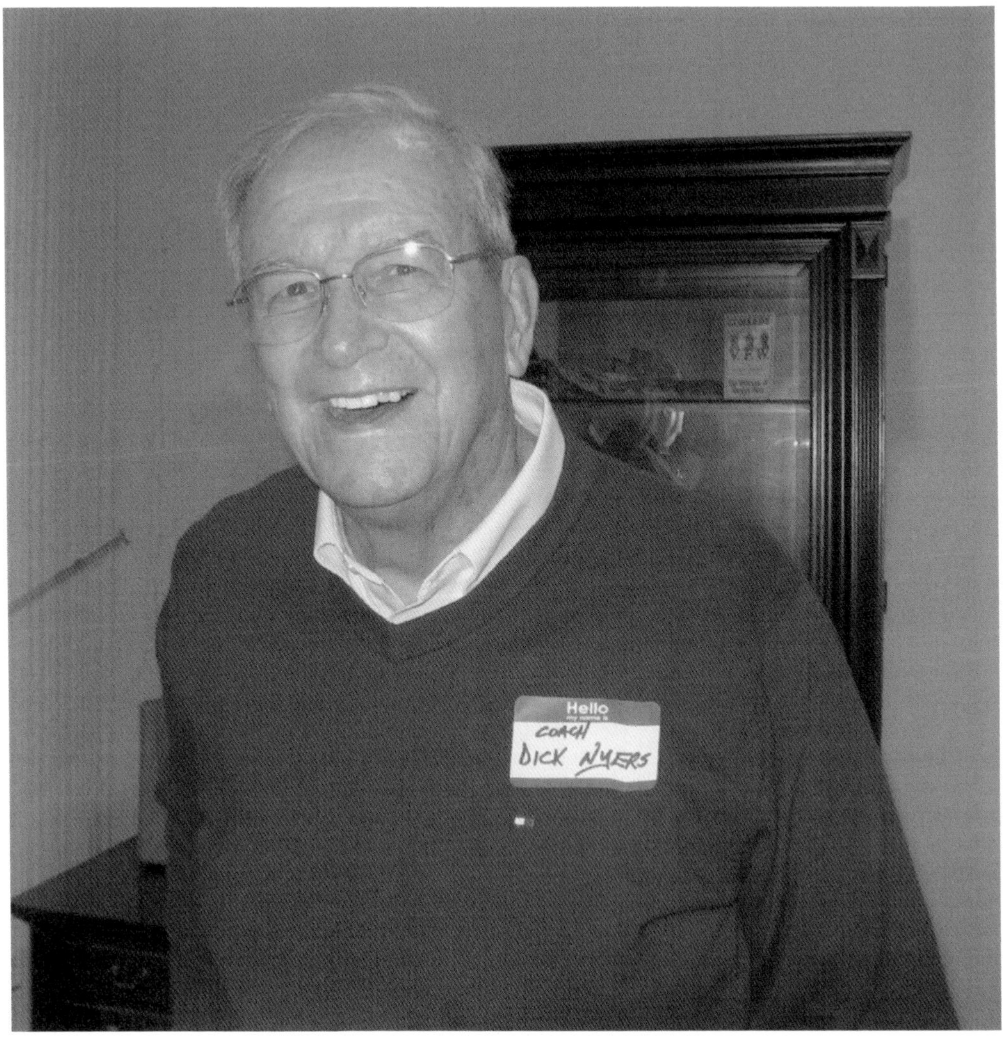

Mark D. Herrmann (1959–)

Carmel High School senior Mark Herrmann poses with his parents, Don and Doris, after being named the recipient of the Arthur L. Trester Mental Attitude Award in 1977. Carmel had just won its first state basketball championship. A three-sport letterman at CHS, football quarterback Mark attended Purdue University, where he was named an All-American and took Purdue to three postseason bowl games, winning all three. After college, he was drafted by the Denver Broncos and then traded to the Baltimore Colts who soon moved to Indianapolis. Further trades would finish out his 11-year career in the NFL. Mark was elected to the College Football Hall of Fame in Atlanta, Georgia, in 2010. (Courtesy of *The Carmel Topics*, 1977.)

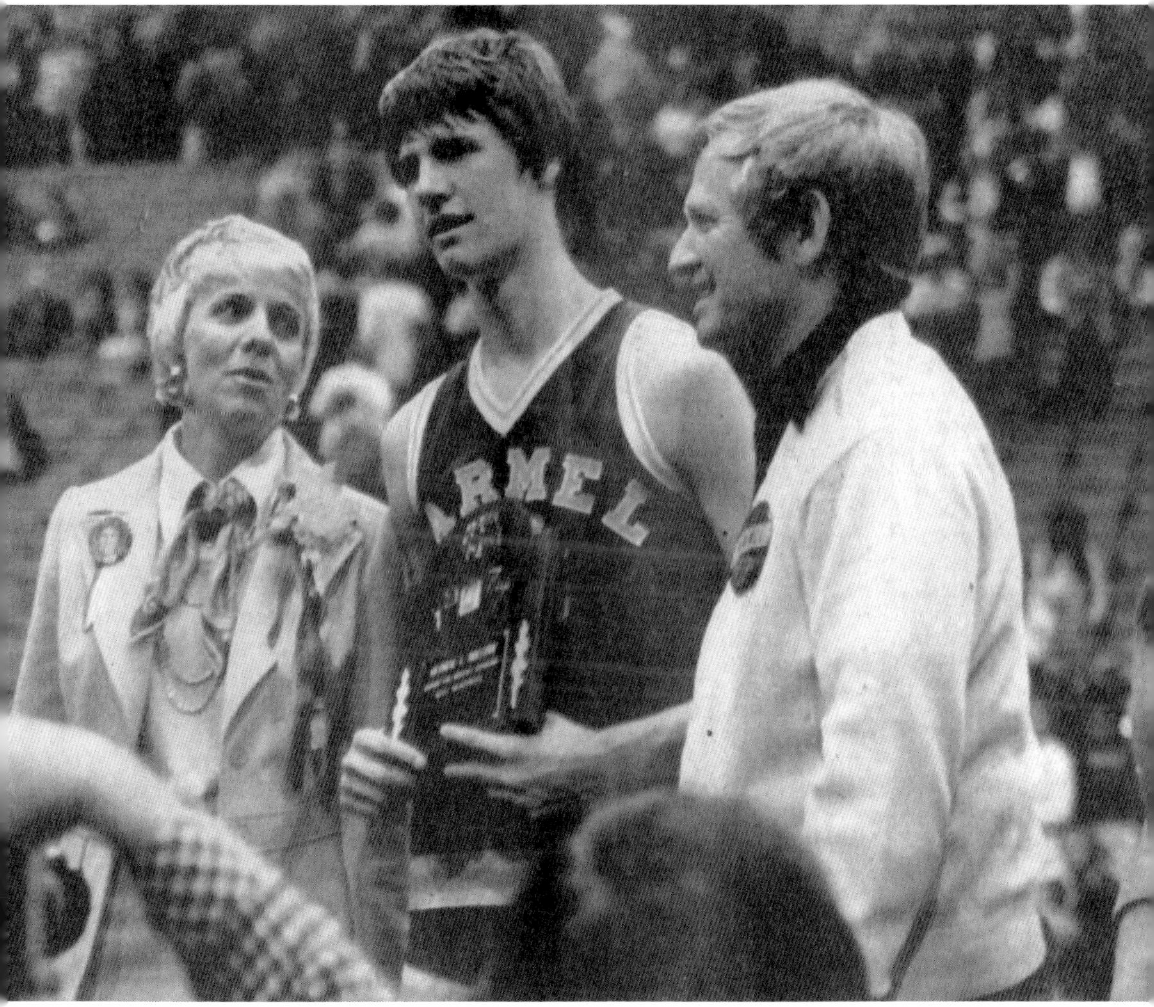

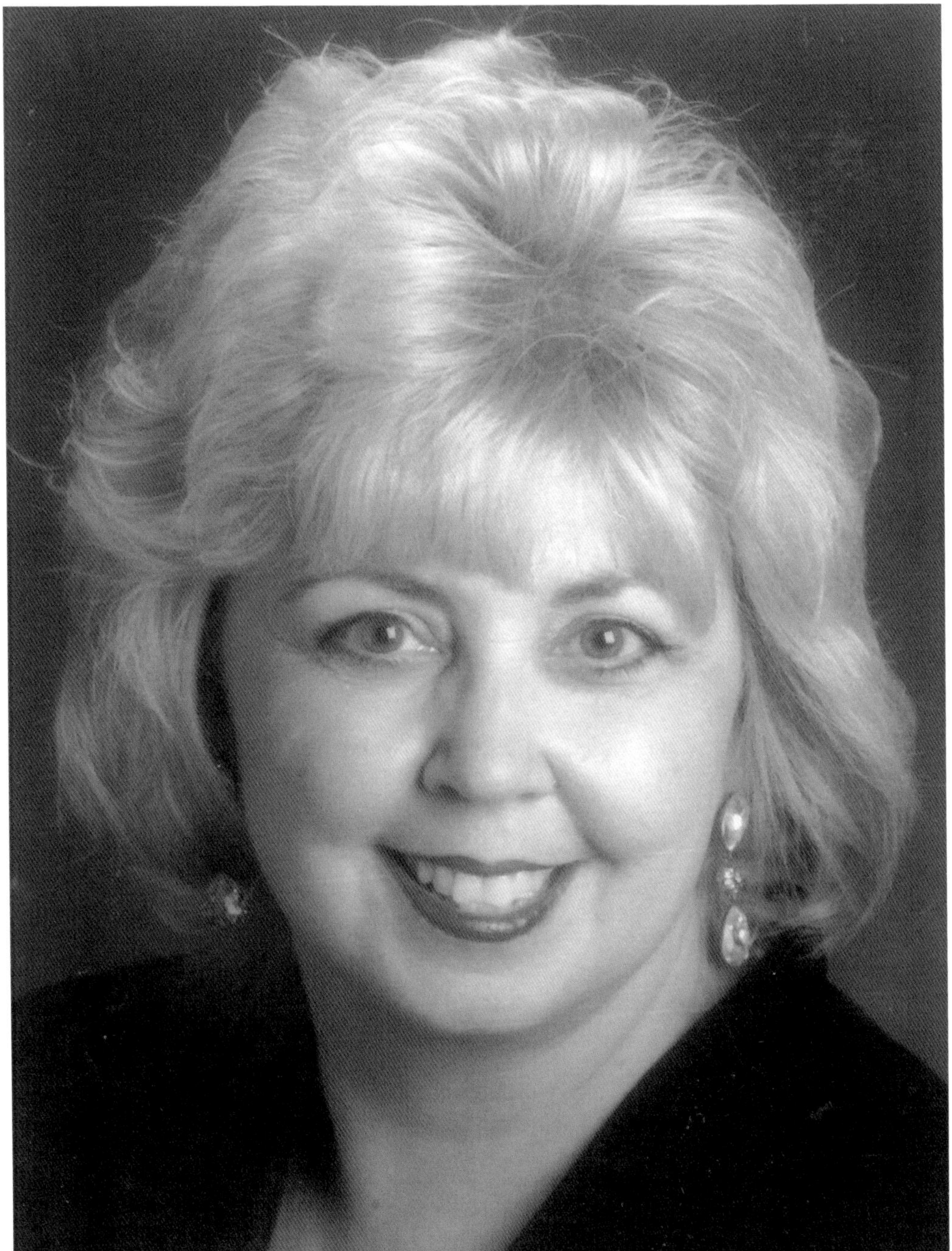

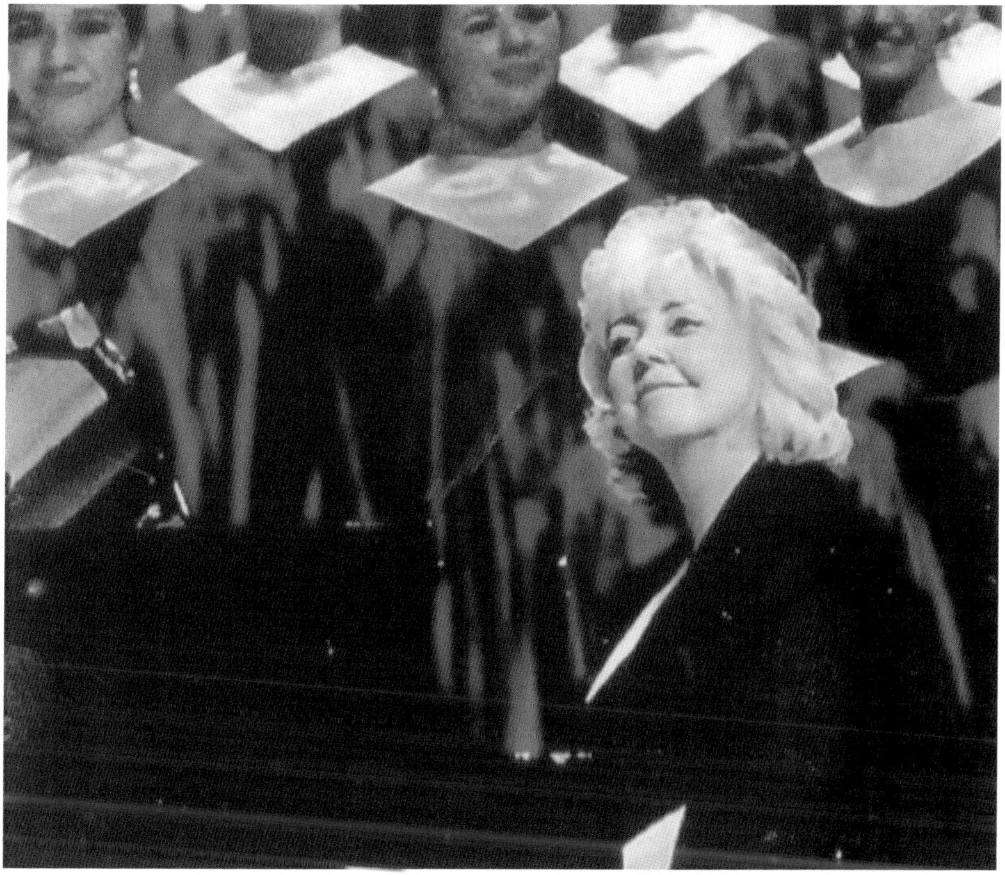

Ann (Calvert) Conrad (1954–)

Retired Carmel High School choral director Ann Conrad reflects at the piano during a performance of the widely attended *Holiday Spectacular*, the school's annual holiday musical pageant put on at Christmastime. A graduate of Arlington High School in Indianapolis, Ann's love of music started at an early age, as her father was a band director that was held in high esteem. Fresh out of Ball State University, Ann was hired in 1976 at Carmel High School, where her career would span 38 years. Encouraged early on to dream big dreams by Principal Dale Graham, Ann built the choral program at CHS from 64 students in three choirs her first year to 525 students in 11 choirs at her retirement in 2014. Ann is the 2010 recipient of the James B. Calvert Outstanding Music Educator Award presented by the Indiana Wind Symphony. This award is especially meaningful to her since it is named to honor her late father. When Ann and her husband, Charles, came to Carmel in 1976, their intent was to stay two years and then relocate to Sarasota, Florida, where there is a vibrant arts community. The years tell the story. Ann has a 38-year legacy at Carmel High School, where she will not be soon forgotten, and Charles is currently the music director for the Indiana Wind Symphony, a resident company at the Center for the Performing Arts. Ann now teaches private voice lessons and serves as the music director for the young adult program at the Booth Tarkington Civic Theatre, which is also a part of the Center. (Both, courtesy of Ann Conrad.)

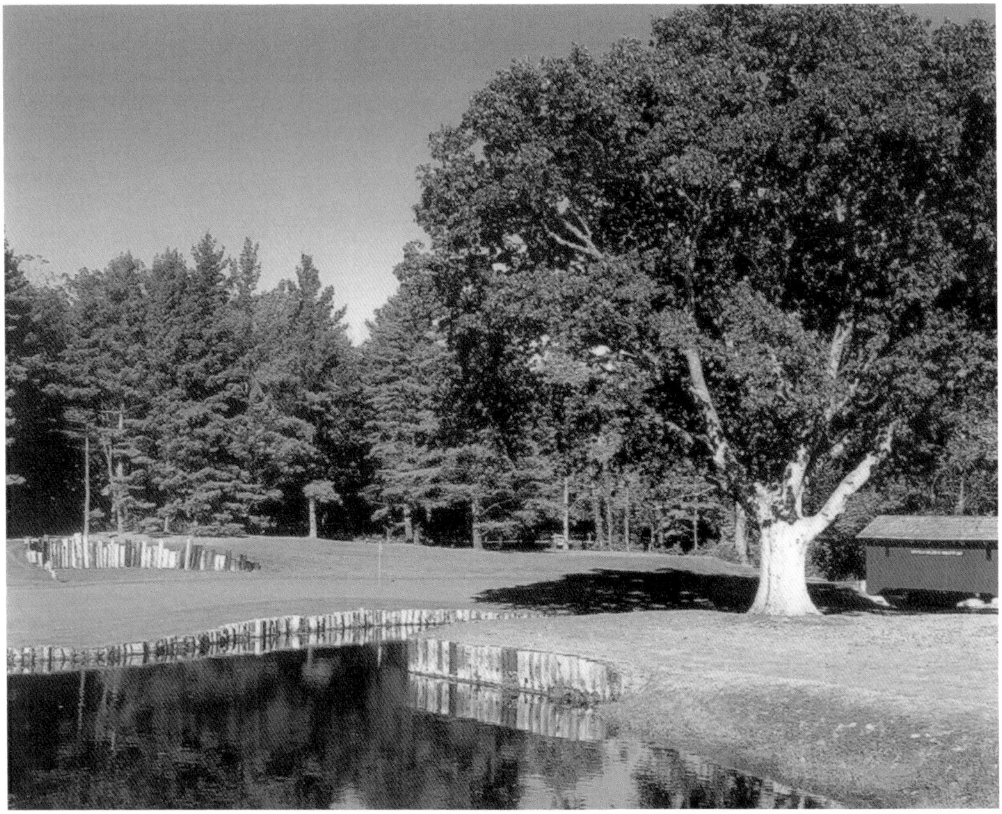

Paul B. "Pete" Dye (1925–)

An insurance salesman with a penchant for golf, which was inherited from his father, Pete Dye would be a great influence on Carmel and the surrounding landscape. His interest in golf led Pete's father to build a nine-hole course on property they owned outside of Urbana, Ohio, and it went on to become the Urbana Country Club. Pete was a competitive golfer in high school, winning the title of Ohio State High School Golf Champion and Ohio State Amateur Golf Championship. In 1944, Pete joined the US Army Airborne School in Fort Benning, Georgia, in the hopes of becoming a paratrooper. The war ended, and that never happened, but he did find himself stationed at Fort Bragg, North Carolina, where he cared for the base golf course. He met his wife at Rollins College in Florida, and they relocated to Indianapolis. Resuming his amateur career, he won amateur titles in Indiana and played in the 1957 US Open. Coming to the decision of wanting to be a golf course designer, he embarked on a career of which he would become widely known. Pete has designed golf courses in nearly every state. Crooked Stick Golf Club in Carmel sits among lavish homes and is a members-only club. It can only be played by invitation. Voted one of the top 100 best courses in the United States, it has been host to the 1991 Professional Golfers' Association (PGA) Championship, the 1993 US Women's Open, 2005 Solheim matches, and the 2012 BMW Championship, which will return in 2016. Pete has been honored to be recognized by the World Golf Hall of Fame and to receive the PGA Tour Lifetime Achievement Award. He designed the Club at Chatham Hills in Westfield, which is under construction. (Courtesy of Crooked Stick Golf Club.)

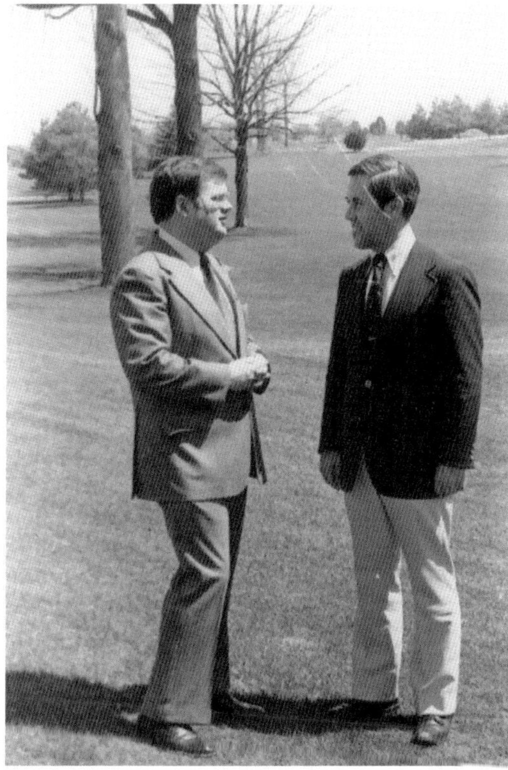

James D. Garretson (1945–)
Jim Garretson, Hamilton County campaign chair for Richard Lugar, discusses political issues with the newly elected senator in 1977. Jim was hired by Carmel Clay Schools to teach social studies. He became department chair and held that position until his retirement in 2002. Jim's resume puts others to shame as he is a community servant to the core. (Courtesy of the Carmel Clay Historical Society.)

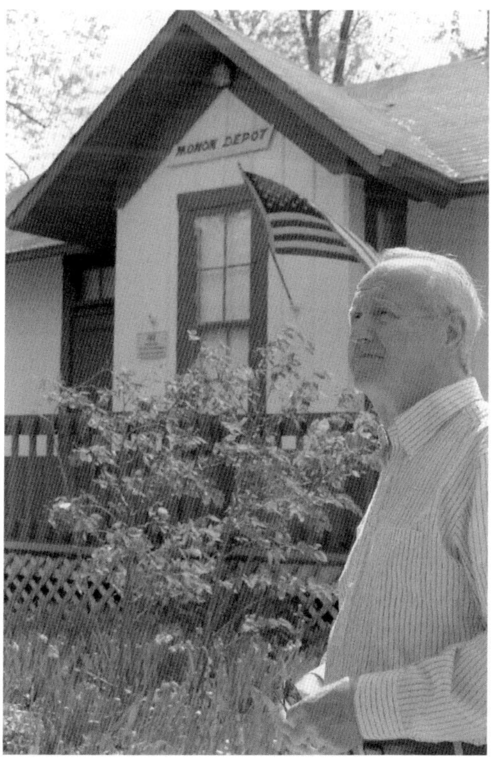

Thomas A. Rumer (1942–)
Here, former Carmel Clay Historical Society executive director Tom Rumer stands outside the Monon Depot Museum reflecting on how fortunate the community is to have an organization to preserve, protect, and share its history. Tom is an accomplished author of several books as well as numerous trade and university works. During his tenure as director of the Carmel Clay Historical Society, he recognized the importance of document and memento preservation for future generations. (Photograph by Jennifer D. Hershberger.)

Steve A. Couts (1946–2003)

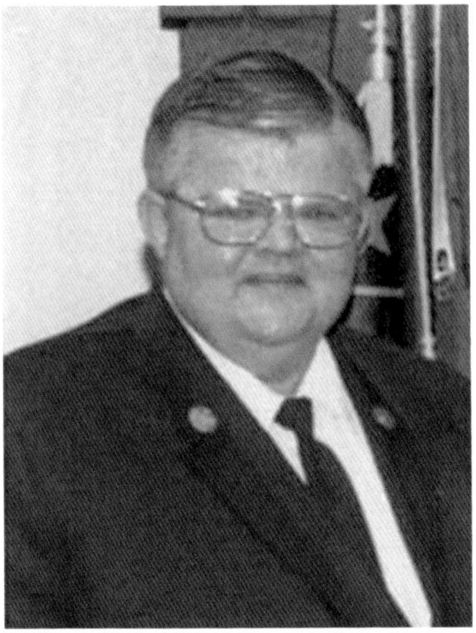

It is remarkable how many of Carmel's community servants today were rooted in the Carmel Fire Department. Carmel recognizes these individuals in ways that are appropriate to their service. Carmel High School class of 1964 graduate Steve Couts was appointed to the position of fire chief by Mayor Jane Reiman in 1982 upon the death of longtime chief Donald Swails. Steve saw great change throughout his term, not only in the department, but also in the community. He saw the development and construction of the new fire headquarters that would be located at 2 Civic Square. That building would eventually bear his name to honor his spirit and dedication to the Carmel Fire Department and the city. Steve retired in 1995 and went on to manage the city's hazardous waste facility. (Right, courtesy of the Carmel Clay Historical Society; below, courtesy of Deborah Swails Collins.)

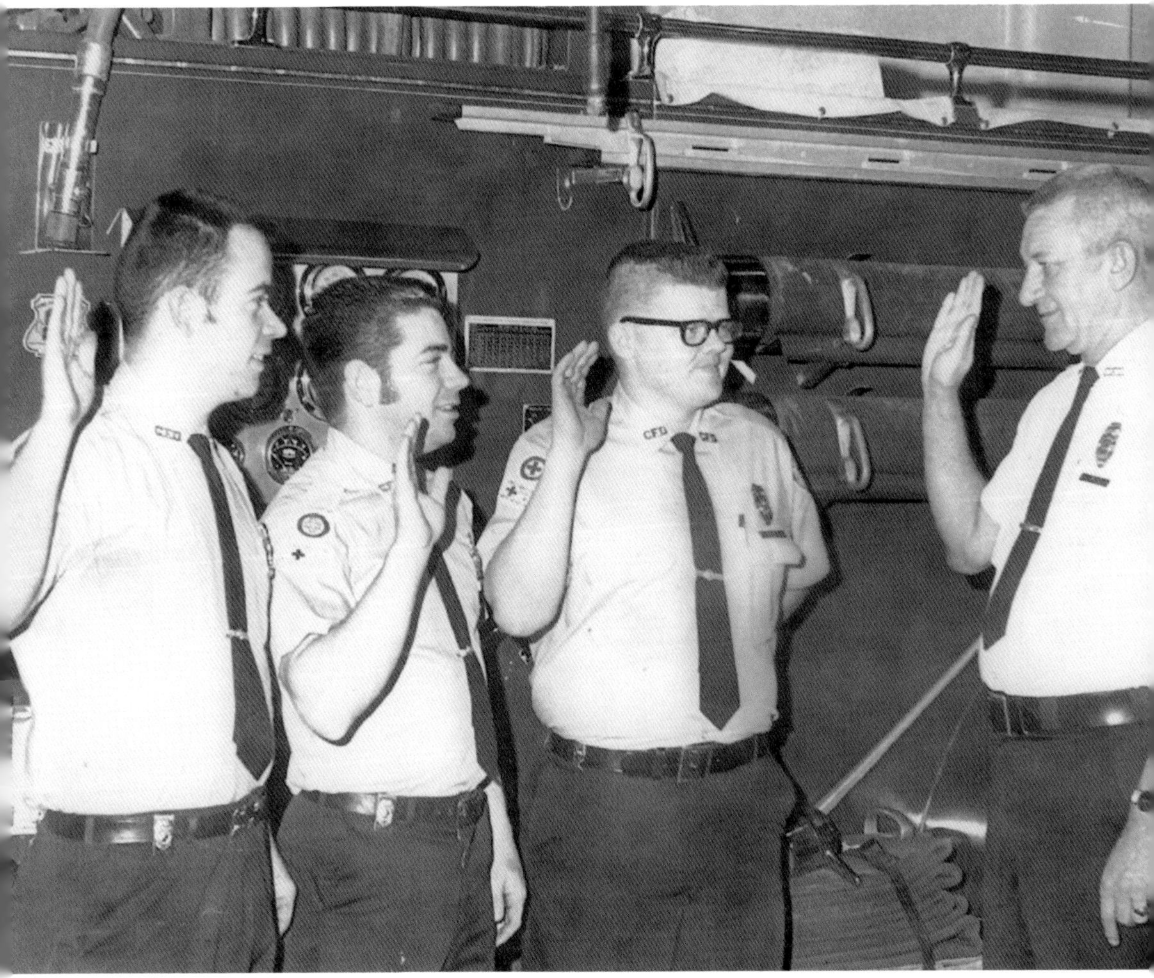

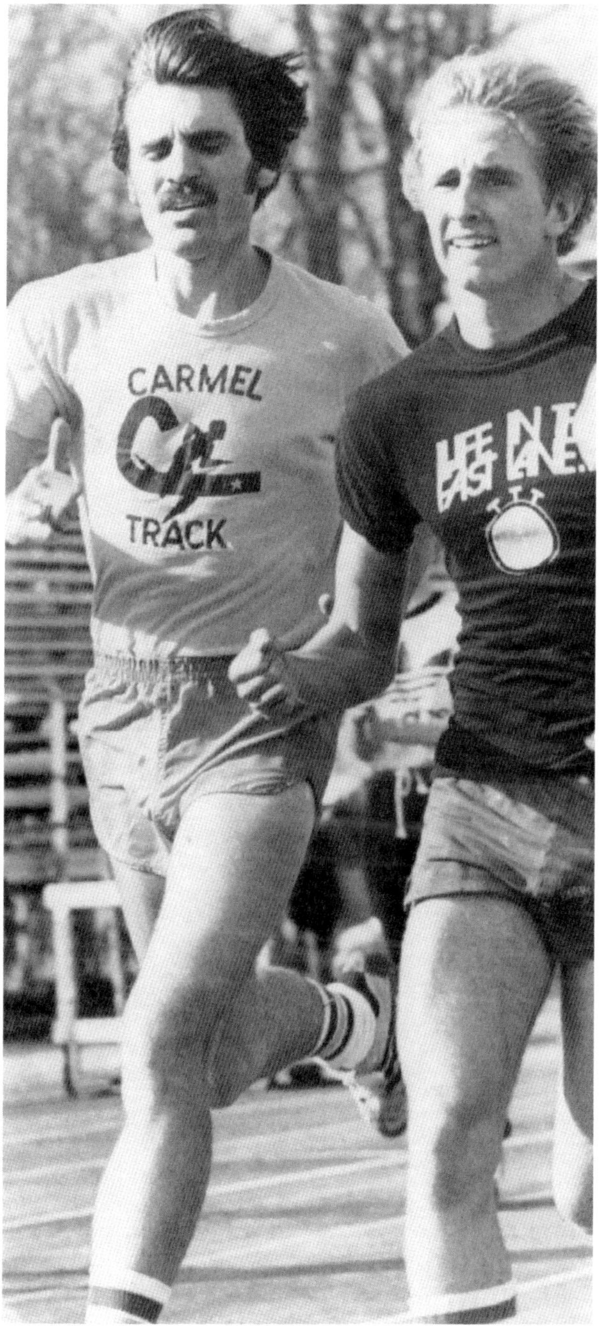

Charles W. "Chuck" Koeppen IV (1946–)

Over a 20-year span, a familiar sight around Carmel after school and on weekends is Carmel High School's cross-country team running on the city streets, sidewalks, and trails. If one lived in Carmel during the 1970s to 1990s, he or she likely saw the coach running with them. Chuck Koeppen developed CHS's cross-country program into one of the best in the country. A graduate of Valparaiso High School, Chuck attended Ball State University and set six school records as a runner while there. His coaching career began at Wapahani High School in Selma, Indiana, in 1968. Hired at Carmel in 1972 shortly after participating in the Olympic Trials, he began a career that would assist in propelling Carmel to the ranks of holding some of the best sports programs in the state. Beginning in 1976, the CHS boys' cross-country team would win five of the next six state championship titles under Koeppen's training and leadership. By his retirement, Carmel would have attained 11 state boys' cross-country championships and 11 state girls' cross-country championships with five of those years being dual. Coach Koeppen oversaw the cross country team at Carmel High School for 37 years. Today, after one successful career, he coaches the Indiana University–Purdue University Indianapolis (IUPUI) Jags. He was entered into the The Valparaiso High School Athletic Hall of Fame in 1989. In 2013, he was inducted into the National Federation of State High School Association's National High School Hall of Fame. His list of honors and achievements is long. (Courtesy of the 1978 Carmel High School yearbook, *Pinnacle*.)

K. Eric Clark (1935–2009)

Assistant coach Eric Clark and son David cut down the nets after Carmel's sectional basketball victory in 1971. Carmel defeated Hamilton Southeastern High School by a score of 72-65. A 12-time letterman at Earlham College, Eric Clark was not one to ever sit still. He was a man of small scope and simplicity, but that scope overflowed with his love of family, sports, and community. After graduating from Carmel High School and Earlham, where he was a stand-out athlete participating in football, basketball, track, and volleyball, his next stop was Butler University, where he earned a master's degree in education. He would begin and end his professional career at his high school alma mater, educating and influencing thousands of Carmel's adolescents for 39 years. He was a beloved teacher, a coach, a counselor, and an assistant principal during his tenure at CHS. The Eric Clark Activity Center at Carmel High School is named in his honor. (Both, courtesy of Deborah Clark Gangstad.)

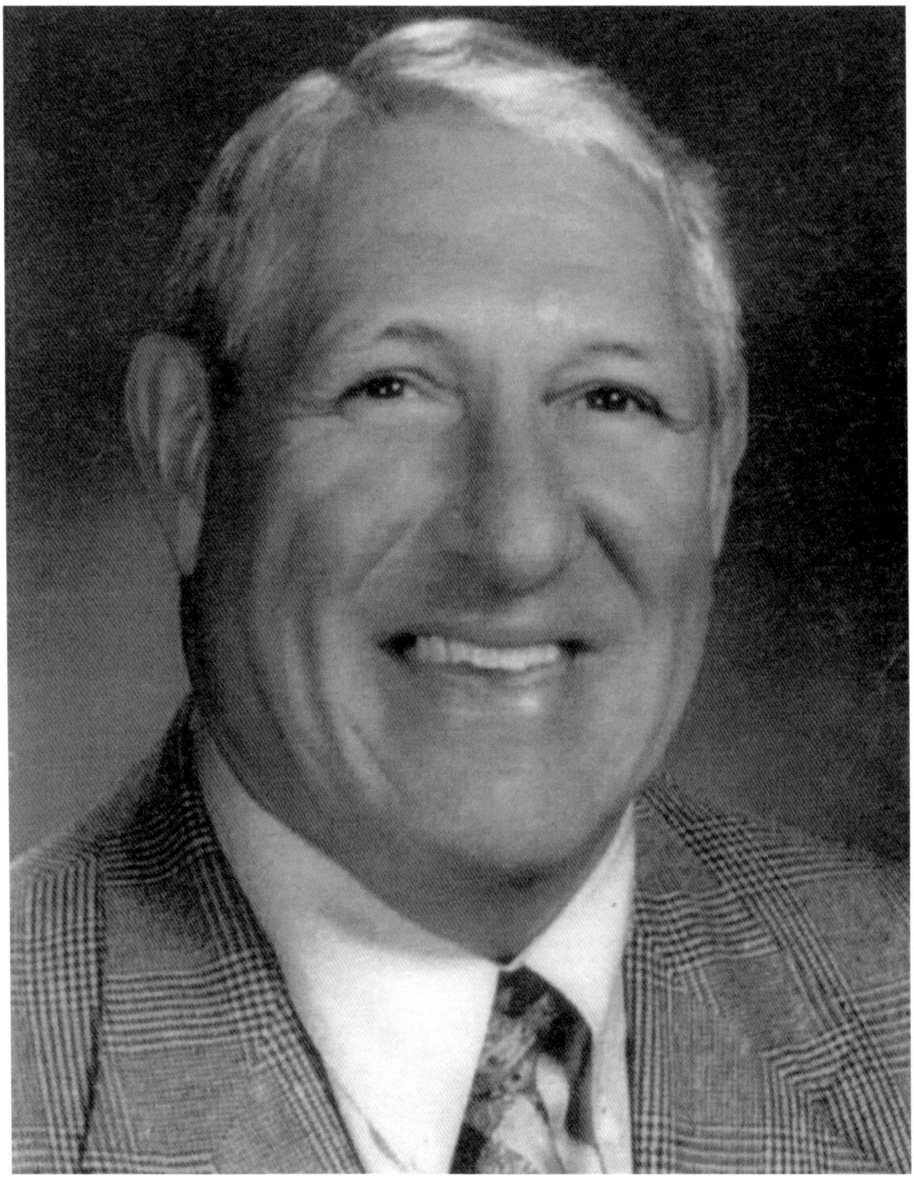

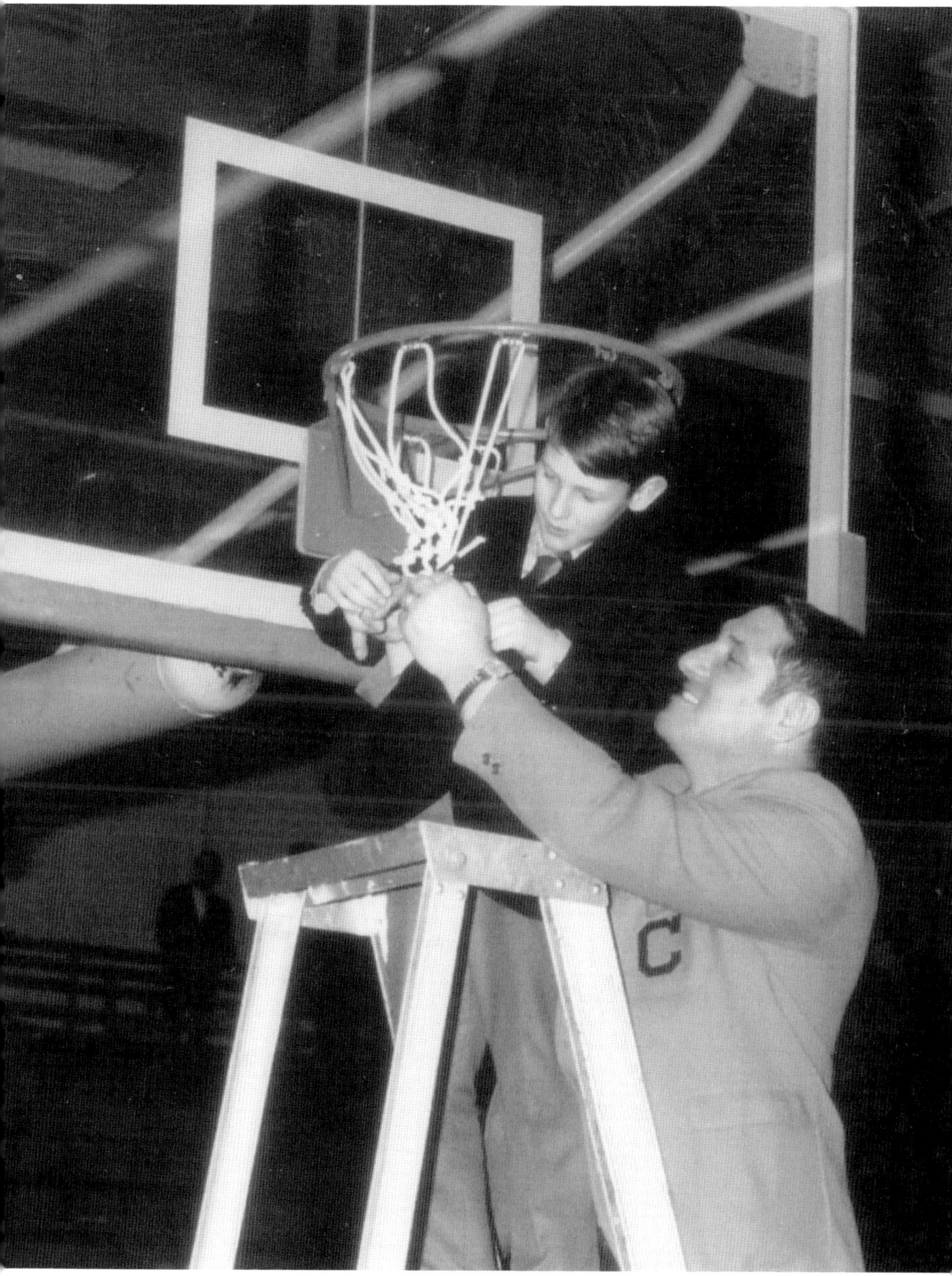

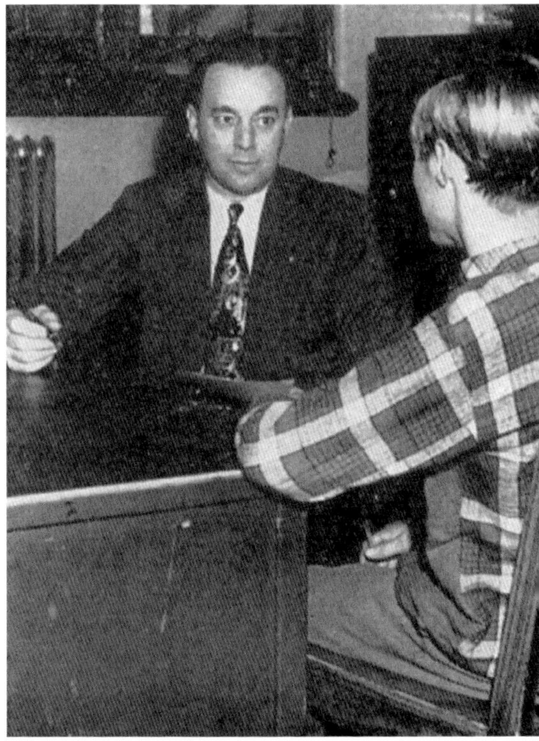

Earl F. Lemme (1907–1973)
World War II Navy veteran and Illinois native Earl Lemme began his 40-year teaching career in Indiana after receiving his master's degree in education from Butler University. After stints at a few other schools, he found himself at Carmel High School in the role of principal. In the late 1950s, he started a ham radio club at CHS. Within a few years, interest in broadcast communications had grown so that money was raised to start a radio station at Carmel High School. WHJE 91.3's first public broadcast was August 6, 1963, from the log cabin on Fourth Avenue NE that held the school administration offices, known as Pattison Hall. It would move into the new school building in 1967. Today, it is one of 200 high school radio stations in the United States. (Right, courtesy of the 1959 Mount Summit High School yearbook; below, courtesy of the 2006 Carmel High School yearbook, *Pinnacle*.)

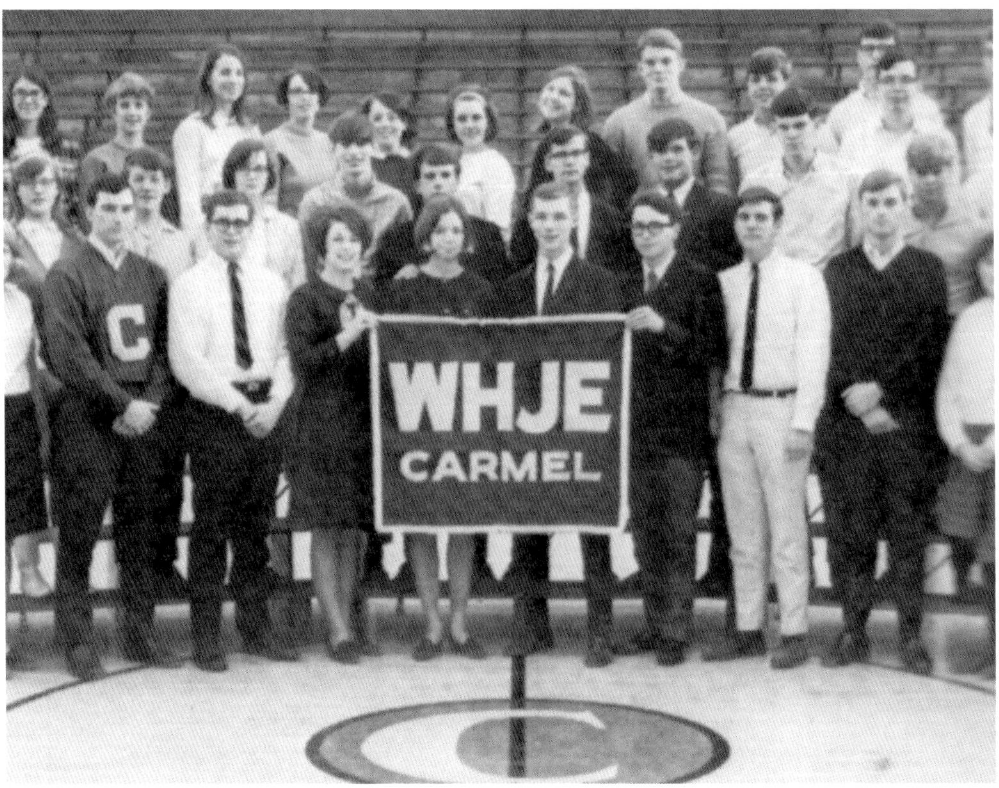

CHAPTER FIVE

Best Place to Live, Work, and Play

One must wonder what Carmel's early residents would think of the thriving, vibrant city today. Its physical size would likely be incomprehensible to them, and they would walk in awe the streets of downtown. Some storefronts are the same but restored. Others are gone. Others are gone and replaced.

CNN's *Money* magazine voted Carmel as American's Best Place to Live in 2012. Carmel was number three on the list in 2014. Mayor Jim Brainard's vision of the city continues to bring a sense of pride to residents, new and old. Today, Carmel covers 48.5 square miles, with each square mile being equally important to the city. There is still farmland in the township, but less and less is farmed each year. Farms that have sat dormant for years are being snatched up by developers to add attractions for residents and visitors to the modern city.

The Center for the Performing Arts includes the Palladium, the Tarkington Theater, and the Studio Theater. Residents can choose their type of entertainment from world-class performers at the Palladium to a community theater production at the Tarkington. Michael Feinstein's Great American Songbook brings in acts such as Shirley Jones, Liza Minnelli, and Rita Moreno to name a few.

The rejuvenated downtown area known as the Arts & Design District holds shops, galleries, and restaurants. Outdoor dining has become extremely popular with the revitalization of downtown. There is never a lack of something to do with festivals such as Artomobilia and the International Arts Festival. On the first Tuesday evening of every month, a gallery walk is held. The galleries in the district stay open late, and downtown comes alive with foot traffic. Live music is a draw to many of the downtown restaurants. Blair Clark's the Warehouse, a refurbished machine shop, is a destination to hear local and national talent. One might even hear Blair himself. Wednesday nights in the summer months, the place to be is on the common area at city hall for the Concerts at the Gazebo. Musical acts, such as the Wright Brothers, play for free, and attendees bring chairs, blankets, and food and drink.

On the common area of the Center for the Performing Arts, the Carmel Farmers Market is held every Saturday morning from May through September. The market features goods and wares all produced in Indiana. Ron Carter, Doug Dolen, Jennifer Hershberger, and Sandra Long are just of few of the dedicated volunteers that make this event possible. And if that is not enough, Carmel has a Winter Farmers Market that runs November through March at Founders Park.

Carmel now has a reputation for its roundabouts, a circular traffic regulator at road intersections that eliminate stoplights, resulting in less traffic accidents and less emissions from idling vehicles. Officials from cities and towns all across the country visit Carmel to learn more about them, and the idea is catching on nationwide.

Even if astounded, those early residents would surely be impressed with how their little town has grown up.

Jeffrey W. Worrell (1958–)

As longtime chairman of the event, Jeff Worrell and his wife, Shari, travel in style supervising all aspects of the Carmelfest Fourth of July Parade and its related events. When a willing spirit meets a community's need for service, the community will always come out the biggest winner. Such it was for Carmel when it met Jeff Worrell. Jeff and his wife landed in the Indianapolis area from Iowa in 1986. They soon discovered Carmel and settled in with work and raising a family. Jeff's father was his example in giving back, and those instincts run deep. As a businessman and a member of the Carmel Chamber of Commerce, Jeff found himself volunteering on the Carmelfest Committee, Carmel's Fourth of July celebration. Soon, Carmelfest broke away from the chamber to become an entity of its own, and Jeff went with it at the request of Mayor Ted Johnson. Carmelfest has not been the only organization to benefit from Jeff's time and talents. He has served on numerous boards of directors with St. Vincent Carmel Hospital, Carmel Rotary, Carmel Clay Parks & Recreation, and Our Lady of Mount Carmel being only a fraction of the list. Elected to Carmel's city council in May 2015, Jeff claims a flaw in his character is his inability to say, "No," and for that flaw, a community is grateful. (Photograph by Jennifer D. Hershberger.)

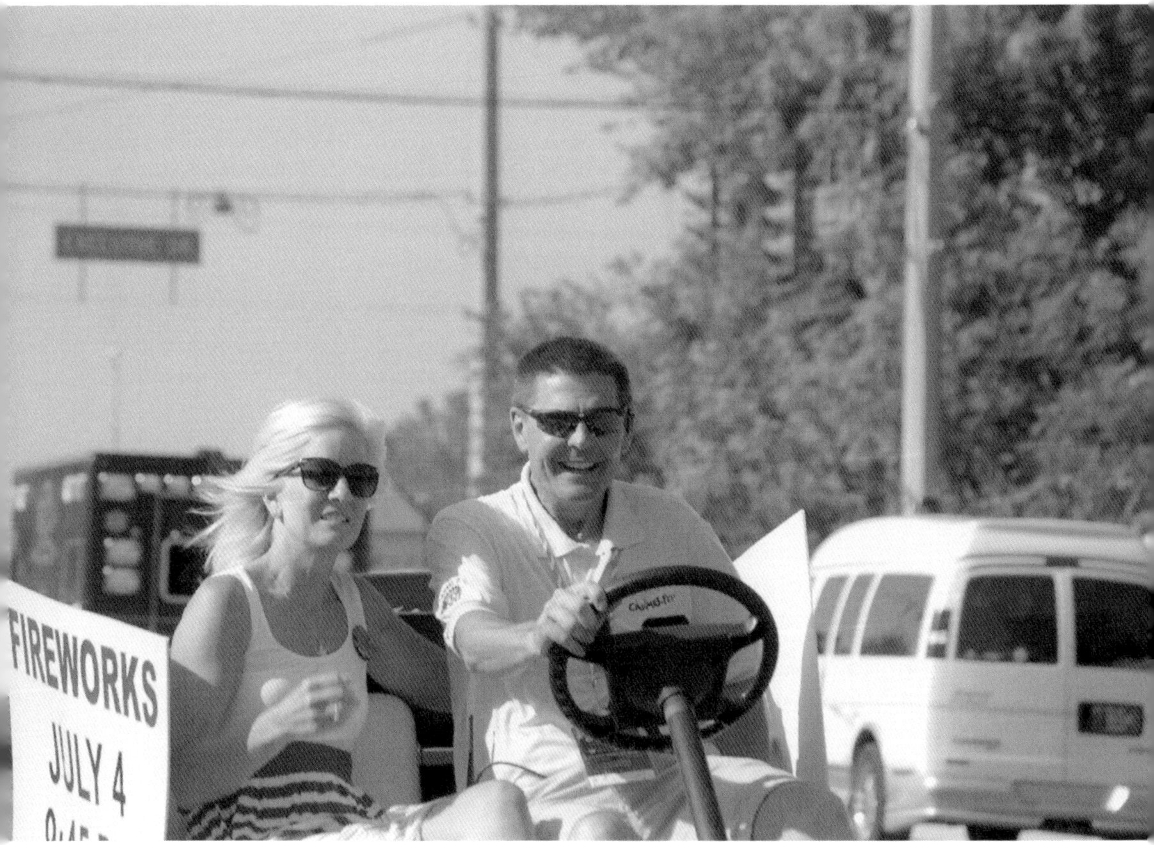

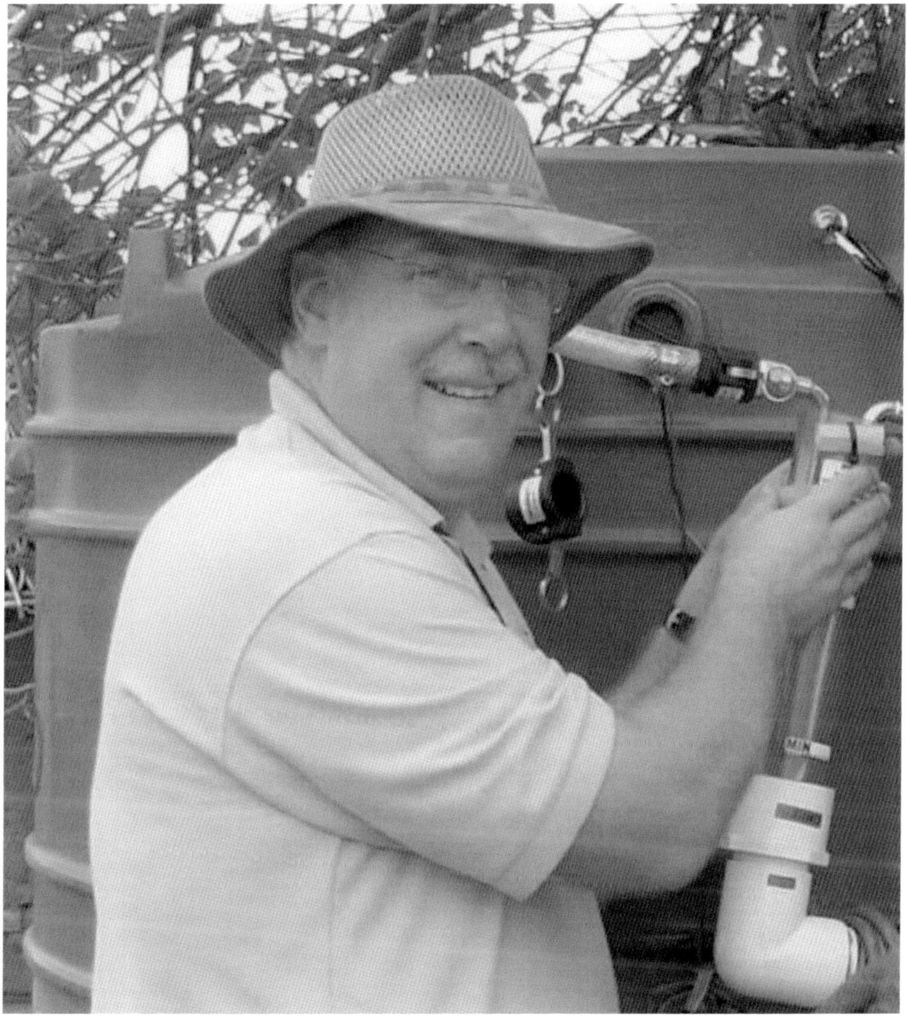

William D. Farrar (1960–)
Bill Farrar, founder and executive director of Fountains of Hope International, tests the water from a newly installed water purifier in Haiti. Born in Washington, at 12 years of age, Bill's family found itself in Carmel due to his father's job. Throughout his high school years, he attended the weekly MYF meetings (Methodist Youth Fellowship) under the direction of Rev. Warren Saunders at Carmel United Methodist Church. Bill quickly found that he had a passion for helping people and making a difference when he participated in work camps (mission trips). He graduated from Carmel High School in 1978 and went to Purdue University, where he earned degrees in aviation technology and aviation maintenance technology. He also achieved his fixed-wing and helicopter pilot's licenses. During college, he volunteered as a counselor for his church MYF work camps. He worked for Allison Engine Company. Bill's love of helping others and his love of mission trips came together in his creation of Fountains of Hope International, a nonprofit he formed that travels to less-fortunate countries to install water purifiers so that people nearby can have clean drinking water. Bill has a patent on a four-pound water purification system that generates chlorine from a quarter cup of table salt, water, and a 12-volt battery. One of these systems can provide 3,600 gallons of purified water per hour for up to 5,000 people. He has traveled to over 15 countries and installed over 180 miniature water treatment systems, saving the lives of many who would die from waterborne diseases. (Courtesy of Bill Farrar.)

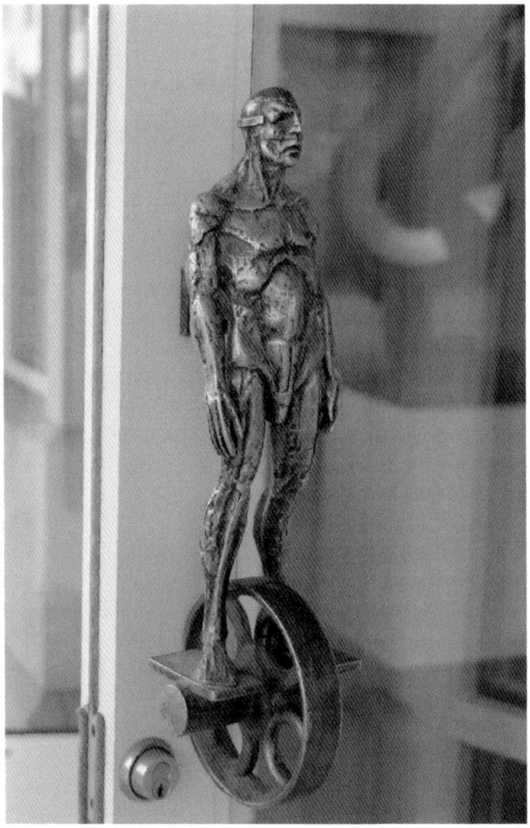

Evan Lurie (1966–)

New York City native and artist Evan Lurie took a chance on the attraction and success of Carmel's up-and-coming Arts & Design District. In 2009, while older residents bemoaned such a drastic change in the Carmel skyline, an art gallery complete with a penthouse apartment opened in the middle of downtown, and, surprisingly, it works well there. Situated between a long-standing music store and an antique mall housed in a refurbished garage, the four-story brick building appears to have always been there. Only its brazen door handles give any indication that it was not around during Carmel's Quaker days. Lurie relied on Carmel's affluent residents, such as physicians, chief executive officers, attorneys, and professional athletes, to become clients in his young, urban-professional customer base. Artists from around the world are featured, and most works are sold on consignment. (Photographs by Jennifer D. Hershberger.)

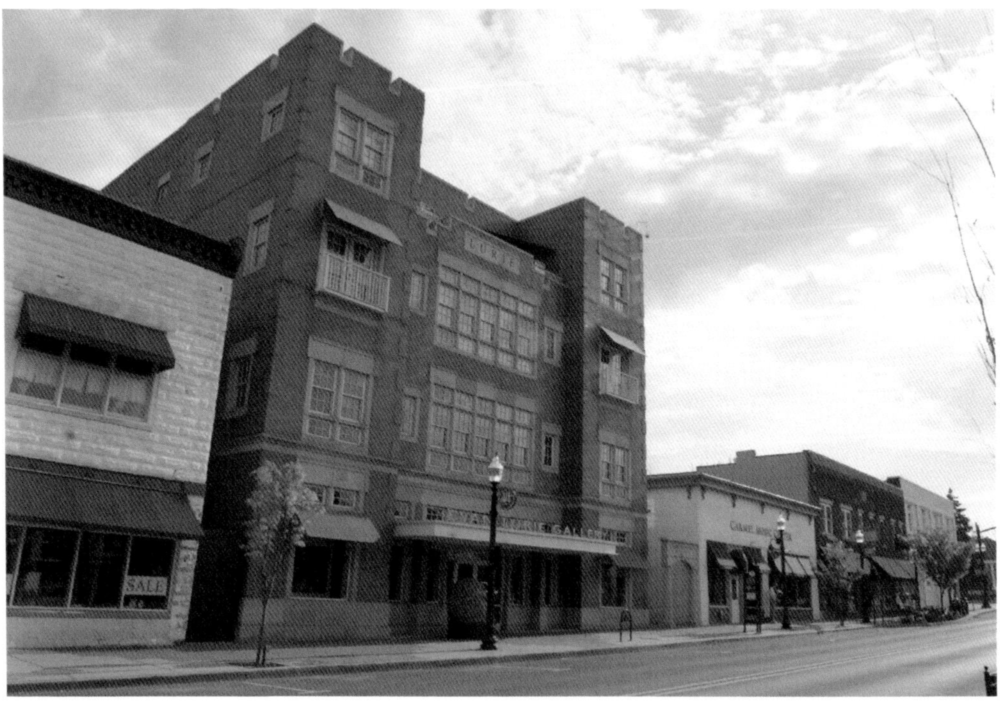

R. Carol Skinner (1942–)

Kentucky native R. Carol Skinner stands outside the Metropolitan Museum of Art in New York City while visiting an exhibit on cubism. Carol's natural talent as an artist became Carmel's gift in 1971 when she took up residence there. In the 44 years since, the Herron Art School graduate has created lasting detailed depictions of Carmel landmarks, businesses, and distinctive homes. Carol claims that she found her niche with the Carmel Clay Historical Society. She has been commissioned by entities such as Eli Lilly, Purdue and Butler Universities, Conner Prairie, and the City of Carmel to render accurate, appealing images of their businesses and organizations. Her works have been exhibited both nationally and internationally, and she has also won numerous awards. (Right, courtesy of R. Carol Skinner; below, courtesy of Carmel Clay Historical Society.)

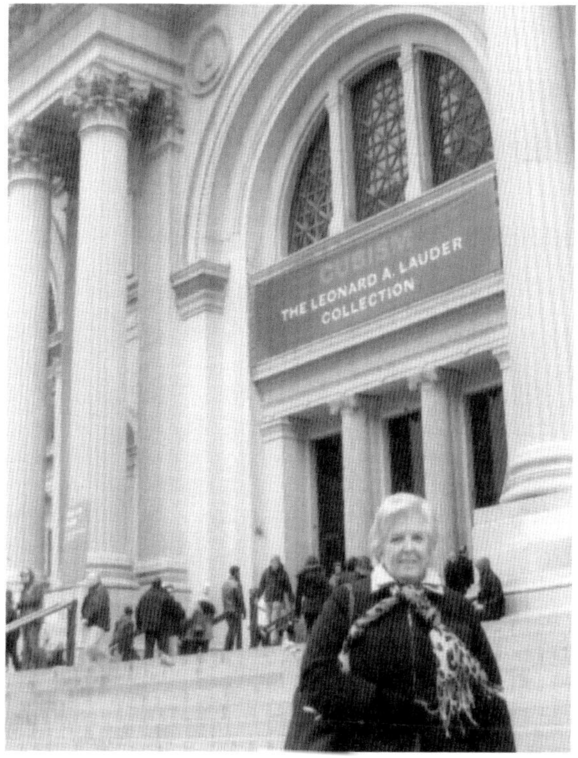

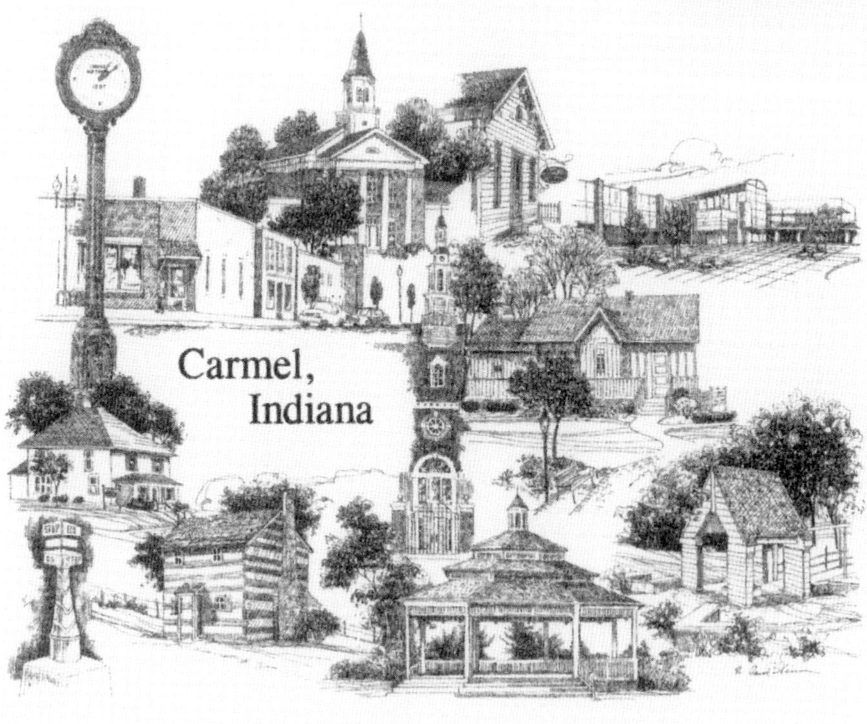

Michael J. Feinstein (1956–)

Michael Feinstein and Mayor Jim Brainard perform together on the stage at the Palladium in the Center for Performing Arts on its opening night in 2010. Before the age of five, Columbus, Ohio, native Michael Feinstein began playing the piano. In 1976, his talent and interest in music led him to Los Angeles, where he secured a job cataloguing the unpublished works of George and Ira Gershwin. Recognized as a proponent of the Great American Songbook, Michael would go on to be a multiplatinum, two-time Emmy-winning, five-time Grammy-winning performer. In 2007, he founded the Great American Songbook Foundation whose purpose is to preserve and promote the music of the Great American Songbook. With accomplishments too numerous to name, Michael Feinstein was appointed artistic director of the Center for the Performing Arts in 2009, and his foundation found a permanent home. As director, he has brought stellar, world-class names in vocal and musical performance to what was once a sleepy Midwest farm town. (Photograph by Jessica Hoffman.)

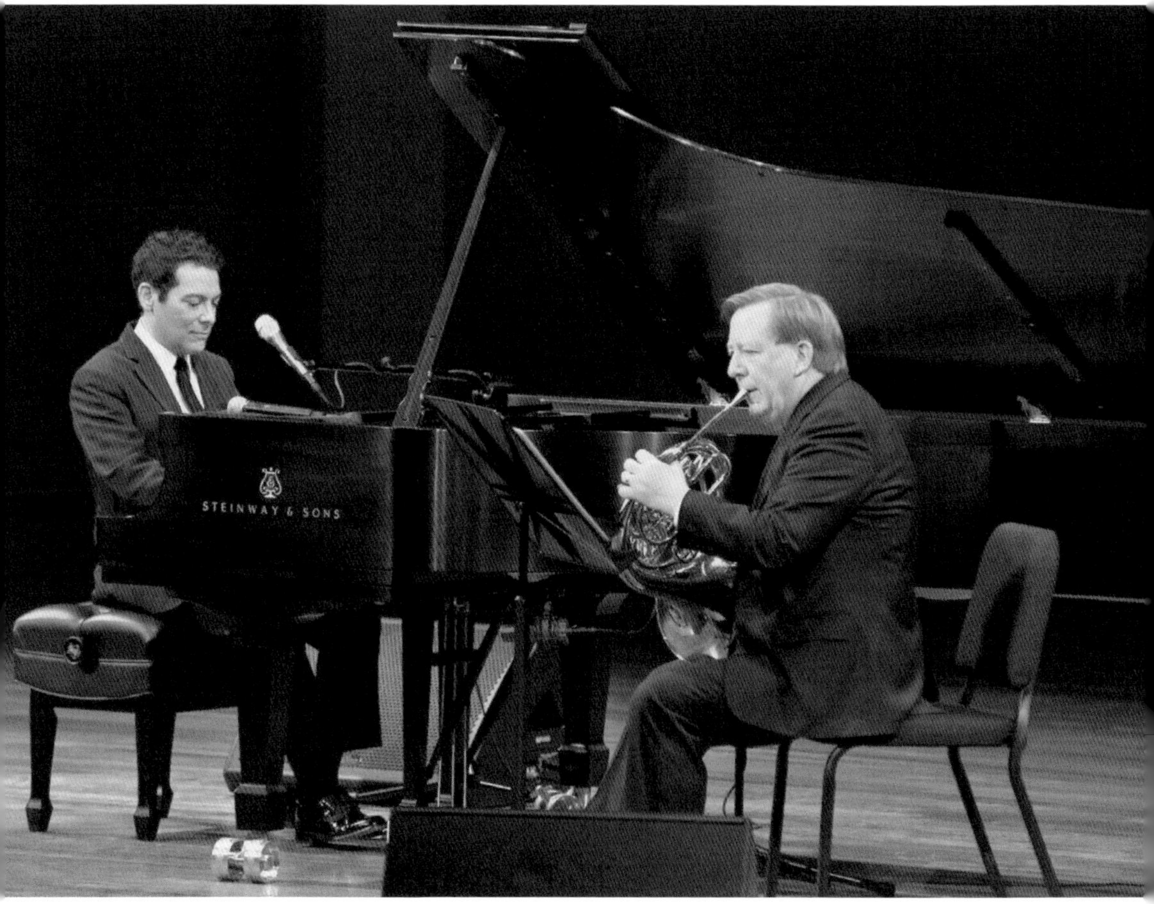

Winston H. Long (1946–) and Sandra J. (Monroe) Long (1945–)

Winston and Sandra Long found themselves in Carmel after some serious recruiting by Betty Grossman, Carmel resident and dean of the Indiana University School of Nursing, to get Winston to accept a position as director of media for the school. Both graduates of Woodlawn High School in Birmingham and the University of Alabama, the native Alabamians needed a good reason to move north. Betty sold them. In 1975, Sandra gave up her job teaching and moved with Winston to Carmel. Sandra became involved in the community in very short order, securing signatures on a petition to change Carmel's status from a town to a city. In this process, she met Jane Reiman. When Jane became mayor, she appointed Sandra to the Carmel Plan Commission and Winston to the Carmel Police Commission. In 1987, Winston and Sandra opened the OMNI Centre for Public Media, and it took off in 2000 when the City of Carmel asked them to produce a video regarding hazardous waste that would be aired on Carmel's government access television channel. The response to the video was overwhelming, prompting them to pull it from the air until the hazardous waste facility could expand to accommodate all the dropped-off items. Since that video, the OMNI Centre has produced many videos for the City of Carmel and Clay Township. They attend and record major events and attractions happening throughout the city, ranging from business/project ribbon cuttings to the Great American Songbook at the Center for the Performing Arts. The OMNI Centre (a nonprofit) began winning national awards only recently. The most recent being the 2015 Hometown Media Award for Overall Excellence in Government Access Programming from the Alliance for Community Media. They only recently started submitting videos and video samplings for awards, and so far, it looks like the awards will keep coming. In their spare time, Winston and Sandra volunteer with several organizations including the Carmel Farmers Market. They have been active in their church since 1975. Winston and Sandra's contributions to the community will go beyond this lifetime with the history of a thriving, vibrant city being recorded and shared for all future generations. (Photograph by Jennifer D. Hershberger.)

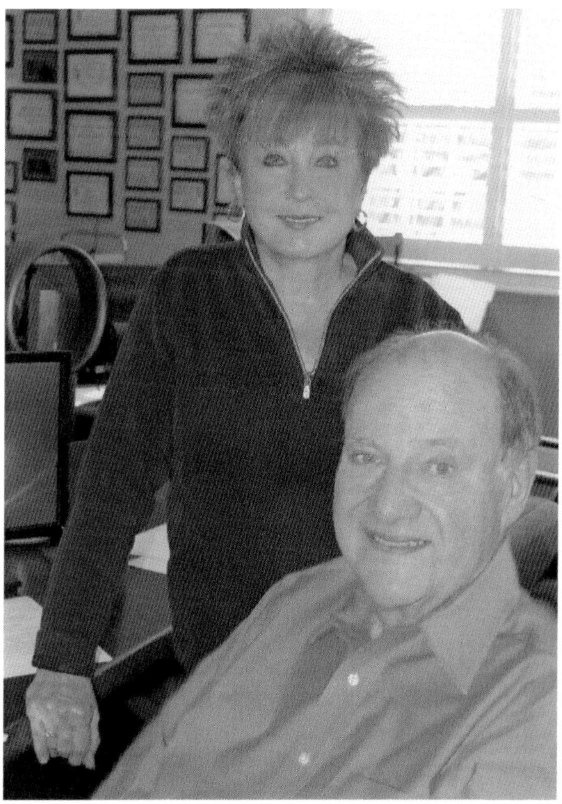

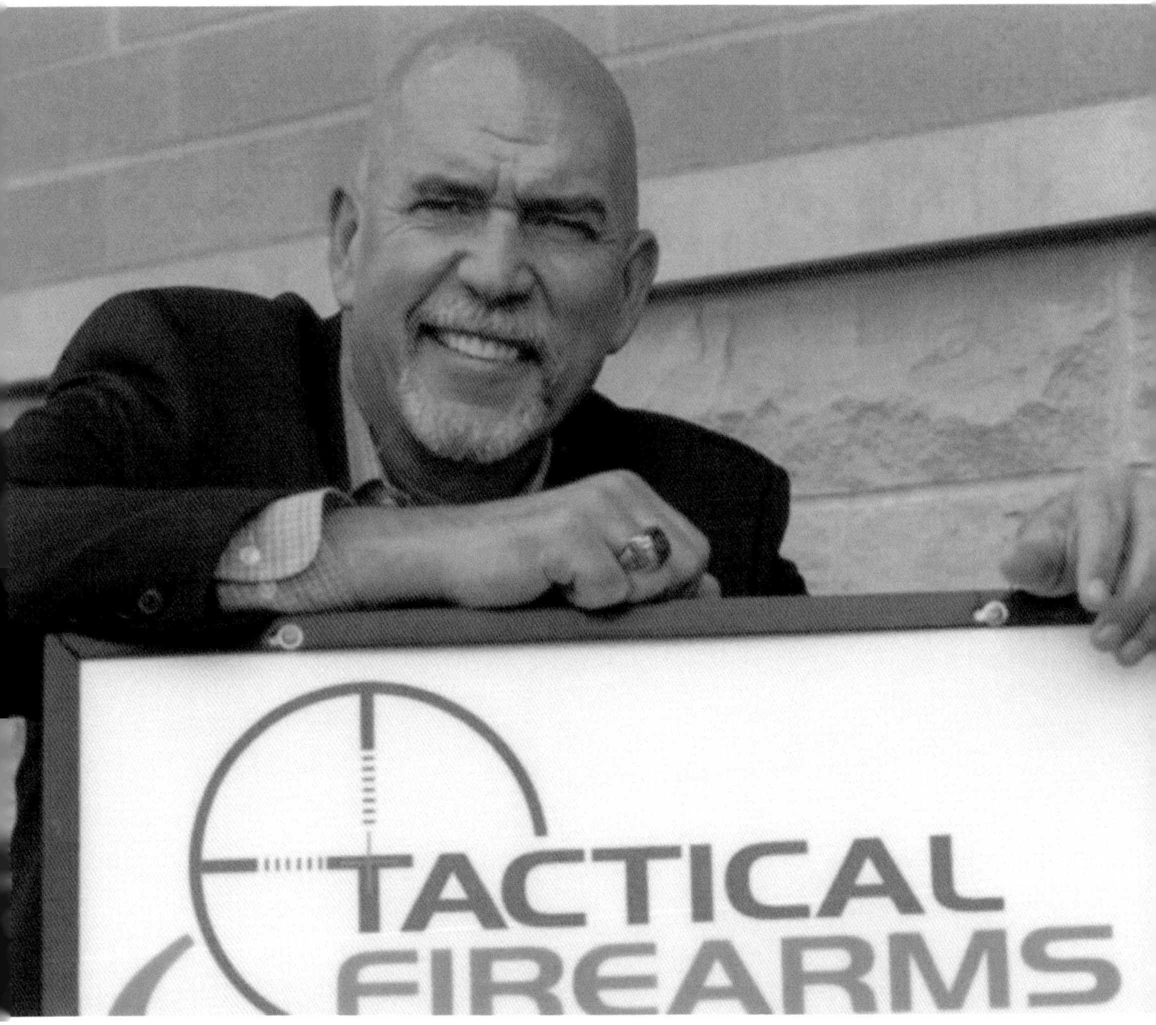

Guy A. Relford (1958–)
Guy Relford graduated from Carmel High School in 1976 and attended DePauw University in Greencastle, where he earned a bachelor's degree in political science and psychology. He then attended the Indiana University School of Law in Indianapolis, where he received his law degree cum laude. Working as an attorney for a law firm and then a litigation attorney for the Dow Chemical Company, Guy opened a private practice in Zionsville in 2009, which relocated to downtown Carmel in the Arts & Design District. Guy's specialty is also his passion, guns and gun safety. His practice specializes in the Second Amendment and Indiana gun laws. Guy also owns and operates Tactical Firearms Training, LLC, in Indianapolis, which offers training in gun safety and handling. He has been a National Rifle Association–certified firearms instructor since 1998 and is qualified to instruct firearm classes in various categories. He is also director and chief range safety officer at Eagle Creek Pistol Range in Indianapolis. (Courtesy of Guy Relford.)

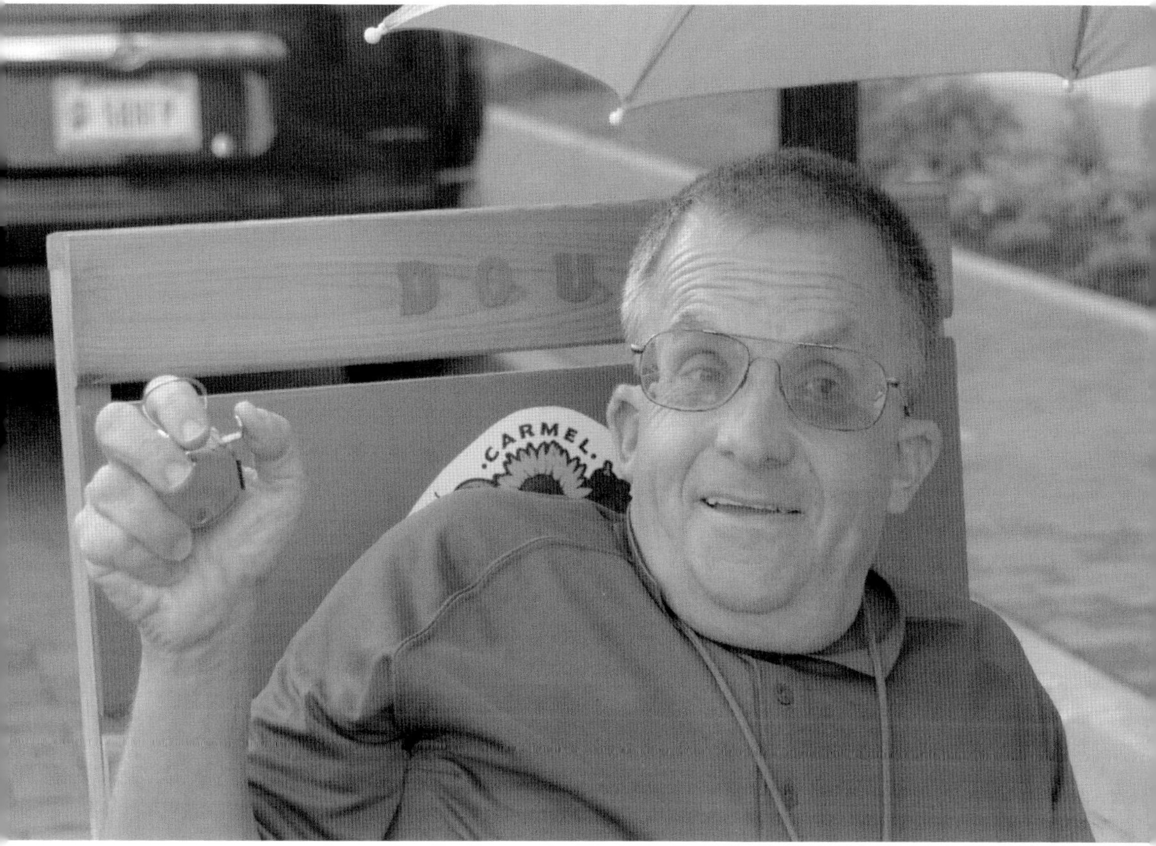

Douglas L. Dolen (1960–)
A welcoming figure at the entrance to the Carmel Farmers Market is lifelong resident Doug Dolen. A Carmel High School alumni and retired Carmel Clay Schools employee, Doug can be found at most any community event that is held at any time during the year. He will not be an attendee—he will be a volunteer. His family's Carmel roots date back to the early 1800s and give him his solid foundation in Carmel, as well as his strong need to give back. Having been a custodian at Carmel Elementary, he has a following of former students as large in number as any retired teacher or administrator. The eldest son of a former Carmel police chief and a registered nurse, Doug loves working with and being around people. Many organizations are the beneficiaries of Doug's generosity, devotion, and time. Those on the receiving end are Carmel Friends Church, where he coordinates the usher schedule and greets, Carmel Clay Historical Society, Carmel Farmers Market (both summer and winter markets), and the Carmel Fire Department, where he serves in the public education division, educating school-age children on fire safety. The Carmel Rotary Club honored him in 2009 with its ROSA Award (Rotary Outstanding Service Award). (Photograph by Jennifer D. Hershberger.)

Todd C. Young (1972–)

Born in Lancaster, Pennsylvania, Todd Young moved to Carmel with his family and settled down. Todd graduated from Carmel High School in 1990. He became interested in the Naval Academy while in high school and soon found himself there graduating cum laude in 1995 with a bachelor's degree in political science. Todd was commissioned in the US Marine Corps and became a naval intelligence officer. Honorably discharged as a captain in 2000, he began work on a master's degree in American politics, which he earned from the University of London. He went to work in Washington, DC. He earned his law degree in 2006 from Indiana University and worked as a deputy prosecutor. In November 2010, Todd was elected to the US House of Representatives, where he speaks for the Ninth District in Indiana. He gives selflessly to organizations such as Big Brothers/Big Sisters, Indiana Sports Corporation, the American Legion, and more. He and his wife have four children and live in Washington, DC, and Bloomington. (Courtesy of Todd Young.)

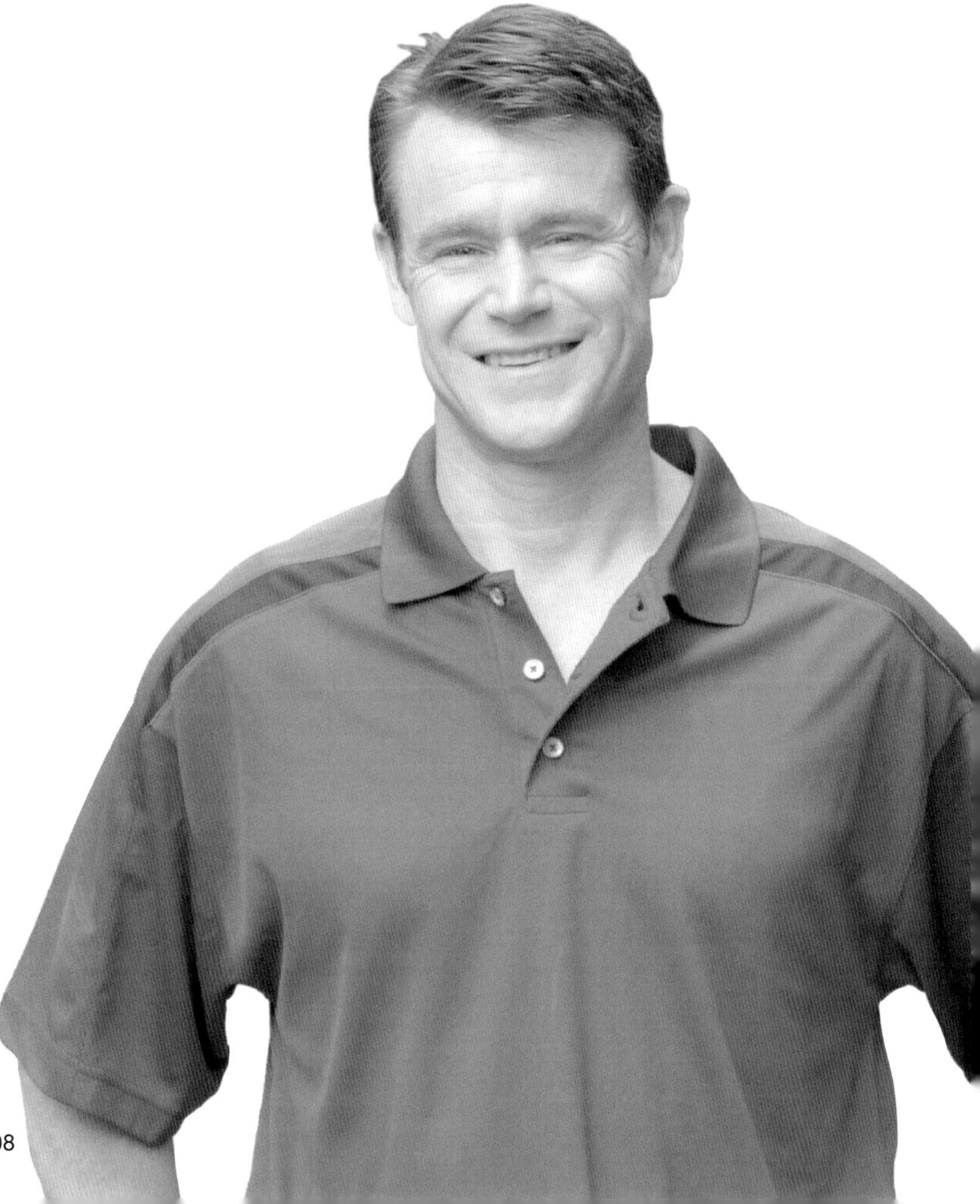

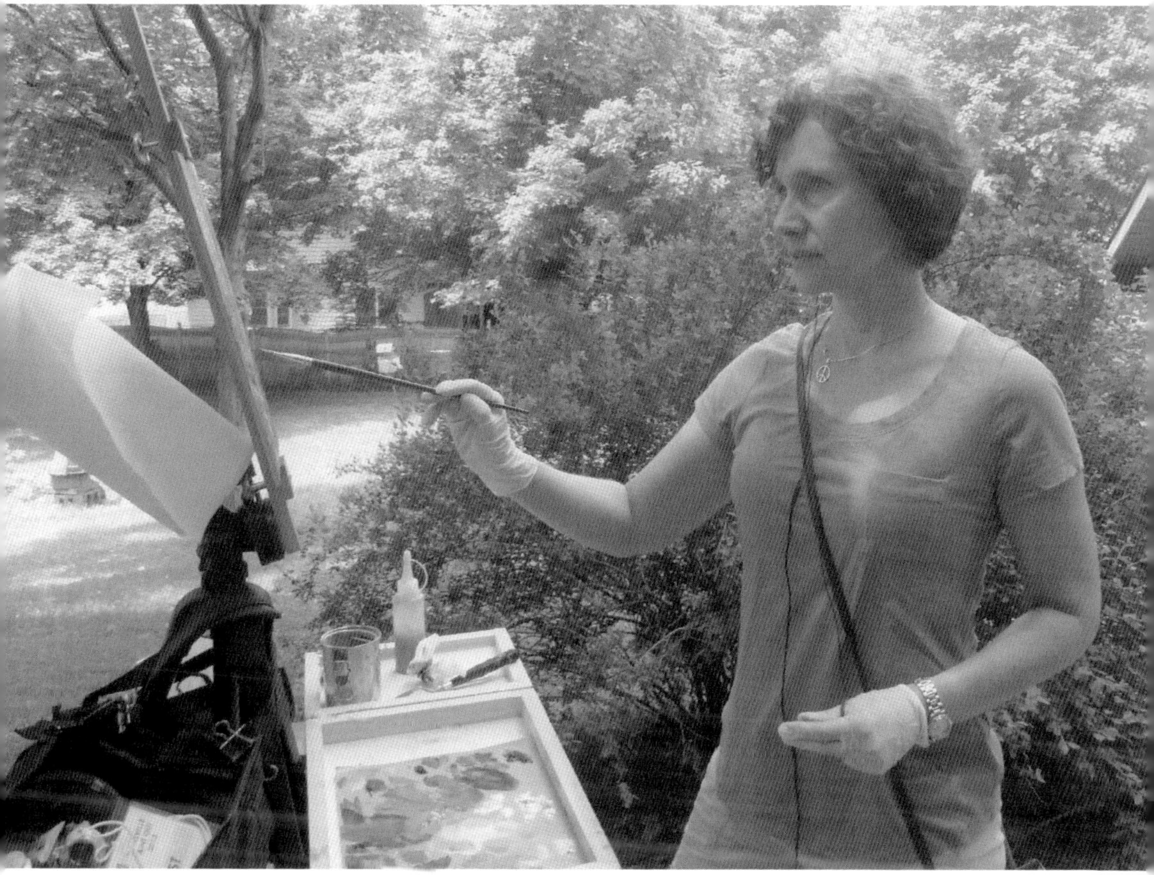

Shawn A. (Fowler) Deitch (1959–)
Local plein air artist Shawn Deitch sizes up her subject as she puts it on canvas. (Plein air means "in the open air" in French.) Accomplished in business with a law degree from Indiana University and licensed as a certified public accountant and realtor, contemporary impressionist artist Shawn Deitch never picked up a paint brush until she was 50 years old. Drawing on the encouragement of family, Shawn began painting in oils and discovered that she had a passion for it and a talent for composition and color. Shawn's paintings have been donated as fundraisers to Guilded Leaf Book & Author Luncheon and Silent Auction benefitting the Carmel Clay Public Library and to the Tippecanoe Watershed Foundation Auction in support of clean rivers and lakes. The Carmel Arts Council and the Indiana University Dance Marathon to benefit Riley Hospital for Children have also been the recipients of Shawn's gift and generosity. She belongs to the Carmel Clay Public Library Guild, Hamilton County Artists' Association, Indiana Plein Air Painters, Hoosier Salon, and the American Impressionist Society. She is drawn to plein air for the challenge—"creating the composition, simplifying the scene, capturing the light, and mixing the colors all while the scene changes before your eyes"—but can see herself in the future painting large, abstract paintings. Shawn's work is regularly on display and available for purchase at the Carmel Clay Public Library. (Courtesy of Shawn Deitch.)

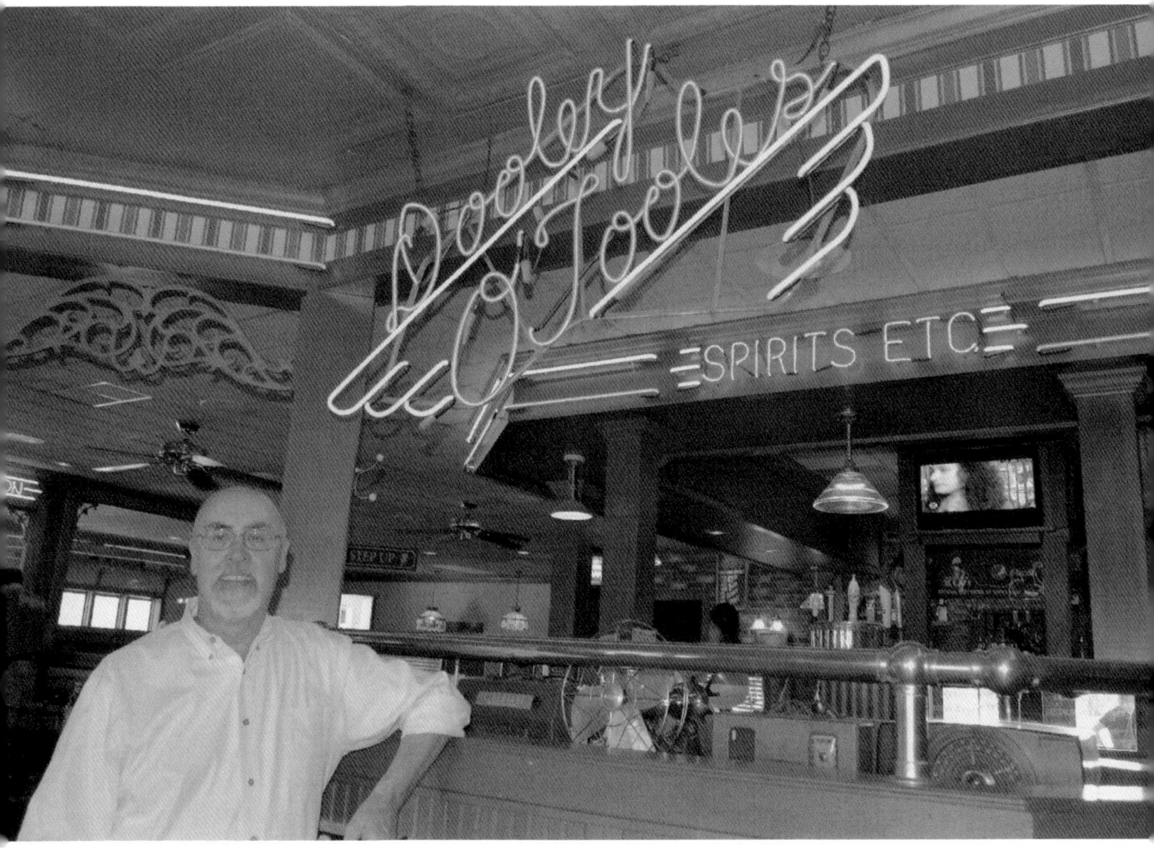

Douglas R. Kemp (1956–)

Thirty years ago in 1985, Dooley O'Toole's Restaurant opened in Carmel. It is a favorite place for the locals who love Tenderloin Tuesdays, as any true Hoosier should. Ellettsville native Doug Kemp graduated from Lawrence Central High School in Indianapolis in 1974. He attended Purdue and Ball State Universities. Food service interested him when still in high school, which was when he worked at Shakey's Pizza. While attending college, he was a bartender. Drawing from his experience and willingness to serve, Doug went to work at Dooley's when it opened. He became its general manager within six months. It can be said that he believed in his career choice and future when he relocated to Carmel in 1990. Eight years after starting at the restaurant, Doug was part owner and eventually bought out his last remaining partner in 2001. On any given day, one can drop by for lunch or dinner and he is most likely there. He works in the kitchen and out on the floor. He might greet and seat guests. He might take people's order. He might bus tables. Whatever task it is, Doug knows it is all a part of the overall dining experience, and he wants patrons at Dooley O'Toole to have the best. (Photograph by Jennifer D. Hershberger.)

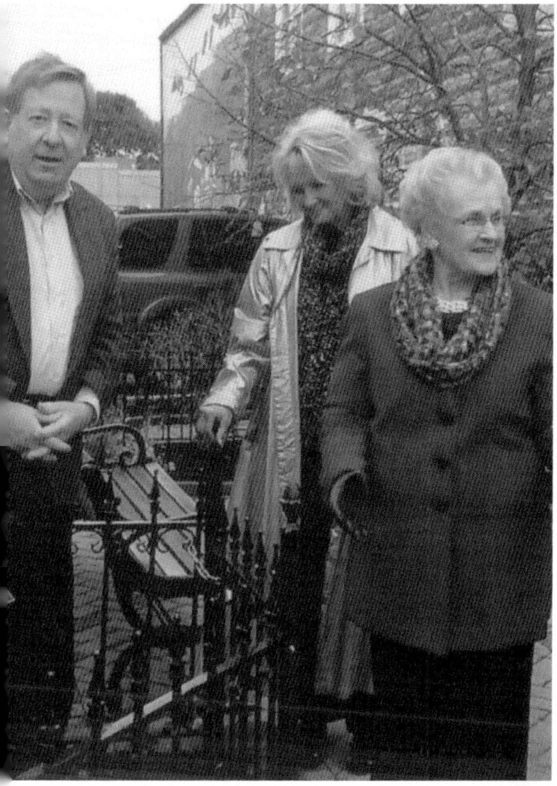

Doreen Squire Ficara (1927–)
Doreen Squire Ficara, executive director of the Carmel Arts Council, is honored upon her retirement in 2014 by having the small garden next to the World's Smallest Art Gallery named on her behalf. Doreen, a native of Devonshire, England, met her husband during World War II in a donut shop where she was volunteering for the American Red Cross. When the war was over, she relocated to New Jersey and started their family. Landing in Carmel in 1983 after living in Indianapolis, Doreen was appointed executive director of the newly formed council in 1994. She held this position until her retirement 20 years later at the age of 86. The 20-year period brought Carmel into the spotlight for its appreciation of the arts with the many galleries that dot the Arts & Design District in the heart of its downtown. (Both, courtesy of the Carmel Arts Council.)

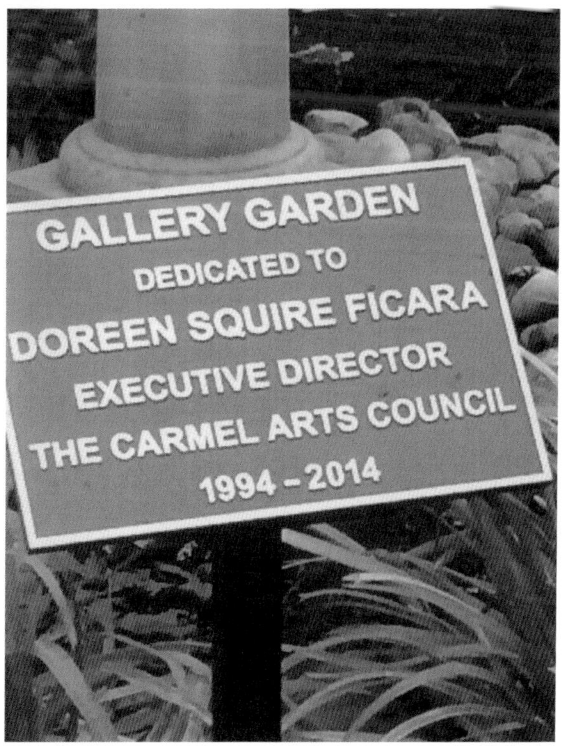

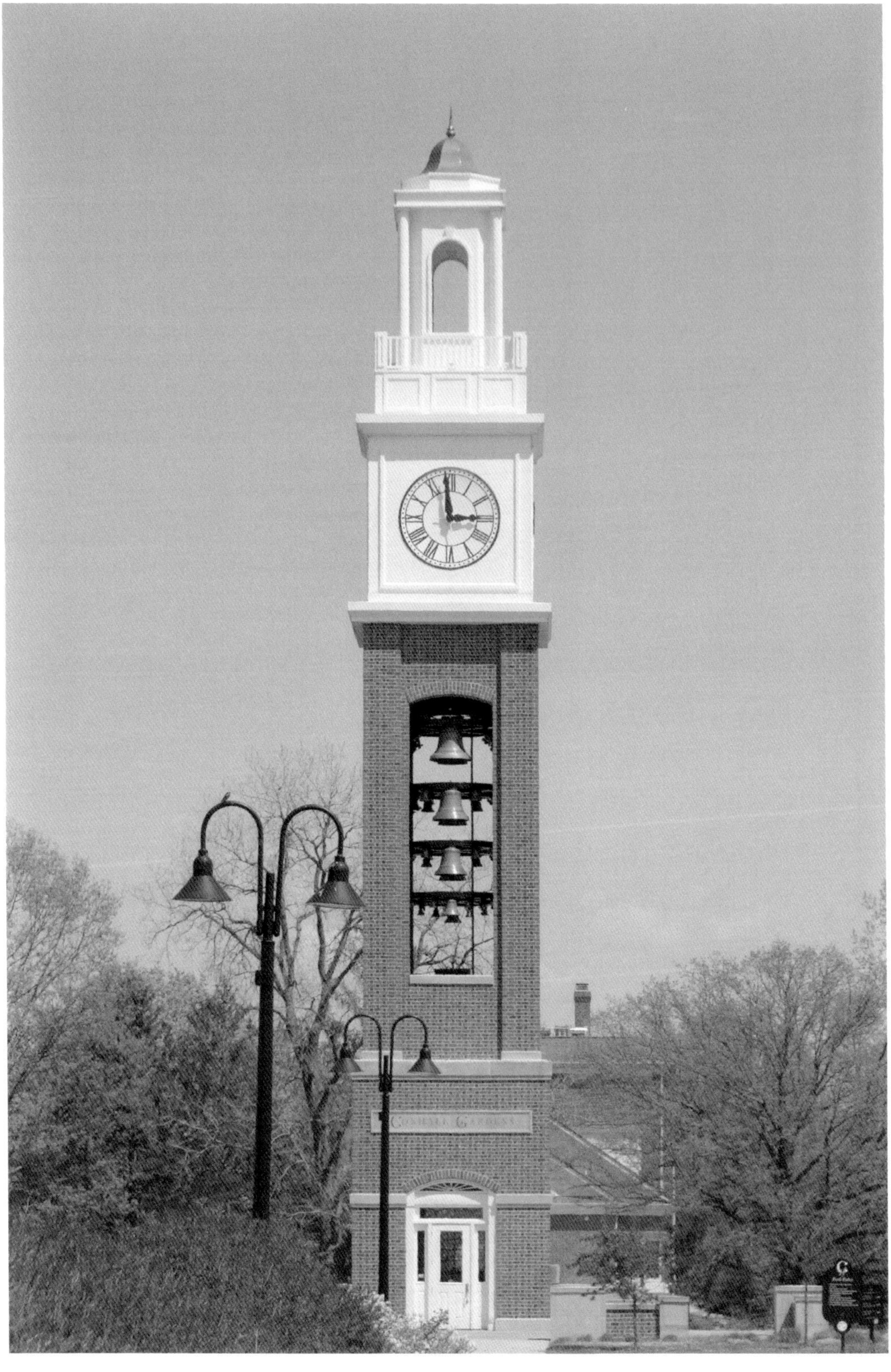

Jesse H. Cox (1918–2008) and Beulah R. (Chanley) Cox (1918–1999)

Businesspeople and philanthropists Jesse and Beulah Cox believed in giving back. An Indiana University graduate, Jesse founded J.H. Cox Manufacturing Company in 1946, which was the parent company of longtime Carmel business Aero Drapery. Both Jesse and Beulah served on several boards and gave monetarily to multiple organizations. Indiana University being one entity with the Jesse and Beulah Chanley Cox Scholarship Fund and the Cox Pavilion in Bloomington. Their greatest gift to Carmel came in 1999 when they gifted their 125-acre farm located on 116th Street at Towne Road to the Hamilton County Parks Department. Today, the Cox farm is known as Coxhall Gardens and is one of the county's premier parks. The property holds Jesse and Beulah's 1974 dream home, which is a replica of the Virginia governor's home in Williamsburg. It has twin 90-foot bell towers that are the only two matching towers of such height to be known. The towers chime to mark time and special occasions such as weddings, as Coxhall has become a favorite for such. There is also a nine-acre lake, a greenhouse, a conservatory, and a multitude of beautiful gardens all named. (Opposite, photograph by Jennifer D. Hershberger; below, courtesy of Hamilton County Parks and Recreation.)

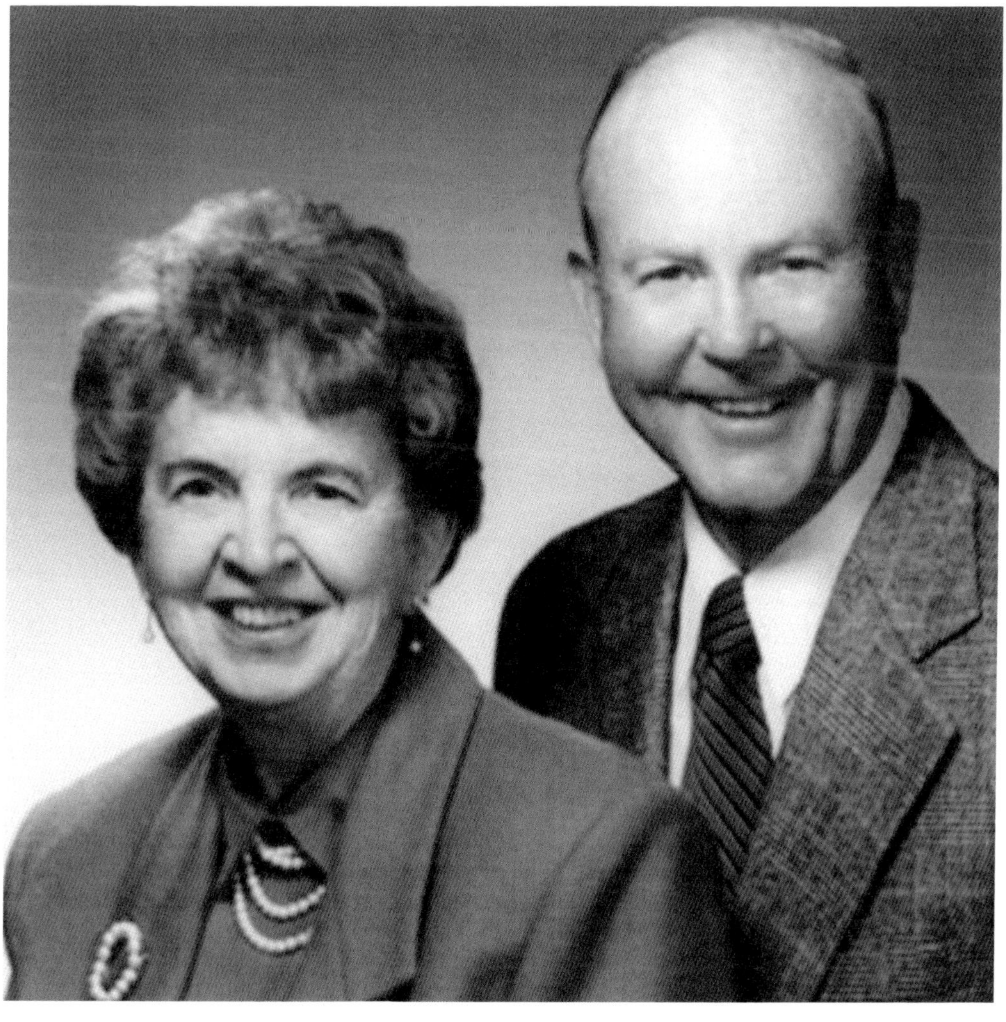

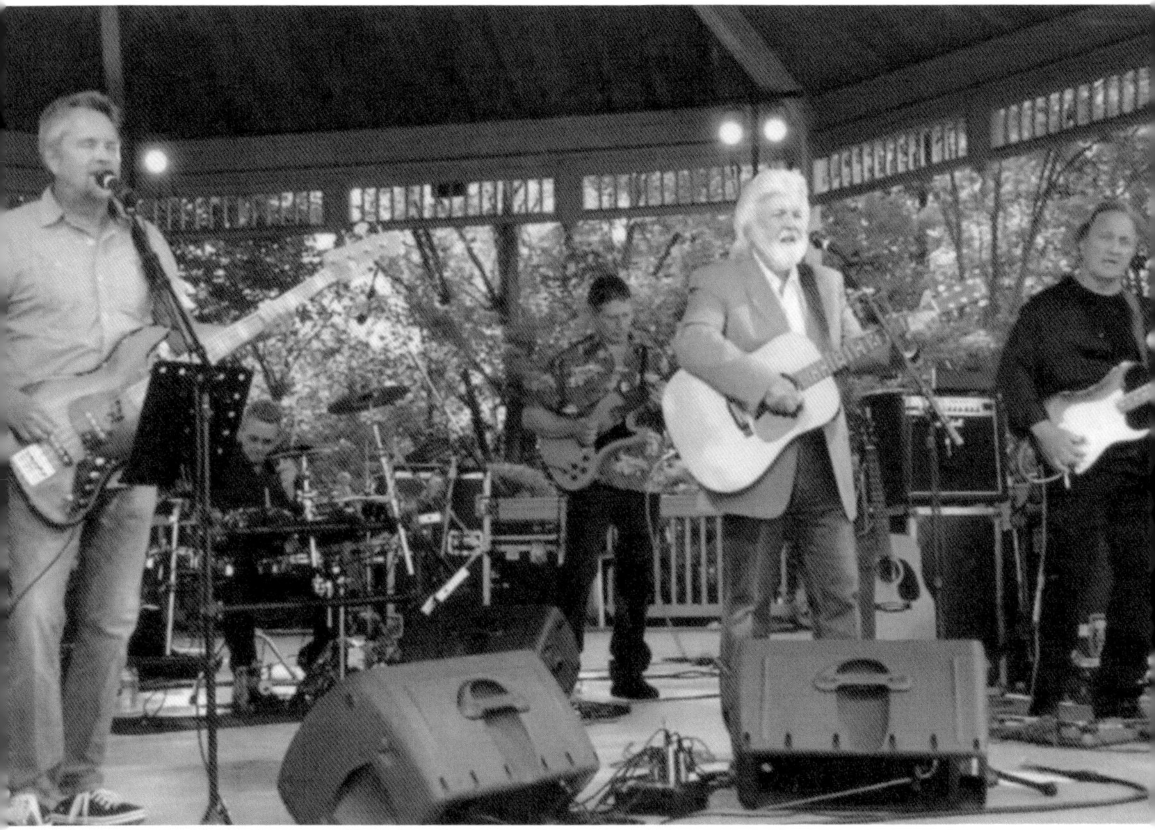

Wright Brothers Band

The Fourth of July is a cause for celebration in Carmel, and Carmel does it up right with Carmelfest. A staple on the gazebo stage during the celebration is the Wright Brothers Band. Established in 1972 as the Wright Brothers Overland Stage Company, brothers Tom and Tim Wright and John McDowell make up the band, which started performing on college campuses and at state fairs and has withstood the test of time. Covering songs from decades long ago, they have created a phenomenon in Carmel that will likely last as long as they do. Regular performers at Carmelfest Fourth of July celebration each year and occasionally at Concerts at the Gazebo on summer Wednesday nights, the band draws in large and dedicated crowds. The band has had nine singles reach the top of Billboard's Hot County Singles Chart, and band members have toured with multiple performers. In 1987, the Goldie Hawn movie *Overboard* featured their music on the soundtrack. (Photograph by Jennifer D. Hershberger.)

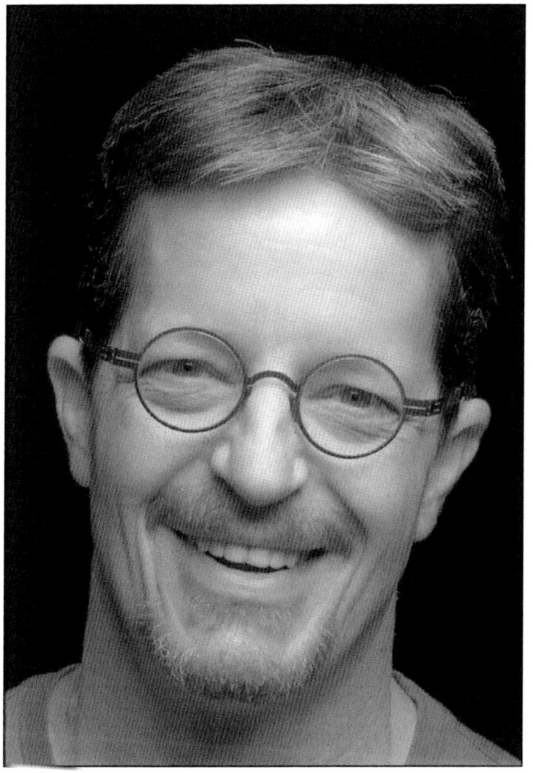

Timothy T. Campbell (1958–)
Born in Indianapolis and a Carmel resident since 1990, Tim Campbell creates editorial cartoons for a weekly feature in the local newspaper, *Current in Carmel.* They are usually timely with local or national events and drive the point home. His ability was recognized at an early age, and after graduating from the Columbus College of Art & Design in 1980, he settled in to make his passion his career. Tim's cartoons have been featured on CNN, which is his proudest accomplishment so far, and his awards are numerous. He has earned the "Best Editorial Cartoon" in the state of Indiana four times. Tim does artwork for charity for the Children's Museum of Indianapolis and other organizations. (Both, courtesy of Tim Campbell.)

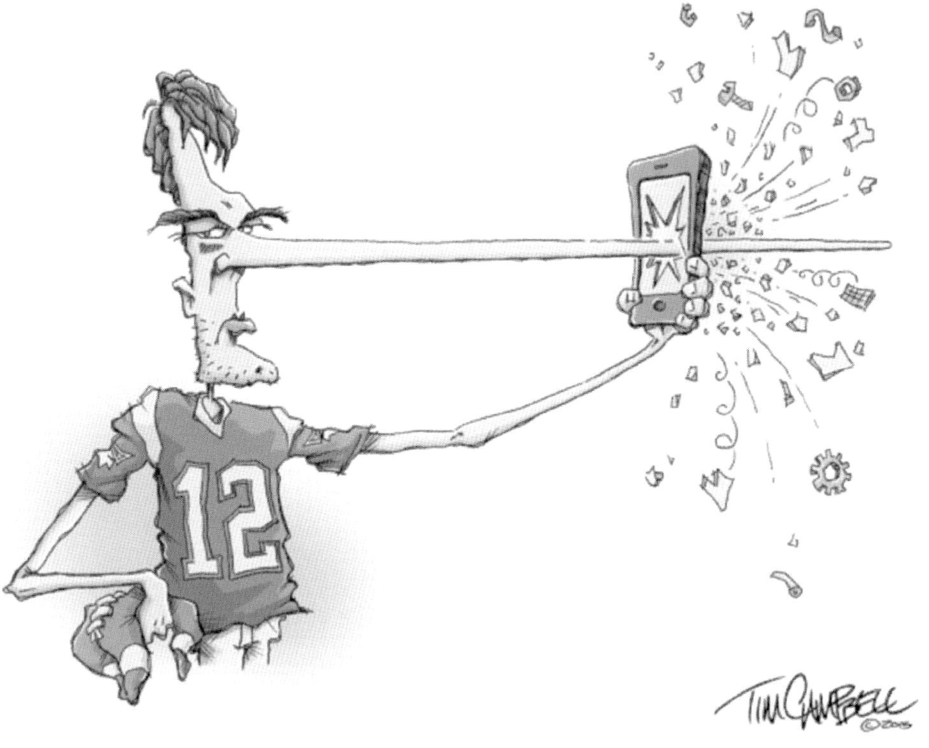

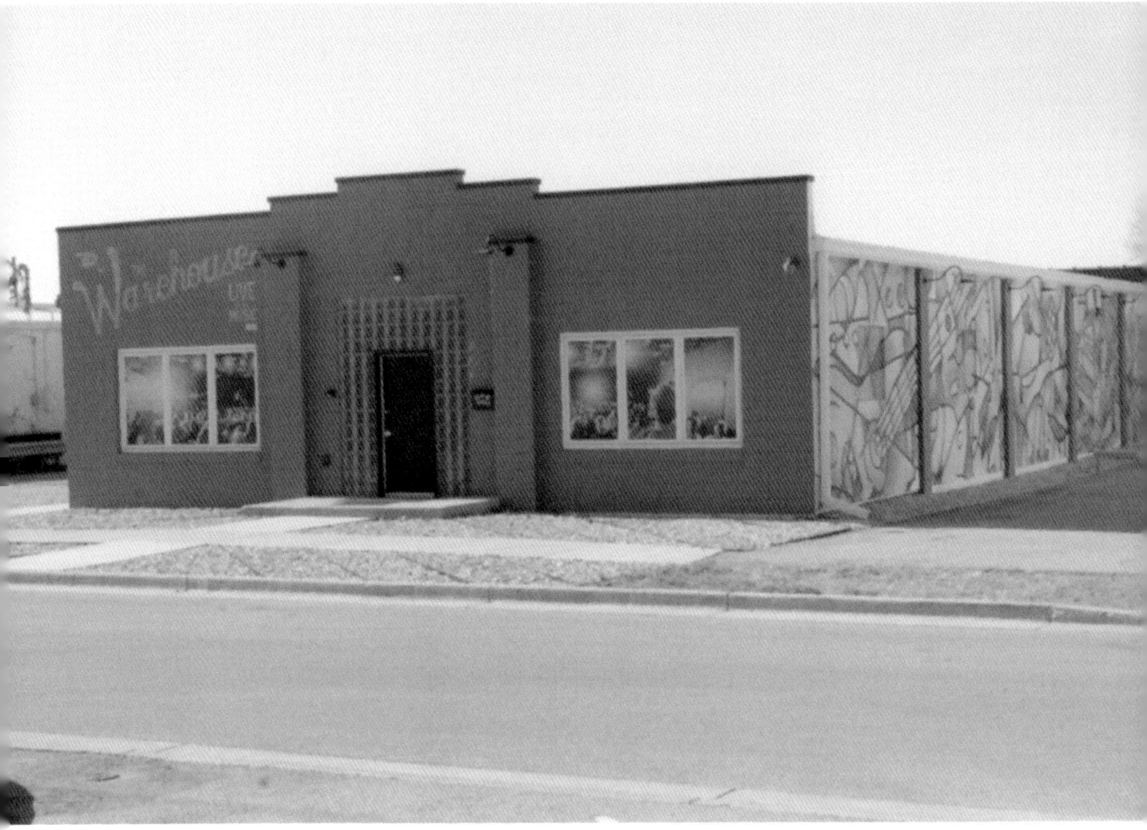

Blair E. Clark (1955–)

Singer/songwriter Blair Clark's smooth voice can be heard at most every public event in Carmel that includes live entertainment. In 1990, looking to partner in business with a friend, the native of Michigan and veteran of the United States Army landed with his family in Carmel looking for a place with great schools to raise a family. Carmel would be a perfect fit for a man with Blair's talent and the growing interest in arts in the community. He claims that Carmel is an "artist's dream come true." Blair's father was a folk singer that played multiple instruments, and his brother was an actor who performed in musical theater. They were both great influences in the direction he would take. Blair is co-owner of the Warehouse, a venue for live music in the Arts & Design District that is in a converted machine shop. He is cofounder of Midwest School of Voice, where a talented staff evaluates, teaches, and shapes vocal performers of every age. (Above, author's collection; opposite, photograph by Jennifer D. Hershberger.)

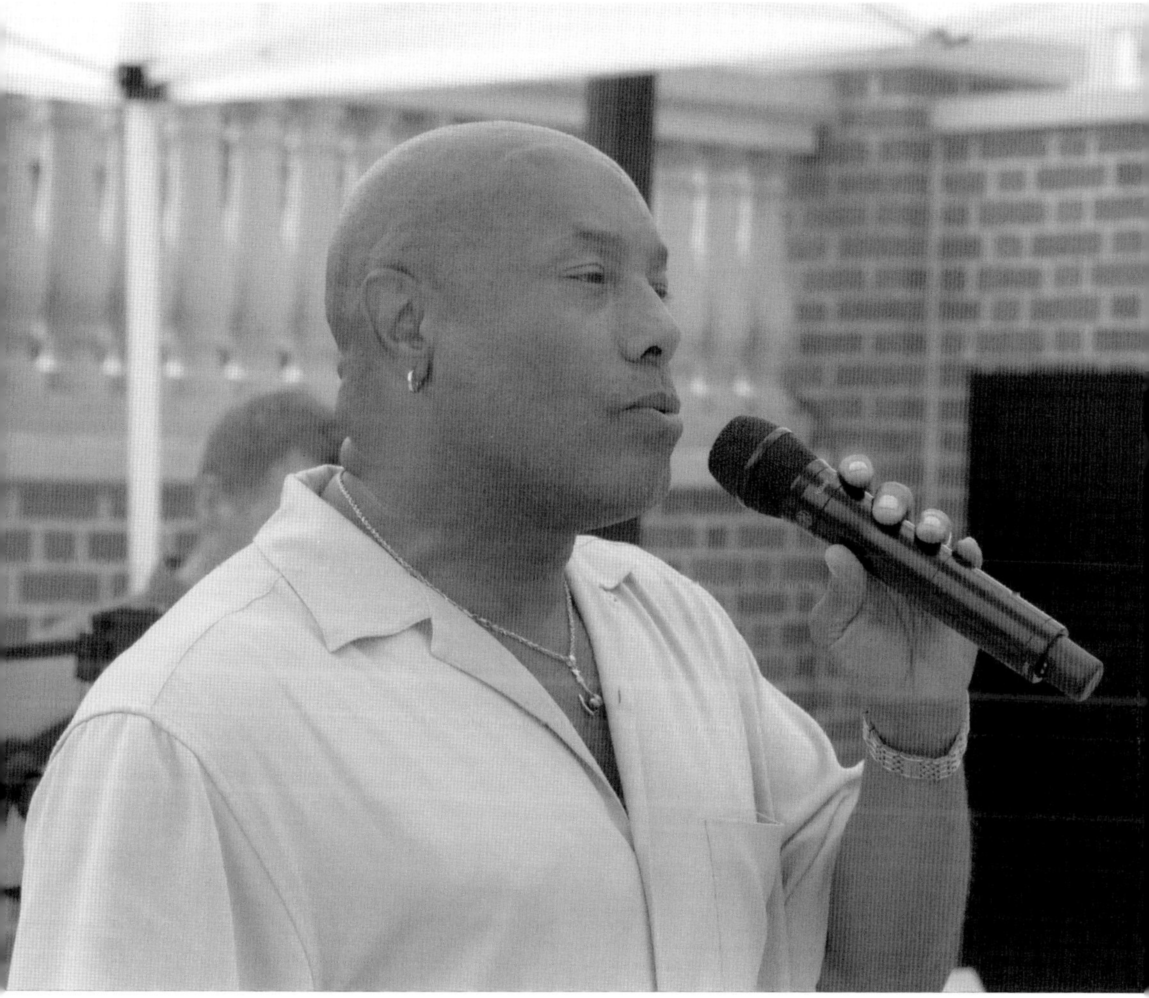

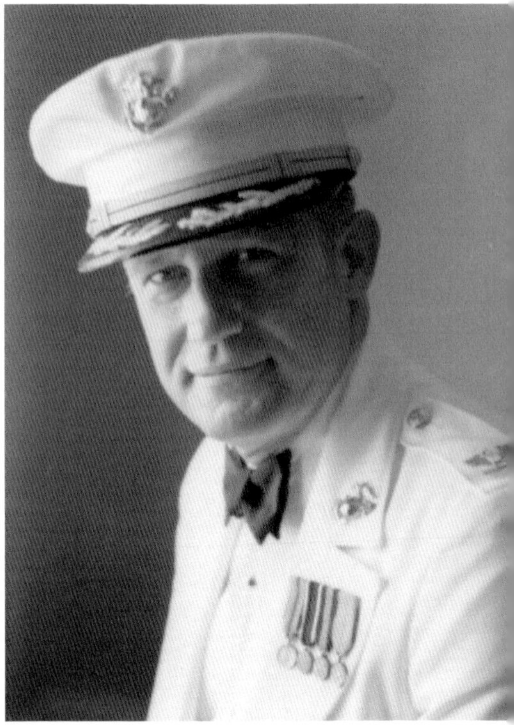

Col. Robert M. Book USMCR (1929–2012)
Carmel's Col. Robert Book salutes the colors as they are brought into the gymnasium at Carmel Elementary School's Veterans Day program where he spoke several times to the students about serving in the armed forces. Colonel Book spent 31 years in the US Marine Corps and Marine Corps Reserve, retiring in 1982. During that time, he was the driving force behind Eli Lilly's division called Elanco Products Company. For 29 years, he served the community on the Clay Township Board and the Clay Township Regional Waste District. When St. Vincent Hospital decided to expand to Carmel, he saw the project through from groundbreaking to serving on its board of directors until 2012, as one-time chairman. He was instrumental in the development and construction of the Carmel Clay Veterans Memorial. (Right, courtesy of J. Bart Book; below, photograph from the 2001 Carmel Elementary yearbook.)

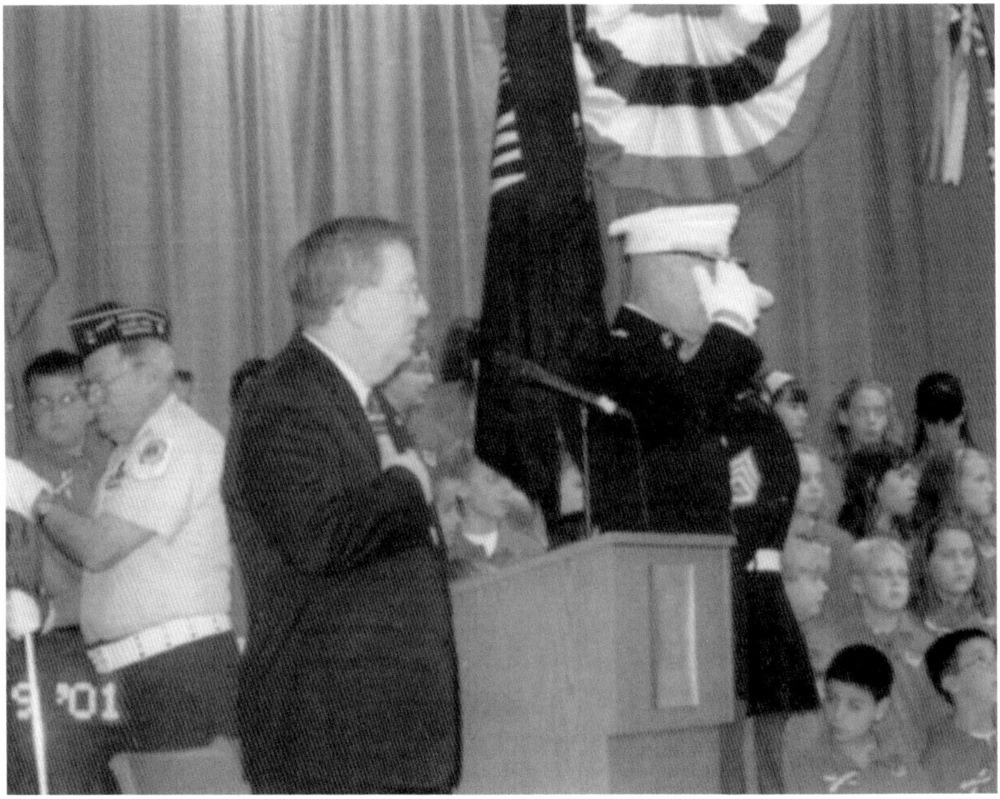

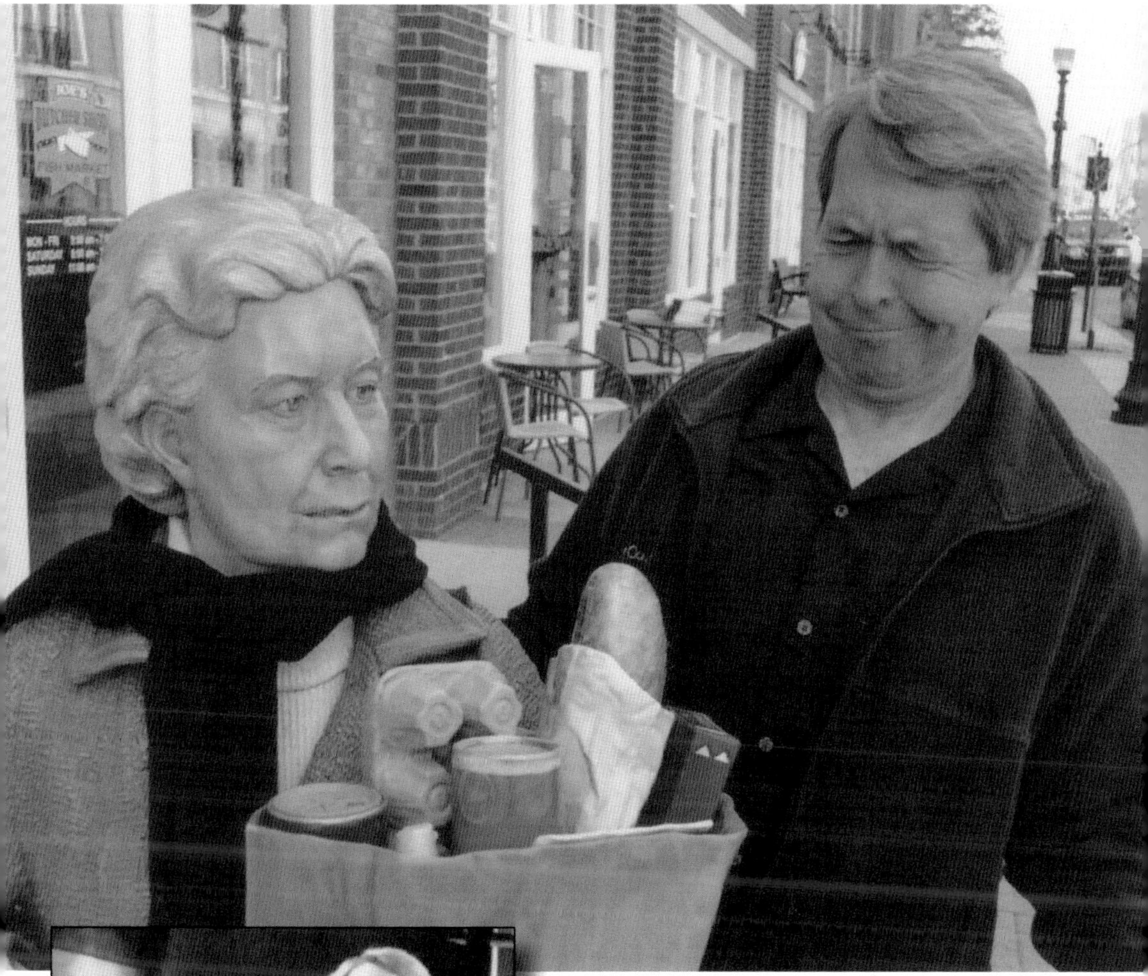

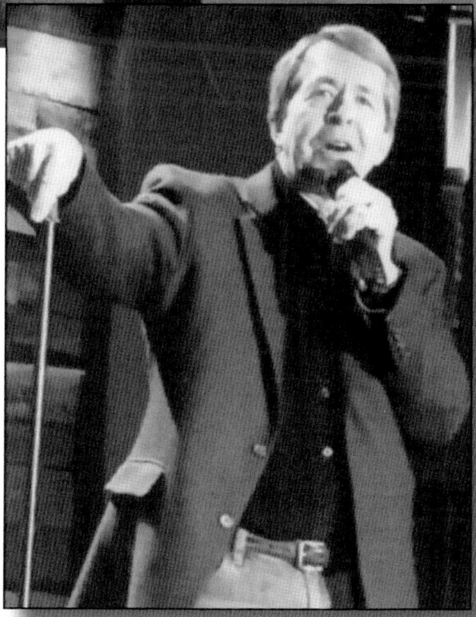

David M. Dugan

Dave Dugan moved to Carmel in the early 1960s from Indianapolis. He graduated from Carmel High School and Ball State University. He found his passion for music leading him to CHS's student-run radio station, WHJE. During his time there, he found a love for doing voiceovers. A pivotal point for Dave would be finding out how humor alleviated his nervousness when presenting in speech class. Today, he can boast of being a regular at The Comedy Store in Los Angeles, appearing on national television shows including *The Arsenio Hall Show* and *The Bob and Tom Show*. Even though his career would take him away, he returned to Carmel to raise a family. He tours regularly and continues to entertain both locally and nationally. (Above, courtesy of John Cinnamon; left, courtesy of Dave Dugan.)

Jennifer D. Hershberger (1950–)

Jennifer Hershberger and Mayor James Brainard celebrate his reelection to a sixth term at his election headquarters after the May 2015 primary. After high school graduation in Carmel in 1968, Jennifer spent her career teaching in Cincinnati after graduating from Ball State with further degrees from Miami and Xavier Universities. Upon her retirement, she returned to Carmel to spend her free time giving back to the community in which she grew up. A lover of history and preservation, her volunteer positions would include serving as president of the Carmel Clay Historical Society and holding a seat on the Historic Preservation Commission. She is an avid genealogist and attends clinics and workshops. Her keen eye for subjects comes out through her camera lens as she records for history most events that Carmel hosts throughout the year. They include, to name a few, the Carmel Farmers Market, Carmelfest, and International Arts Festival. (Author's collection)

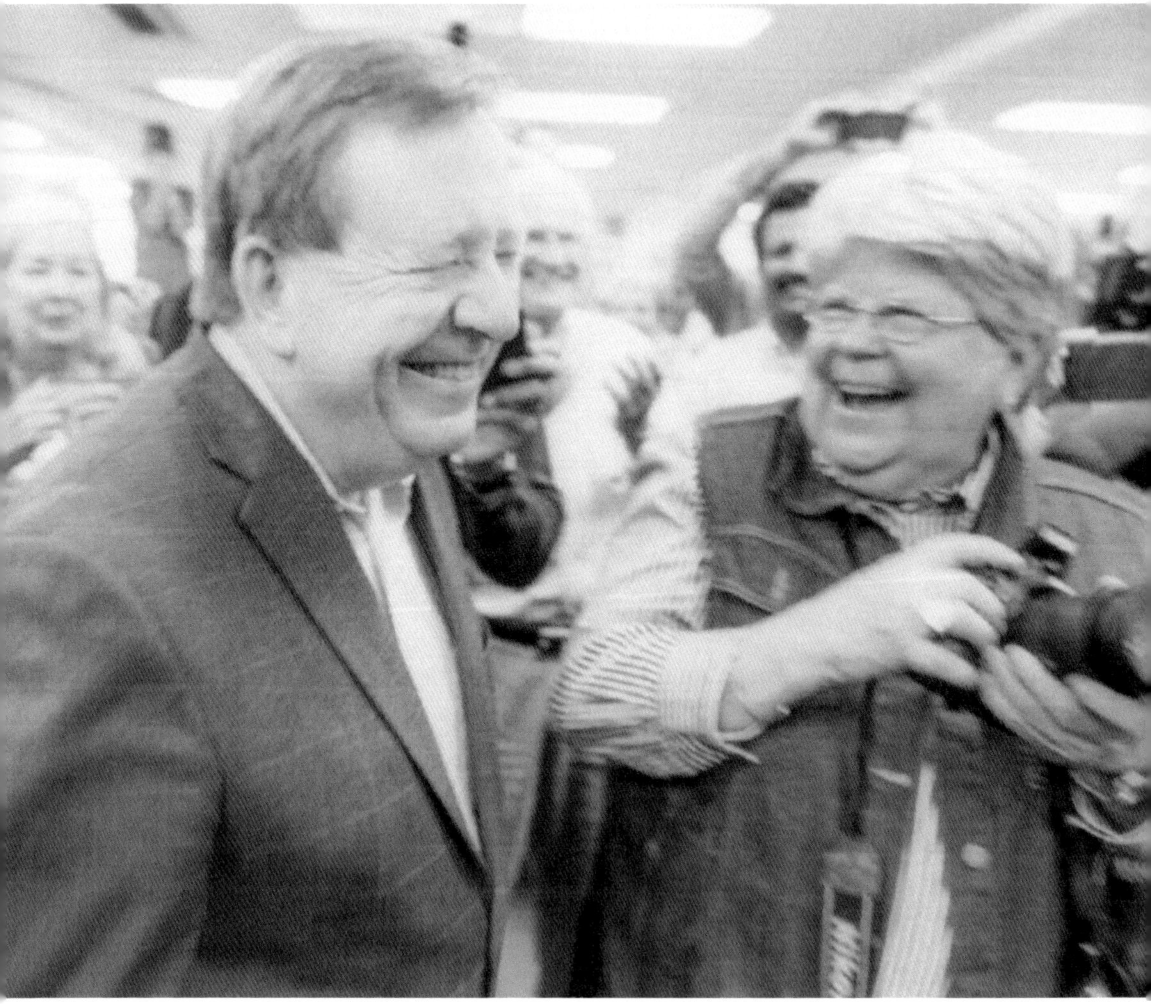

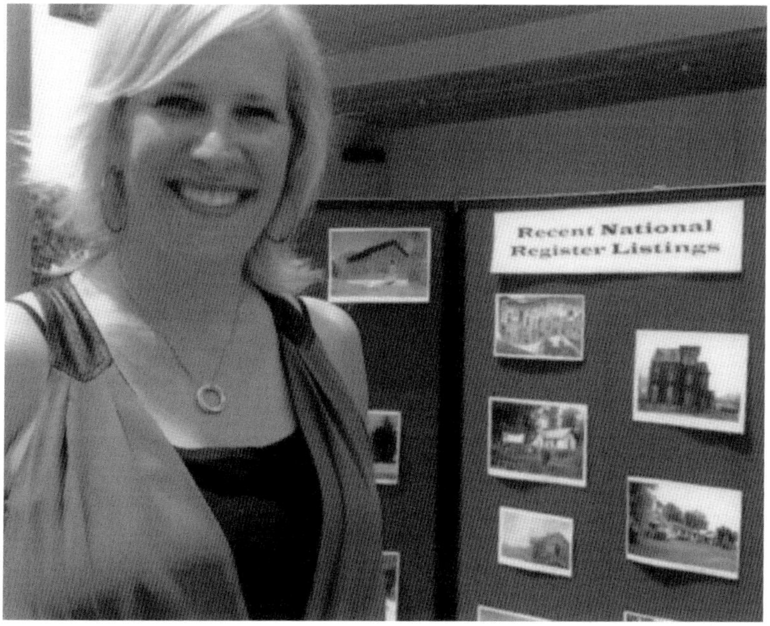

Katherine (Kuntz) Dill (1973–)
Former executive director of the Carmel Clay Historical Society Katherine Dill poses by the list of the 2013 Indiana inductees to the National Register of Historic Places being honored at the Indiana State Fair. The list included Carmel's own restored Monon depot that serves as the museum on the campus of the Carmel Clay Historical Society. Katherine worked with devotion and emotion to get the building placed on the prestigious register. From Vincennes, where history is rich, she grew up to appreciate it and pursued post-secondary degrees in journalism and history. After serving as CCHS executive director from 2011 to 2014, her time was spent volunteering for the organization where she was curator. She now volunteers for the Indiana State Archives. (Photographs by Jennifer D. Hershberger.)

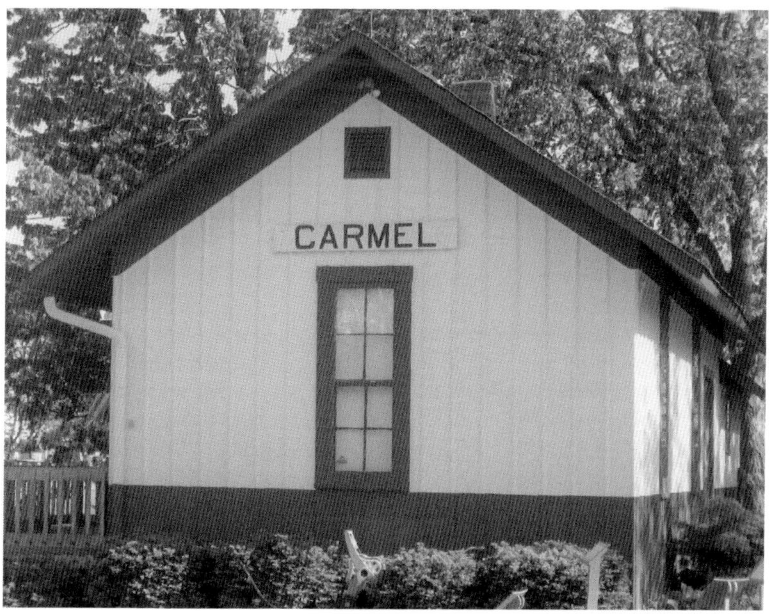

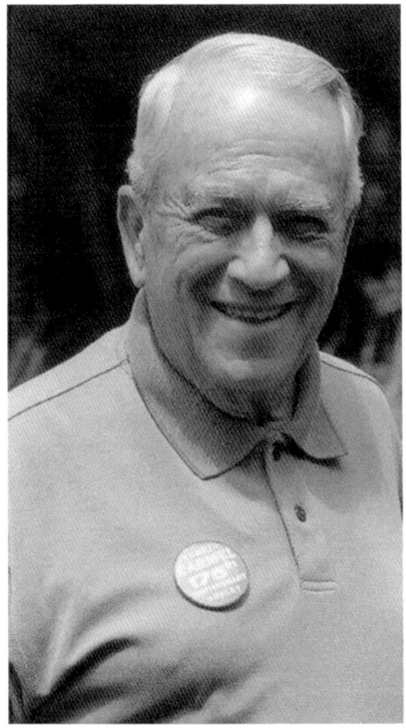

Jack G. Badger (1937–)

Jack was instrumental through the Carmel Dads' Club (CDC) in securing the 39-acre site on East Main Street to build a premier youth sports park in 1977. His son Mark would be memorialized by the CDC a few years later when he succumbed to cancer at age 10. Jack's most recent recognition was being the inaugural recipient of the Pillar of the Community Award in July of 2014. He was honored with the 1998 Rotary Outstanding Service Award by the Carmel Rotary Club and the Range Line Pioneer Award in 2011. Countless hours over the years have been given to numerous organizations. To help fund Carmel's annual fireworks show for the Fourth of July, Jack decided six years ago to sell Spark Buttons. This concept of fundraising caught on, and in 2014, over 3,000 were sold in packets with coupons from local merchants. (Right, photograph by Jennifer D. Hershberger; below, author's collection.)

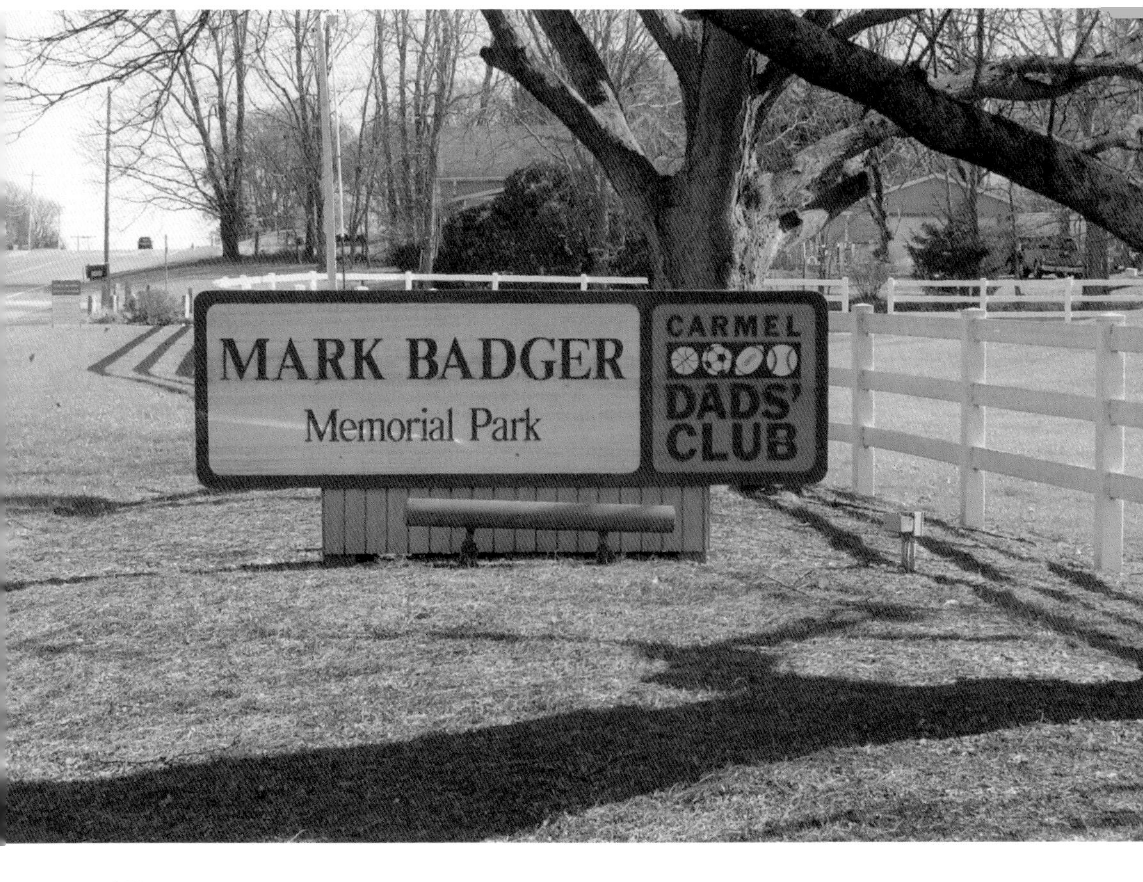

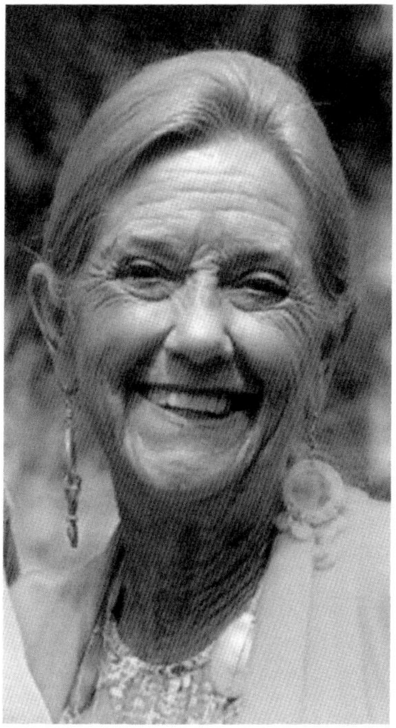

Ila M. (Reeve) Badger (1938–)
Not at all by coincidence, Jack Badger's beautiful, adoring bride of 55 years gives back to the community as well. During the early years of raising their children, Ila was content to volunteer at church and the children's schools. In 1980, she was asked by then Carmel mayor, Jane Reiman to serve on the Carmel Plan Commission and subsequently the zoning appeals board. Surviving breast cancer twice and undergoing a liver transplant in 2001, one can find Ila speaking on behalf of the Indiana Organ Procurement Organization. She educates the public on how lives can be saved by organ donation. Jack and Ila are two steadfast fans who have witnessed great change in the community, have given countless hours of service and shown everyone their courage and strength with boundless enthusiasm along the way. (Both photographs by Jennifer D. Hershberger.)

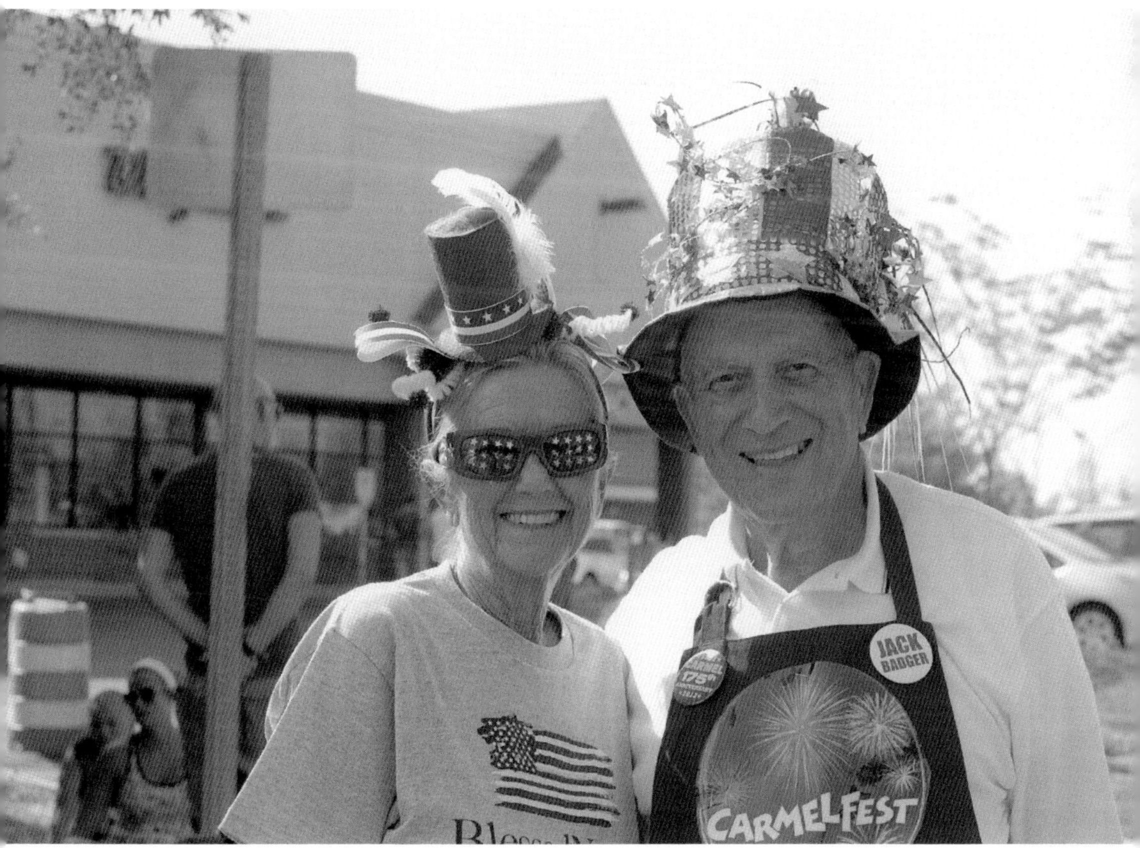

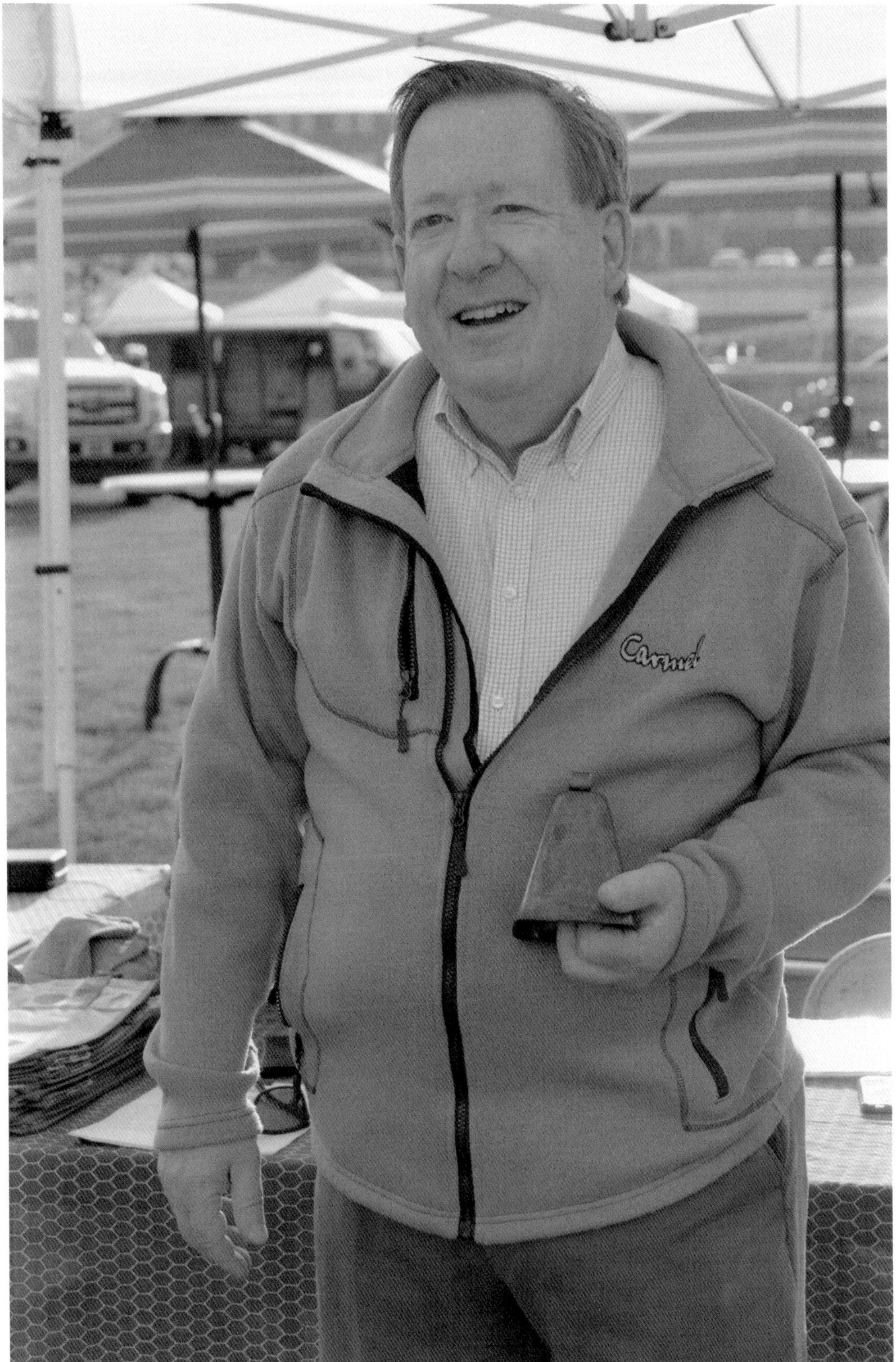
Carmel

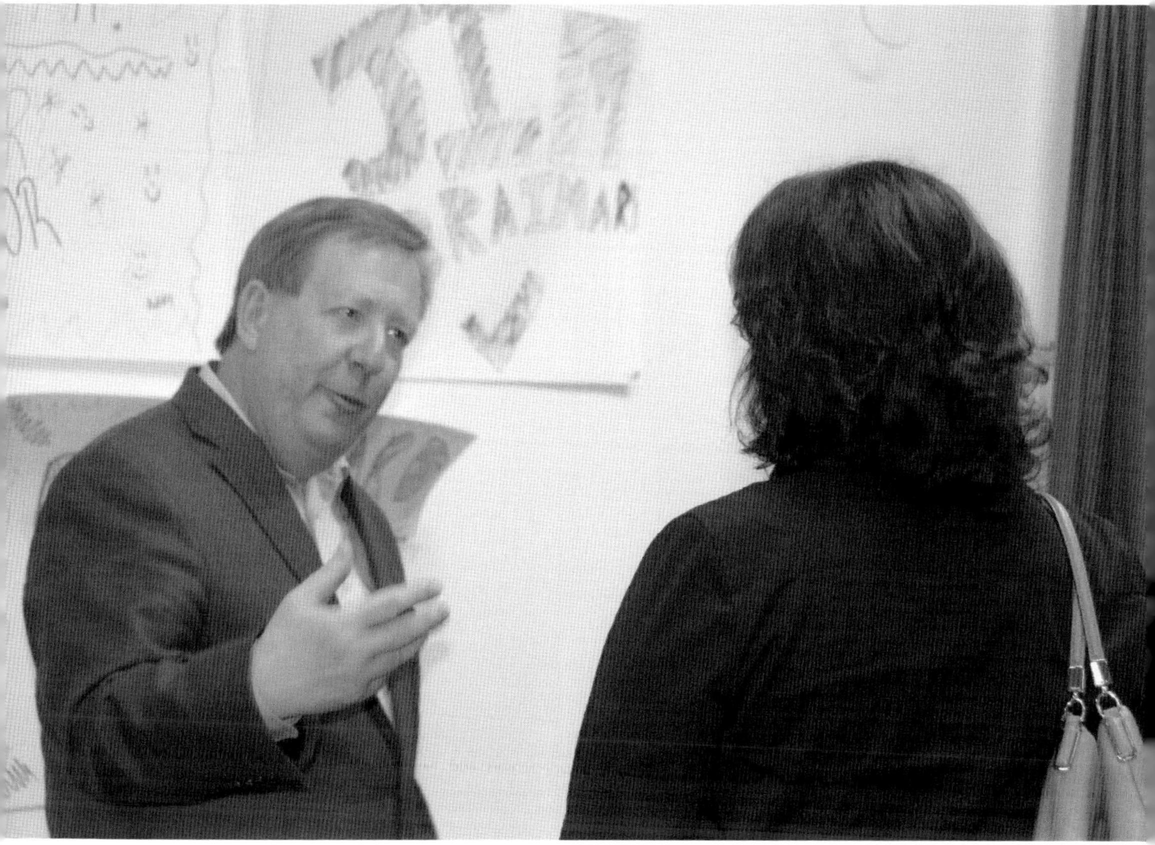

James C. Brainard (1954–)

At left, Mayor James Brainard will ring the bell to signify the opening of the 2015 Carmel Farmer's Market season. Above, he talks with a supporter at his campaign headquarters after his reelection. Since Carmel attained city status with a governing city council and mayor in 1975, five individuals have held the position of mayor. Carmel's fifth mayor holds a record of which no other mayor in the country can boast. James Brainard is the longest serving city mayor in Indiana's history of 200 years. He was elected to an unprecedented sixth term in 2015. Originally from Bristol, Indiana, Mayor Brainard had a vision for Carmel and has confidently taken the community into the 21st century with redevelopment, sustainable growth and livability efforts, and economic development—all with low taxes. His vision of making Carmel a great city has been more than successful and has put the small farm town of just 50 years ago on the map both nationally and internationally.

Brainard's energy saving innovations have won Carmel a number of national environmental awards as well as himself an appointment to serve on the White House Task Force on Climate Preparedness and Resilience. He also has served on the US Conference of Mayors' Energy Independence and Climate Protection Task Force. The widely popular revitalized downtown area known as the Arts & Design District draws visitors from a wide area to the shops, galleries, and special events held throughout the year. Carmel's numerous environmentally friendly roundabouts (replacing stop-signed or stop-lighted intersections) are rapidly becoming popular in cities across the nation and Mayor Brainard takes delight in giving tours for city leaders from around the country. Among the many awards the city has won during his tenure being named CNN *Money* magazine's #1 Place to Live in America rates as a proud accomplishment for him. (Both photographs by Jennifer D. Hershberger.)

INDEX